CW00557814

BRITAINS TOY SOLDIERS

1893-1932

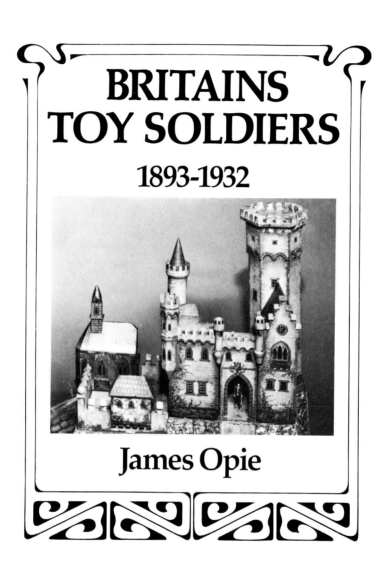

James Opie

LONDON
VICTOR GOLLANCZ LTD
1985

DEDICATION

The man who awoke in me the desire to track down every last variation
ever produced by Britains was the late Len Richards, founding father
of toy soldier collecting. To him I dedicate this book, in the belief
that he would have approved.

First published in Great Britain 1985
by Victor Gollancz Ltd,
14 Henrietta Street, London WC2E 8QJ

British Library Cataloguing in Publication Data

Opie, James
 Britains toy soldiers
 1. Military miniatures-Collectors and collecting
 I. Title
 745.592′82   NK8475.M5

ISBN 0-575-03741-5

Created, designed and produced by
Black Pig Editions Ltd (Justin Knowles Publishing Group),
P.O. Box 99, Exeter, Devon, England.

Text copyright © 1985 James Opie.

Copyright © 1985 Justin Knowles Ltd. All rights
reserved. No part of this book may be reproduced
or utilized in any form or by any means, whether
electronic or mechanical, including photocopying or
recording, or by any information storage and retrieval
system without permission in writing from the
copyright holders.

Editor: Christopher Pick
Design: Elizabeth Palmer
Production: Nick Facer

Typeset by P&M Typesetting Ltd, Exeter.
Printed and bound in Hong Kong by Mandarin Offset Ltd.

CONTENTS

PART ONE
INTRODUCTION

For the 74 years they manufactured hollowcast metal toy soldiers, Britains Ltd were among the most prolific producers of toy soldiers in the world. Over the years, these toys have given immense pleasure to children and adults alike. Even before 1966, when production by the hollowcast method ceased, collectors world-wide were seeking discontinued models. Since then, many people have discovered an absorbing hobby in collecting these souvenirs in miniature of a vanished military pageantry, a hobby at once compelling, arduous, decorative and instructive.

For those who do not yet collect, it is my aim in this book to introduce a fascinating corner of the world of toys: toys whose spectacular and patriotic portrayal of the British Empire at its height has captured the hearts of generations of boys (and girls!). Everyone who appreciates craftsmanship and artistry will be attracted by the intricacy and detail of these toys. Everyone with a feel for the past will be fascinated by the sense of history unfolding itself in miniature.

For collectors, I hope to provide pictures of things they may not have seen and to establish an organization and historical outline upon which further research and collecting may proceed. The illustrations are a crucial part of this book. A large number of figures have been photographed in colour for the first time. About 600 different types and paint finishes are shown on 19 pages of individual recognition pictures. On the remaining 45 colour pages there are approximately 1800 further figures – in boxes, on parade, on campaign or in action: in short, re-creating the evocative spectacle that is the chief attraction of these toys.

The book covers the years 1893, when Britains produced its first hollowcast toy soldier, to 1932, when proper records of the models manufactured began to be kept. In these years the company expanded from a small family concern to a factory based enterprise with an appreciable share of the British toy market. (Britains' other products deserve a book to themselves and are not dealt with here.) Since the early 1930s Britains has remained a major producer, and it is currently the largest privately owned toy manufacturer in Great Britain, although ownership has now (February 1984) finally passed out of the hands of the Britain family. Few records remain from the early years of expansion and experimentation. Such catalogues and source material as are available are discussed on pages 12–13, but a large amount of information must be inferred from the surviving models themselves and from their associated

packaging material. Much of the text is therefore devoted to discussing the items shown in the pictures. A large number of highly decorative box labels are also shown. There are chapters on Britains' commercial organization and practice, on the company's catalogues and its continuity of style and manufacturing techniques, and on collecting terminology and conventions.

Finally, I should make it clear that the contents of this book represent my own ideas and opinions formed over some 20 years of researching and collecting Britains' toy soldiers. Much remains to be done to fill out the intricate details of the company's history, and in many areas I can only put forward hypotheses about events and methods. My thanks are due in advance to those who will correct my ideas and increase my knowledge of my favourite subject.

WOODEN FORT WITH AN ASSORTMENT OF SOLDIERS.

Although not all the soldiers shown with this fort are from the period covered by this book, the fort itself is a magnificent example of a toy symbolic of childhood wars. This particular one was probably made in Germany, and was very expensive in the shops. It is surprising that Britains did not make forts to go with its soldiers during our period. Perhaps it was because they were so easily made at home, or because by tradition they belonged to the large wooden toy branch of the toy trade. Although this book will examine Britains' early output academically, even pedantically, we should never lose sight of the primary purpose of toy soldiers: to be played with, as is happening in this introductory picture. (Phillips, London)

Chapter 1
How to use this book

Organization of the book

Part One, *Introduction*, introduces the subject and gives a short background history of Britains and a summary of how hollowcasting worked.

Part Two, *Research*, deals with source materials, the design of models, set content, painting, boxes, labels and packaging, Britains' competitors and terminology. These are the topics it is useful to understand before examining the models in detail.

Parts Three to Seven are the main illustrative sections of the book, and examples are shown in colour of nearly all the known types of toy soldier produced by Britains during the period 1893 to 1932. The pictures are arranged by subject and usually follow the order evolved by Britains in its catalogues: the British Army first, then the British Empire and, last, the rest of the world. In Britains' catalogues, however, second-grade and small-size figures are always listed separately, whereas in the illustrations in this book these types are shown with the others of their subject.

Most of the chapters in Parts Three to Seven contain a main article on the subject, colour illustrations of the soldiers concerned and a full-length description of the illustrations. The description is normally placed on the reverse of the illustration referred to, but a short caption always gives directions to where the descriptions can be found.

Where the illustration shows similar or sequenced figures, the earlier models are always on the left unless otherwise stated. The descriptions of the figures laid out in rows are identified thus: top row, 2nd row, 3rd row, 4th row, with the figures in each row being numbered from the left: fig 1, fig 2, fig 3 etc. When the parts of a figure are being considered, the words left and right are always used as if the figure itself were speaking. A Grenadier Guard would say, 'I wear my white plume on the left of my bearskin', and most marching Britains figures would say, 'I put my left foot forward'. Seen marching towards the reader, the left foot forward would appear on the right.

The term 'our period' means the years 1893 to 1932, and all information given refers only to that period unless specifically stated otherwise. Occasionally, where an early enough version of figures from sets 1 to 500 has not been available, I have chosen to illustrate a later version rather than show nothing. Dates are given as *c*.1900 if the exact date of an event or figure is unknown. The condition of figures is coded as follows: E = excellent; G = good; F = fair; P = poor. (See page 30 for a fuller explanation.) Set numbers are referred to simply as 'set

111'. In common with modern toy and model soldier practice, even in countries that use imperial measurements, scales are given in millimetres measured from the top of the head (without hat) to the ground in a normal standing infantryman. 'Standard' scale is 54mm (2⅛ inches). (See also page 7.)

At the back of the book are summaries of subjects such as Britains' Paris Office, second-grade and small-size troops. These types of model appear quite widely in the colour pictures, so explanations of them are needed.

Finally come the listings of best-quality toy soldiers produced between 1893 and 1932, first by type of figure, with the sequential development of the versions of each type, and then by numerical order of set and chronological order of production (which normally coincide).

Looking things up

Broad subjects, such as 'Highlanders', can be easily found in the Contents List, as they often form chapter titles in the central section of the book (Parts Three to Seven). All other subjects, such as, for instance, a regiment or country, will be found in the general index at the back of the book (pages 190–2). British cavalry regiments with numerical titles are entered under their generic type: thus the 5th Irish Lancers are listed under

Lancers, 5th Irish. In order to identify a particular regiment of the British Army, the introduction to Part Three contains three pictures showing the uniform differences for those produced by Britains during our period. Technical terms are listed on page 30.

If it is necessary to look up a set by its number, the main military series is listed in the Chronological and Numerical Index of Sets, starting on page 169. Sets above number 500 are not dealt with in this book, since they are either civilian items or were produced after 1932.

If the set number required has a letter in it, it belongs to one of the subsidiary series. All these, including series made outside our period, are listed alphabetically by the letter used on pages 9 and 10, so that the type of set in question can be identified. If the series does date from our period, a further listing of the individual items within the series can be referred to. The alphabetical listing gives a cross-reference if further information is available elsewhere in the book.

Other useful listings are the list of dated figures in date order on page 16, the list of Paris Office figures on page 162, and the list of second-grade figure types on page 164.

A full set of the CFE Army Service Supply Column (see page 119) showing the ingenious display packing. Four rivets hold the card to which the infantry escort and officer are tied to the front flap of the box. The two seated men for the front wagon fell off their seats for this photograph. (Phillips, London)

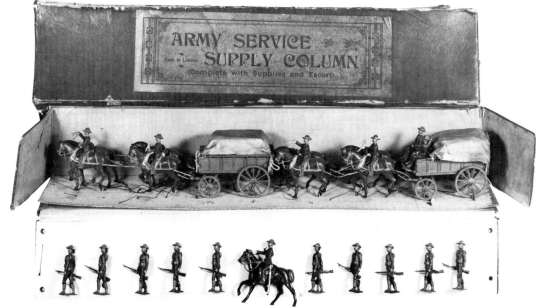

Chapter 2
Bibliography

The original 'Bible' for research in Britains is a series of articles written by the late Len Richards in *The Bulletin* of the British Model Soldier Society. He does not say where he himself obtained his information, but gives a year of first issue for the majority of set numbers. This information has been amplified and extended in articles in the *Old Toy Soldier Newsletter*, a journal specifically for toy-soldier collectors, first issued in October 1976, which devotes about a quarter of its space to Britains. I also issue my own occasional subscription newsletter entitled *The Encyclopedia of British Toy Soldiers*, which has so far been devoted almost entirely to Britains. In this I go into more esoteric mysteries of Britains, as well as providing various listings and comments useful primarily to collectors.

Len Richards also wrote a book, *Old British Model Soldiers 1893–1918*, published in 1970 but now unfortunately out of print, to which I refer occasionally in my text. This included photographs of Britains and other contemporary figures on a similar pattern to this book, but in black and white and without much text. To gain most from them, Len Richards' articles and his book should be read together. We should remember that he was writing before many collectors became interested in toy soldiers, when little research had been done.

After Len Richards' death in 1980, his collection was sold by his widow, and I was privileged to write the auction catalogue. The catalogue is quite useful in amplifying Len Richards' written work, and contains many photographs of otherwise unrecorded figures, some of which are reproduced in this book. Copies of this catalogue are still available from Phillips Auctioneers, London, at the time of writing.

Joe Wallis, probably the foremost researcher into Britains in the United States, has published privately an excellent book, *Regiments of all Nations*, which gives virtually complete details of all production after the Second World War. The book is usually available from toy soldier dealers and specialist shops.

In his capacity as curator of the fabulous Forbes Toy Soldier Museum in Tangiers, Peter Johnson, who has directed publicity for Phillips Auctioneers throughout the 16 years they have been running toy soldier auctions, has produced a book entitled *Toy Armies*, about half of which is devoted to Britains. It includes an extremely worthwhile account of the fortunes of the Britain family, much of it gained from extensive conversations with Dennis Britain, the grandson of the founder and son of William Britain Junior. Although not an analytical book, it contains a great deal of essential information.

John Ruddle, another very knowledgeable collector, has written a *Collectors Guide to Britains Model Soldiers*. The introduction contains some good material, and an extensive selection of figures appears in the photographs, many of which cannot be seen elsewhere. Unfortunately the book is plagued with printer's errors, but it is nevertheless well worth buying.

In the United States Joanne and Ron Ruddell have published a *Britains Collector's Checklist*. These three pamphlets list nearly all the Britains set and individual numbers, as well as many pictures and points of view.

An additional book, due for private publication at about the same time as this one, will be of considerable use to collectors. Colonel Donald Pudney, a noted Bermudian collector, has obtained from Britains the rights to publish its complete factory records which were compiled retrospectively in about 1933 and maintained from then on. His book consists of numbered listings of the composition of each set, cross-referenced to mould numbers and painting style numbers.

Here are the bibliographic details of the works discussed above.

Johnson, Peter, *Toy Armies*, Batsford, London, 1982
Pudney, Donald, *Britains Ltd, Master Lists of Toy Soldiers and Models, 1893–1966*, private publication, 1986
Richards, L W, *Old British Model Soldiers*, Arms and Armour Press, London, 1970
Ruddell, Joanne and Ron, *Britains Collector's Checklist*, vols I, II and III, private publication, 1980–2
Ruddle, John, *Collectors Guide to Britains Model Soldiers*, Argus, Watford, 1980
Wallis, Joe, *Regiments of All Nations*, private publication, 1981
Bulletin of the British Model Soldier Society; all enquiries to the Secretary, Mr D Pearce, 22 Lynwood Road, Ealing, London W5 1JJ, United Kingdom
Old Toy Soldier Newsletter, 209 North Lombard, Oak Park, Illinois, USA
The Encyclopedia of British Toy Soldiers; all enquiries to James Opie, c/o Justin Knowles Publishing Group, PO Box 99, Exeter, Devon EX2 4TW, United Kingdom
The following are excellent introductory reading:
Garratt, John G, *The World Encyclopaedia of Model Soldiers*, Muller, London, 1981; an exhaustive survey of toy and model soldiers past and present
McKenzie, Ian, *Collecting Old Toy Soldiers*, Batsford, London, 1975; an introduction to collecting
Opie, James, *British Toy Soldiers 1893 to the Present*, Arms and Armour Press, London, 1985; a book similar to that by Len Richards with new illustrations
Opie, James, *Toy Soldiers*, Shire Publications, Princes Risborough, 1983; an introduction to every aspect of the world of toy soldiers
Useful reference material can be found in the following reprints of catalogues:
Gamage's Christmas Bazaar, David & Charles, Newton Abbot, 1974
Mr Gamage's Great Toy Bazaar 1902 and 1906, Denys Ingram, London, 1982.
Many of Britains' original catalogues have been reprinted, and some should be available from dealers.

Two of William Britain Senior's early toys. His speciality was mechanical toys with cast metal moving parts, powered by a variety of clockwork, gyroscopic and other methods. These pictures are from a catalogue attributed to 1880, and show items that foreshadow later developments in toy soldiers: a mechanical machine gun capable of firing at a rate of 200 dried peas a minute, and 'the General', a figure of a soldier on a hobby horse. At this time, and until 1907, the firm traded as William Britain and Sons, offering 'Celebrated Automatic and Scientific Clockwork Models, Toys Etc'.

THE MACHINE GUN.

THE GENERAL.

Chapter 3
Britains: a brief history

 The business of Britains Ltd, incorporated on 4 December 1907, had been started some 60 years earlier by William Britain (1828–1906), an ingenious toymaker from the Midlands. Moving into a large house at 28 Lambton Road, Hornsey Rise, in north-east London, he started to build a small but reasonably thriving trade.

Then as now, the toy trade was a fairly risky business, and there was strong competition in mechanical toys, which were produced both in Great Britain and on the continent of Europe. In the early 1890s William Britain and his sons cast about for some speciality that would bring them a real advantage over their rivals. One idea they considered was toy soldiers, in which there was a substantial import trade from Germany.

It is William Britain Junior, the eldest son, who is credited with having invented, after some experimentation, the hollowcasting process for manufacturing toy soldiers. Hollow parts were already used in a number of existing Britains' toys, and doubtless this experience helped enormously. Applied to the manufacture of toy soldiers, however, hollowcasting was totally revolutionary and gave the Britain family just the sort of competitive edge it had been looking for.

In 1893, when the Britain family put its new toy soldiers on the market, the younger generation consisted of two daughters, Emily, the eldest child, and Annie, and five sons, the eldest of whom was William Britain Junior (1860–1933), followed by Alfred, Frederick, Frank and Edward. In the early years they all took part in the business, although later, when success was assured, the daughters and the two youngest sons went their own way.

Imports from Germany dominated the toy soldier market, and, as often happens nowadays, it was difficult for a new type of model from an unknown source to gain a commercial foothold. No doubt William Britain's connections with the toy trade stood him in good stead, and after an understandably slow beginning the problem soon became to produce enough models to satisfy the demand – a new experience for the company since it had previously traded in a small way.

Albert Gamage and his celebrated store in Holborn, then one of the largest outlets for toys in the country and especially well-known for its Christmas displays, played a crucial part in Britains' success. Gamage immediately started to stock the new Britains' lines. Following his usual policy he sold the toy at well below the recommended price, tenpence halfpenny instead of one shilling. As Britains extended its range, Gamages

continued to buy, reducing its stock of German imports, and by 1906 the toy soldiers featured in its catalogue were almost all made by Britains. A notice at the top of the first page devoted to toy soldiers read:

English Made Metal Soldiers – We hold a stock of 500,000 Soldiers of all nations, but owing to the exceptional demand at Christmas time Customers are urged to give their orders as early as possible so as to prevent any possibility of delay.

In this same year Britains introduced giant display boxes, which were an immediate success.

Another quotation from the same catalogue indicates a second, and equally important, reason for Britains' success.

All our soldiers are made exact to scale, that is a Foot Soldier is the same size as a Horse Soldier, and Horses are in proportion to the men; whilst the Uniforms and Colourings have been most carefully considered and will be found perfectly correct in all details.

From the start, the soldiers were standardized on a scale equivalent to the most popular size of toy train at that time, known as gauge 1. This meant producing a man 54mm (2⅛ inches) tall. It is a measure of the influence Britains had on the entire toy and model soldier world that this measure is still known as the standard scale; all toys and models are now measured in millimetres as the height of an ordinary infantryman without headgear. Britains also manufactured a smaller size measuring 43mm (1⁷⁄₁₀ inches), a little smaller than the '0' gauge trains for which they were intended. In 1912 the height of these smaller models was increased by 2mm so that they conformed exactly with the trains.

Britains did indeed go to great lengths to get the uniforms right, and was successful on the whole, as this book shows. The firm's accuracy made a sharp contrast with the German sets on sale through wholesalers in the 1890s.

The first years of hollowcast production, between 1893 and the turn of the century, were characterized by rapid changes in models, unstandardized box labels and a relatively low level of production. The new century brought expansion and greater standardization. The original house in Lambton Road was extended; then the house next door was acquired, and another extension built. Even that was to prove insufficient and the whole lot was torn down and replaced by a factory, warehouse and office complex occupying the entire side of a block, with a floor area of 36,000 square feet. Some 300 people were employed. Between 1900 and 1916, when the factory was converted to war production, standard dated figures were introduced and kept in production for many

years. The export trade to the USA and continental Europe was developed, and a consistent product image established, Fred Whisstock being appointed to design the box labels in a single style. (Some idea of the detailed expansion of the company's product range can be obtained from the Chronological and Numerical Index of Sets (pages 178–89), which shows the new sets and ideas introduced each year.)

Normal production resumed in 1918, at the end of the First World War, and in response to the prevailing popular mood, which turned aside from the horrors of the war, the Home Farm range was introduced. In retrospect the 1920s can be seen as a period of consolidation and preparation for the astonishing performance of the 1930s. A new factory, known as the North Light building, of no less than 20,000 square feet, was planned and erected in Walthamstow, north-east London, in 1931, and the entire production of the Home Farm range was moved there. Exports were increased, especially to the USA, and production facilities expanded.

The models described and illustrated in this book were made no later than 1932, but a brief look forward to the present day is not inappropriate. In the 1930s, Britains survived economic depression by going for every money-earner it could think of. New types of model proliferated – zoo, garden, circus, motor vehicles and so forth – and many different grades of quality were produced. The 1940 range, marketed just before the company had to go over to war production once again, was the largest ever.

The return to normality after the Second World War was slow, and it was not until 1953 that a reasonable range was offered. Box labels were standardized to a single 'Regiments of All Nations' design. Almost immediately, plastic began to pose a serious threat. By the mid-1960s, it had almost entirely taken over, and in 1966 the era of the hollowcast toy soldier finally came to an end – although not before some 1000 million had been manufactured.

However, the company itself remains prominent. Herald, the leading manufacturer of plastic toy soldiers, was acquired in 1959, and with it considerable expertise in the new material. In the 1980s, Britains' success continues, and its ranges of plastic farm animals and complementary die-cast vehicles are both worthy upholders of the standards set long ago. A new range of die-cast metal toy soldiers in the old, traditional uniforms is being made at the time of writing to satisfy the expanding collectors' market – and some of these collectors happen to be children!

Chapter 4
Hollowcasting

Hollowcast models were produced as a hollow shell of metal with an empty interior, rather than as a solid moulding. The mould was made of brass and held by hand resting on a narrow stand. It consisted of two or more parts attached to a pair of long handles. These were hinged together at the top like a pair of nutcrackers, so that the operator could open and close the mould extremely quickly. When closed, the mould looked like a solid block of brass with a large funnel-shaped opening in the top.

In operation, the mould was heated to the right temperature, a little less than the melting-point of the alloy being used. The alloy, normally a mixture of lead, tin and antimony, was then poured in with a ladle. As the alloy cooled, a skin formed round the edge of the shape. When the mould was turned upside down, the rest of the molten metal streamed out through the funnel, leaving the complete hollow figure in the mould. The mould was then opened and the model extracted with pliers. The skill of the operator lay in heating the mould to exactly the right temperature so that the molten metal would cool fast enough to form a figure quickly but not so fast that the metal would solidify before it could be poured out again.

Air holes were left at strategic points to ensure that the metal reached all the extremities of the mould. The thinner parts – rifle barrels and horses' legs, for instance – were solid to prevent breaking. The antimony in the alloy caused the metal to expand slightly as it cooled, producing a crisp casting that expanded into the engraving of the mould.

Skilled hand-mould operators could achieve more than 300 infantry castings an hour, though inspection was generally very rigorous. Sometimes casting errors were missed both at casting and during painting. I have one such model, of a 17th Lancer in foreign-service order, which has come out not quite right in the head (see page 20).

Low production costs were vital to Britains' competitiveness and success, and the hollowcasting method used only half as much metal as solid casting. The models themselves were half as heavy on average, which also reduced transportation costs. After manufacture, to cut costs further, all the models were weighed in batches; very overweight castings were removed and their metal used again.

Collectors often come across unusually heavy models which must have passed inspection either by mistake or because the batch in which they were weighed was not overweight as a whole. Very light models also turn up from time to time, although these get crushed rather easily because of their very thin skins. According to one theory, the standard weight of metal per figure was reduced during the First World War because of scarcity of raw materials. But this would have resulted in a plague of 'light' soldiers, and I have never found enough to substantiate this idea.

The master models from which the moulds were prepared were usually the work of William Britain Junior, although other members of the family were quite prepared to lend a hand: witness the beautiful models in 70mm scale by Alfred Britain (see page 64). All the dated figures apart from these are 'signed' by William Britain Junior. After the First World War more people became involved in preparing the masters, family members, employees and even freelance pattern-makers.

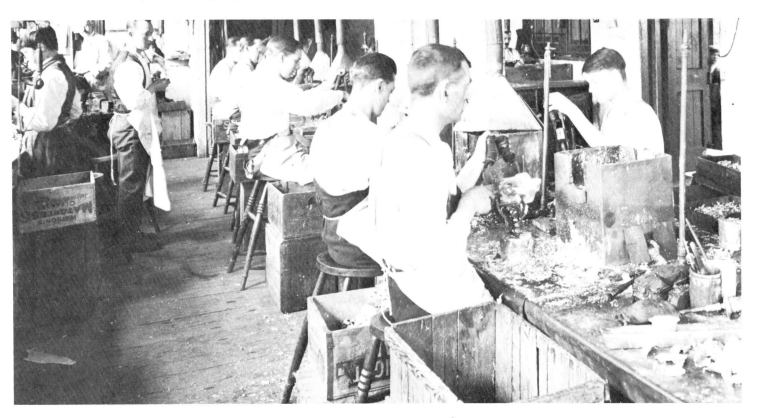

CASTING HOLLOWCAST FIGURES
A general view of the casting shop at Britains'. Notice how the mould is being rested on a stand and manipulated in one hand while the other hand wields the ladle and pliers. The castings are being put to into the big box to the right of the operative. (Britains Ltd)

PART TWO
RESEARCH

 Knowing from my everyday office job how difficult it is to determine exactly what went on last year sometimes makes me appalled at my audacity in trying to learn about what went on so many years ago at Britains. The only approach for the early period is to derive empirical conclusions and probabilities from the surviving toys, boxes and catalogues, and to listen to the reminiscences of those who worked for the company.

When no complete answer is available to a mystery in Britains' corporate behaviour, we have to guess at what might have happened, on the basis of commercial expediency – 'the easiest way of solving a problem with the available resources'. I do this quite often, and whenever I do make such a guess I show ICP – Inherent Commercial Probability – in brackets. (See also page 12.)

The purpose of the research done by myself and many others is to become so familiar with the working methods and products of the company through the years that any figure can be dated as closely as possible and put in a collection in its proper context. Britains' normal practice in regard to set numbering, messages on the underside of bases, design of heads and arms, painting, packing and labelling all give pointers to the date of production and therefore to where a particular figure might fit into the jigsaw of the total output.

Chapter 5
Company policy and catalogues

The set numbering system

 In the very early days, sets were not numbered, and they were ordered by name, as had always happened with the company's mechanical toys. However, as their range of toy soldiers grew, some form of numbering system became necessary, since it was tedious to differentiate between regiments with the same title but depicted in different poses, and awkward that the only way to order display sets was to write out their contents in full. In either 1897 or 1898, therefore, Britains started to number its boxes. The earlier boxes have no number printed on the label. Set 83, Middlesex Yeomanry, is the highest-numbered box I have seen without a number on the label. As this set is most likely to have gone into production in 1897, this suggests the year numbering began – although the sets might well already have had an internal number, for use solely within the factory. (For a further discussion of early numbering, see the article in the Chronological and Numerical Index of Sets on page 178.)

Once the numbering system had been established, all boxes were carefully numbered on the label. The new sets introduced each year were fairly consistently allocated the next higher numbers available. This simple numbering sequence was used for the main, best-quality series. When second-grade, novelty or other non-standard lines were produced, Britains either started a new number sequence suffixed by a letter or else simply did not number at all. Gilt figures and other items which were often unmarked and sold in unmarked boxes, for instance, had no catalogue number before the First World War.

When the Home Farm series was launched in 1923, the military sets had yet to reach number 250, and the new lines were allocated main series numbers from 501 upwards. Clearly, Britains had no idea that within nine years all the spare military numbers would have been used up. As a result, some new military lines issued in 1932 had to start at 1201, to leave room for the expanding civilian side. The jump from 500 to 1201 makes a convenient point at which to break off this survey of the first 40 years of Britains' military production, and hence in this book only main series sets numbered 1 to 500 are discussed.

The main military series had reached set number 1919 when the Second World War stopped production. Post-war numbers started at 2001, and by 1960 number 2189 had been reached, after which the metal series began to be discontinued. In 1962, all Britains' products were completely renumbered, and the surviving metal soldier sets went into a series in the 9000s. And so set 1, which had been in continuous production since 1893, became set 9206 until it was discontinued along with all the other remaining metal sets in 1966.

Subsidiary series

The contents of subsidiary series produced between 1893 and 1932 are described in detail elsewhere. Here the type of product of which each series consisted is outlined. Until the late 1930s, Britains usually wrote letter suffixes in lower case: thus, a. From about 1935 onwards, capitals were normally used.

A Series This series of second-grade sets was started soon after the end of the First World War and was continued with additions and deletions until 1941. A considerable number of sets was made up from a comparatively small number of basic models to meet the requirements of the inexpensive end of the market. By 1932, numbering had reached 274a, although plenty of unused gaps were left in the sequence on offer in the catalogue. During the rest of the 1930s, sales were high, and the highest number in the 1940 catalogue is 1088A. Whether all the intermediate numbers were in fact allocated is not yet known, but Britains' normal practice suggests that they were. Not all of them would necessarily have been featured in the general catalogue, however, since many were special lines for particular shops or for overseas markets. (See also page 163.)

After the Second World War, the A suffix was used for the range of spare parts, shells, wheels etc available from Britains' stockists.

B Series This series, which was issued between 1896

and 1916 and reached set number 26b, consisted of smaller-scale sets (43mm, later increasing to 45mm). The painting on these sets was best quality. (See also page 166.)

Between the two world wars, B suffixes were used for a number of miscellaneous lines, including individual road signs, gnomes, circus items and Snow White and the Seven Dwarfs, and usually meant B for Bulk, ie available in dozens. In 1941, even the standard railway personnel were given a B suffix.

After the Second World War, the Picture Pack series of individual boxed figures, available from 1954 to 1959, was catalogued with numbers with a B suffix. But these numbers referred to the paint style reference number within Britains' factory and had no connection with the B series.

C Series This consisted of individual second-grade figures in standard scale and was available between about 1928 and 1934. Towards the end of the series, some non-standard items were included: the highest number I have recorded, 85c, is a small-size Egyptian Camel Corps figure.

The various series of figures that Britains sold by the dozen to the wholesale trade were confusing, to say the least, and were renumbered twice between the wars. The 1926 catalogue lists the C series in a numbering system that runs 4a, 4b, 4c etc – very muddling, since 4a was of course also used in the A series. By 1935 the entire C series had been renumbered in an entirely different order as the N series, in a separate leaflet that was not part of the main catalogue. (See also page 163.)

D Series This series was equivalent to the C series, but had smaller-size figures. The last three cavalry figures in the series were dropped in 1934, but the Armoured Car (27d) and the Gun Mounted on Wheels (26d), the two highest military numbers in the series, remained popular and stayed in production until 1941, as did the models used to play race games.

After the Second World War, a number of miscellaneous items in the catalogue were given the suffix D. Thus the Race Game Jockey on horse was numbered 19D, the Miniature State Coach 44D, the Coronation Chair 86D and the Large Jockey on Horse 96D. The Coach and Throne had no connection with the earlier D series, but the 19D Jockey had been in the original series.

E Series The sole item in this series that appeared in a catalogue seems to have been 65e, the set of a Stag and Doe in a presentation box.

F Series This was reserved for Home Farm sets, whose individual pieces were numbered from 501 in the main sequence.

G Series This suffix was given to assortments of smaller-size second-grade figures made up in boxes for customers who did not require a dozen at a time of a single figure.

H Series H was reserved for figures of larger than standard size. These were available throughout the 1920s and 1930s in gilt or second-grade paint. There were three

70mm scale military models, an Infantryman of the Line, a Highlander and a Fusilier, all at the slope.

In 1935 an even larger series, known as HH, was introduced, in 83mm scale. This too had three models, an Infantryman of the Line, a Foot Guard and a Highlander. As they were only current from 1935 to 1941, and were not very popular, they are rather rare today.

Some novelties – dogs in large scale, for instance – were also given an H suffix, as were the individual Mickey Mouse set models. The highest number the H series reached was 22H. After the Second World War the number 54HU was used for the toy Electric Iron.

J Series This suffix was used for Garden Ornaments after the Second World War.

KS Series A series of five Kitchen Sets of utensils produced in the late 1930s was given this suffix.

L Series L, LB, LP or LV suffixes were used for the Lilliput 00 gauge series after the Second World War.

M Series M suffixes identified a short series of 47mm second-grade cavalry a little larger than the normal smaller size. The series was current between 1934 and 1941; the highest number reached was 5m.

MG Series This suffix stood for Miniature Gardening.

N Series This was the old series C, which was renumbered in 1935 and added to until 1941; the highest number was 93N.

P Series This series, introduced in about 1932, consisted of individual figures sold for a penny each instead of the usual penny halfpenny for C series figures. The cheap price was made possible by 'third-grade' painting, in which even fewer colours were used than in the C series. Bases were no longer painted green, for instance, and instead the colour of the legs was continued.

After the Second World War the P series continued as individual figures of the Crown range, the highest number being 155P.

R Series In 1940–41 only, 0 gauge railway personnel sold individually were given the suffix R.

RC Series This was used for Racing Colours after the Second World War.

S Series This was used for second-grade sets after the Second World War.

V Series After the Second World War Petrol Pumps were allocated this suffix.

W Series This started life as a series of sets of household utensils in the 1920s, but from set 7w onwards it chiefly consisted of sets of smaller-size military figures, the smaller-size equivalent of the A series. The highest number in the W series appears to have been 201W, the Royal Horse Artillery team, which was transplanted from its original place in the list, set 125 of the main series, and was only available in 1940. (See also page 166.)

X Series This series of pre-First World War second-grade figures is shrouded in mystery, since it appears in no catalogue I have seen. The series itself certainly did exist, since numbered boxes with an X suffix turn up from time to time containing figures of the right age. (See also page 163.)

After the First World War the X suffix was used for Christmas Cake decorations.

Z Series This suffix was allocated to sets of Zoo Animals and Zoo Buildings.

Occasionally, Britains started other series of numbers without either suffix or prefix, usually for items such as novelties or household utensils quite distinct from soldiers. In the 1915 catalogue, there are Gilt Soldiers numbered 1 to 5, three unnumbered second-grade figures and a series of British Army Encampments numbered 01 to 06. The 01 series was used again in 1937, when the Miniature Gardening series was introduced. Although the sets were suffixed MG, as mentioned above, the individual pieces were numbered 01 to 071.

Pricing

From 1893, when Britains first manufactured toy soldiers, to 1914, the retail price of a standard single-row box of eight infantry or five cavalry was one shilling (5p in today's decimal currency). Although Gamages retailed the same article for tenpence halfpenny, discounting was not widespread at that time. In contrast, the set of six Roman Soldiers made by the German manufacturer Heyde and mentioned in the 1913 Gamages catalogue contained twelve infantry and six cavalry in 50mm scale and sold for four shillings and sixpence. At Gamages' prices one could have bought five ordinary Britains boxes for the same money, and so the Dresden company was being undercut by some 45 per cent. Earlier the price difference might have been still greater, before the Germans responded to the new competition.

Small-size and second-grade boxes were normally put out at a retail price of sixpence, although Gamages managed a staggering 25 per cent discount, asking only fourpence halfpenny (just 2p in today's currency).

As inflation increased after 1914, Britains did not reprice all its soldiers but merely announced an overall percentage increase at the beginning of each catalogue. The 1916 list read 'All prices are now advanced 75%', and by 1926 90 per cent was the amount quoted. These increases are almost exactly in line with the Retail Price Index after 1914.

The depression brought some deflation, and prices steadied. In the 1931 catalogue a single-row box cost one shilling and ninepence (the price was now shown for each individual box), and by 1933 the price had fallen to one shilling sevenpence halfpenny. Britains also attempted to specify permissible retail discounts; if these were not observed supplies would be denied to offending retailers – a legal practice at the time. The Second World War brought further inflation, and afterwards Britains found that the large labour costs involved in manufacturing metal toy soldiers forced its prices up faster than the Retail Price Index. At the close of production in 1966, a single-row box of seven infantry cost twelve shillings and sixpence, more than fourteen

times the 1914 price, although the Retail Price Index had only increased by a factor of six. The equivalent box of plastic soldiers issued by Herald cost six shillings and sixpence in 1966.

In the late 1920s Britains tried a variety of different pricing techniques with different-size boxes in an attempt to overcome the effects of inflation. They harked back to the shilling box by using second-grade pieces in various box sizes and tried to bring out first-grade boxes at popular price levels such as two shillings, half a crown and three shillings, from which retailers could discount the odd penny or two. This explains the existence of so many almost identical sets which differ only because some contain one or two additional figures.

Because of the work they required, a few of the most spectacular sets cost more. The Mounted Band of the 1st Life Guards, for instance, which had twelve horsemen, cost five shillings and sixpence, over double the normal price for cavalrymen. And set 69, which cost one shilling, had only seven Pipers of the Scots Guards to the box instead of the usual eight, because of the intricacy of the paintwork.

The top end of the market was not neglected, and a number of expensive sets were offered, ranging up to the giant set 131, whose 275 pieces cost four pounds ten shillings. For that money one could have purchased 90 boxes of infantry – an army of 720 troops. At the time of writing the equivalent retail price of box 131 would be £336.50, on the basis of the increase in retail prices to 1983.

Accuracy

Britains prided itself on the accuracy of its uniforms and made some capital by comparing its figures with imported figures from foreign competitors, one of whom once placed Life Guards on *brown horses*! It would be foolish to claim that Britains was infallible. Nevertheless, it did try to make its toy-painting as accurate as it could, and it attempted to make each uniform a faithful portrayal. Often it used the work of contemporary military artists as reference, especially that of Richard Simkin, from whose prints many early Britains' figures seem to have sprung fully fashioned. Analysis of a few controversial figures will show how Britains did strive for accuracy.

The Rifle Brigade Every military man knows that this regiment never marches at the slope – yet this is how Britains showed it. But correspondence in the *Army and Navy Gazette* reveals that despite regimental tradition the Rifle Brigade was forced to march at the slope for at least six years, from 1897 to 1903, which distressed them a great deal. Photographs show the Rifle Brigade marching in this way. Britains' figure was correct when it was issued in 1897 and remained so for some years.

The South Australian Lancers This was Britains' name for set 49, brought out in 1896 sporting slouch hats. Officially, there was no such regiment. Unofficially, that was the name given to the New South Wales Lancers, who sent contingents to the Dublin and Islington tournaments in 1893 and participated in the Diamond Jubilee celebrations in 1897. From 1891 their official uniform was a salmon khaki jacket. But Britains gave them a blue coat, which they might well have worn, since the uniform differs in no other particular.

In about 1900, Britains changed the uniform of this set to an all-khaki dress with a spiked helmet and a yellow belt with a red stripe. This was the dress of the Adelaide Lancers, a regiment that really did hail from South Australia, so fully justifying Britains' title.

The First Bengal Cavalry (Skinner's Horse) Britains portrayed this regiment in dull ochre rather than in its usual bright yellow. It has been suggested that the Richard Simkin original from which Britains worked faded *en route* to the printers from India and was faithfully reproduced in the dulled colour.

Austro-Hungarian Infantry of the Line Mystery has always surrounded the bright red trousers used on this set, number 177, since red trousers were unknown to the Austrian Army at that time. However, recently a collector found a volume of European military prints containing a number of pictures very like Britains' European models, and in particular a good picture of a little known Hungarian territorial unit in red trousers. From all this it is clear that Britains should not be blamed for 'mistakes' until its source of information for a particular figure has been established. Britains' competitors, both British and European, did not always stop to research their models before they marketed them: but Britains, it appears, always did things for a reason. What a fascinating subject for further research!

11

Complete List of Metal Soldiers

MANUFACTURED BY

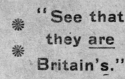

"See that they are Britain's."   "See that they are Britain's."

IN LONDON.

STANDARD SIZE.

British Army.

Artillery.

No.		s.	d.
39	The Royal Horse Artillery	6	0
28	Mountain Artillery	2	6
	Gun of the R.H.A.	1	0

Cavalry.

No.		s.	d.
101	Band of the 1st Life Guards	5	6
1	1st Life Guards	1	0
43	2nd Life Guards	1	0
2	Horse Guards	1	0
3	5th Dragoon Guards	1	0
106	6th Dragoon Guards	1	0
32	2nd Dragoons (Scots Greys)	1	0
31	1st Dragoons	1	0
108	6th Dragoons (Inniskilling)	1	0
23	5th Lancers	1	0
24	9th Lancers	1	0
33	16th Lancers	1	0
81	17th Lancers (active service)	1	0
100	21st Lancers (review order)	1	0
94	21st Lancers (khaki)	1	0
12	11th Hussars	1	0
13	3rd Hussars	1	0
8	4th Hussars	1	0
99	13th Hussars	1	0
83	Middlesex Yeomanry	1	0
105	Imperial Yeomanry	1	0

Infantry.

No.		s.	d.
34	Grenadier Guards	1	0
111	Grenadier Guards (attention)	1	0
120	Coldstream Guards (firing, kneeling)	1	0
37	Full Band of the Coldstream Guards	4	0
75	Scots Guards	1	0
82	Colours and Pioneers of Scots Guards	1	0
69	Pipers of Scots Guards	1	0
107	Irish Guards	1	0
124	Irish Guards (firing, lying)	1	0
7	7th Royal Fusiliers	1	0
109	Dublin Fusiliers (khaki)	1	0
74	Welsh Fusiliers	1	0
9	Rifle Brigade	1	0
98	King's Royal Rifles	1	0
11	The Black Watch (Royal Highlanders)	1	0
15	Argyle and Sutherland Highlanders	1	0
77	Gordon Highlanders	1	0
118	Gordon Highlanders (firing, lying)	1	0
114	Cameron Highlanders (active service)	1	0
112	Seaforth Highlanders	1	0
122	The Black Watch (firing, standing)	1	0
16	East Kent Regiment	1	0
17	Somersetshire Regiment	1	0
18	Worcestershire Regiment	1	0
36	Royal Sussex Regiment	1	0
76	Middlesex Regiment	1	0
110	Devonshire Regiment (khaki)	1	0
113	East Yorkshire Regiment	1	0
119	Gloucestershire Regiment (khaki)	1	0
121	Royal West Surrey Regiment	1	0
104	City Imperial Volunteers	1	0
30	Drums and Bugles of the Line	1	0
27	Band of the Line	2	0
96	York and Lancaster Regiment	1	0

Royal Navy.

No.		s.	d.
79	Landing Party with Gun	2	6
78	Bluejackets	1	0
80	Whitejackets	1	0
97	Royal Marine Light Infantry	1	0
35	Royal Marine Artillery	1	0
	4·7 Naval Gun	2	0

Types of the British Army:

No.		s.	d.
73	Containing the Royal Horse Artillery, 2nd Life Guards, 17th Lancers, Royal Welsh Fusiliers, Scots Greys, Band of the Line, The Gordon Highlanders, and General Officer	25	0
93	Containing complete company of Coldstream Guards, with Officers, Full Band, Colours and Pioneers, and a Squadron of Royal Horse Guards	12	0
29	Containing Mule Battery, 1st Life Guards, 3rd Hussars, 9th Lancers, and Royal West Surrey Regiment	7	0
21	Containing 1st Life Guards, 11th Hussars, West India Regiment, and East Kent Regiment	4	0
22	Containing Royal Horse Guards, 5th Lancers, The Black Watch, and Worcestershire Regiment	4	0
102	Containing the Grenadier, Coldstream, Scots, and Irish Guards	4	0
53	Containing Horse Guards, 4th Hussars, and Grenadier Guards	3	0
54	Containing 1st Life Guards, 2nd Dragoon Guards, and 9th Lancers	3	0
55	Containing 2nd Dragoons, 3rd Hussars, and 16th Lancers	3	0
89	Containing the Cameron Highlanders, in three positions (firing)	3	0
90	Containing the Coldstream Guards in three positions (firing)	3	0
40	Containing 1st Dragoons, Royal and Somersetshire Light Infantry	2	0
41	Containing 2nd Dragoons (Scots Greys) and Grenadier Guards	2	0
42	Containing 1st Life Guards, and Royal Sussex Regiment	2	0
50	Containing 1st Life Guards, and 4th Hussars	2	0
51	Containing 11th Hussars, and 16th Lancers	2	0
56	Containing Grenadier Guards, and East Kent Regiment	2	0
59	Containing the 2nd Dragoons (Scots Greys)	2	0
88	Containing the Seaforth Highlanders and Pipers	2	0

No.	**Indian Army:**	s.	d.
61	The 3rd Madras Cavalry	3	0
60	The 1st Bombay Lancers	3	0
62	The 1st Bengal Cavalry	2	0
63	The 10th Bengal Lancers	2	0
64	The 2nd Madras Lancers, and 7th Bengal Infantry	2	0
45	The 3rd Madras Cavalry	1	0
46	The 10th Bengal Lancers	1	0
47	The 1st Bengal Cavalry	1	0
66	The 1st Bombay Lancers	1	0
67	The 1st Madras Native Infantry	1	0
68	The 2nd Bombay Native Infantry	1	0
123	The Bikanir Camel Corps	1	0

No.	**Egyptian Army:**	s.	d.
48	Camel Corps	2	0
115	Egyptian Cavalry	1	0
116	Soudanese Infantry	1	0
117	Egyptian Infantry	1	0

No.	**Colonials:**	s.	d.
19	West India Regiment	1	0
49	South Australian Lancers	1	0
38	South African Mounted Infantry	1	0

No.	**Miscellaneous:**	s.	d
6	Boer Cavalry	1	0
26	Boer Infantry	1	0
91	American Infantry	1	0
92	Spanish Infantry	1	0
71	Turkish Cavalry	1	0

Inherent commercial probability

When a complete explanation is unavailable, we must take a guess at what went on and why, a guess based on commercial expediency – on what was the easiest way of solving the problem at the time.

A simple example concerns strange arms attached to soldiers. This may reasonably be assumed to result from a temporary shortage of an arm casting combined with an urgent order, for which 'these will do' – something that happens in the best regulated enterprises. Indeed, it is greatly to Britains' credit that such 'wrong arms' are so rare.

I call this factor 'Inherent Commercial Probability' (ICP), and whenever I make a guess on this basis I indicate (ICP) in brackets.

One other general problem is an example of ICP: namely the use of catalogue illustrations. Britains tended to use the same illustrations year after year, long after the version shown in the engraving had been superseded. These engravings were expensive; using the same ones saved money and hardly mattered in the days before the Trade Descriptions Act (ICP).

Catalogues

The main source from which the 'company policy' of Britains can be deduced is the catalogues. The earliest catalogue of which I know is a list inserted into boxes in about 1902. Unfortunately, during our period Britains did not date its catalogues, and so a probable date has to be inferred from the figures appearing in them. The '1902' listing includes sets up to number 126. The date embossed on the team of horses in this set is 1.11.1901, which thus supports the 1902 dating. A similar but slightly longer list including the Russo-Japanese sets exists for 1904. The 1902 list is illustrated on this page.

Recent reprints of the toy soldier pages in Gamages' Christmas catalogues for 1902, 1906 and 1913 are most helpful, since, although the name Britains does not appear, the sets illustrated are recognizably Britains and use the company's numbering system. Every set included in these catalogues must have been current in those years. The reverse does not apply, however: non-appearance of a set does not necessarily mean it was not available, since Gamages did not take the entire Britains' range.

The highest set number in the next Britains' catalogue that has come to light is 161. The 'latest additions' shown on the front cover of the catalogue are Territorials and Boy Scouts, the latter dated 20.7.1909. This list must therefore date from the 1909 Christmas season or from 1910.

Left: Top part of Britains' 1902 leaflet list, showing all the standard-size sets then on offer. The list was completed with the smaller-size sets.

The company itself reprinted the magnificent 16¾-by 11-inch (42 by 28cm) 20-page catalogue from which many engravings are reproduced in this book. As usual the original is undated. At first Britains claimed that this was its 1905 catalogue, but it contains Boy Scouts, and that organization was only founded in 1908. Britains then made a further guess – 1910 – printing an apology on the back page. But the latest number in this catalogue is 191. The highest number in Gamages' 1913 catalogue is 167, and Gamages usually took all Britains' new lines, even if it did not stock the entire range. The balance of probability is thus that this large catalogue dates from 1914 or even 1915, and throughout this book I refer to it as the '1915' catalogue.

To confuse matters further, a half-size reprint of this '1915' catalogue exists, marked 1908 on the front cover and overprinted in the space provided for the retailer 'THE PUFFIN'S PERCH', Alberta. This reprint made me think for some time that the catalogue did indeed date from 1908 and that Britains had listed items 158 to 191 from its future production plans, so that the catalogue would last for some time. This now seems to me unlikely, as retailers would have found it difficult to explain to the public that forthcoming items were listed, and I believe that the '1908' marking on the catalogue is as modern as the retailer's name.

A recently found list of new lines dated 1916 announces sets 192, 193 and 194, and a separately discovered full listing goes up to 197, together with the garrison-mounted 18-inch Howitzer. Many collectors believe that this full listing is post-war, as it quotes some lines 'held up by the war'. But one of these is the Royal Flying Corps, and since the RFC became the RAF in 1918 it probably dates from late 1916, because for most of 1916 to 1918 Britains was manufacturing shrapnel balls. As another pointer, in the list in question prices are marked up 75 per cent on 1914; in 1916 the Retail Price Index had risen 62.2 per cent over January 1914 and was still increasing, whereas by 1918/19 the price rise was over 120 per cent, which makes 1916 more likely still.

The next catalogue I know of dates from 1926 at the earliest, since it refers to a court case concerning piracy of Britains' farm animals by the Pixyland Toy Company which was settled on 18 December 1925. The highest military number listed here is 224, only 27 higher than in 1916, although the Hunting series and Racing Colours, which have slightly later numbers, are also included. This may seem slow progress, but since 1918 Britains had had to restart production and restock all its outlets, and between 1919 and 1922 developed and produced the Home Farm series, which required well over 100 new master figures.

The 1931 catalogue shows far more items, many exported to the USA. Britains was also willing to manufacture boxes to any price and specification for the trade, or even for individual customers. Britains may well have done this before but not included the boxes in its main numbering system. Certainly, not all the numbers that the factory allocated to different sets

No. 102. Types of the British Army.

No. 53. Types of the British Army.

No. 3. 5th Dragoon Guards (Princess Charlotte of Wales), 1/-

No. 22. Types of the British Army.

actually appeared in the catalogue.

After 1930, the compilation and issuing of catalogues became much more systematic, and between them collectors probably own all of them. Much research remains to be done, however, since in 1950 Britains issued what it called its 105th catalogue – which implies more than one catalogue a year since the firm started in business in about 1850 (let alone since toy soldiers were first catalogued in 1898), given that no catalogues were issued in the last years of each World War.

Each year Britains also issued one or more leaflets describing that year's new lines. Whether these announced extra items or merely extracted new items from the catalogue for retailers' convenience is not known. Nor, if Britains' post-1945 record is anything to go by, would many of the lines announced at the beginning of the year be ready for sale by the Christmas season. If these 'New Lines' lists could be collected, they might give a good idea of the company's activities each year.

The most helpful catalogues are those that illustrate set interiors, since they help us to establish set contents. Most pre-1939 catalogues illustrate only a very small proportion of items. The exception is the large '1915' catalogue, which contains high-quality engravings of the vast majority of sets from which the specific version of each figure can be identified. Most of these illustrations, however, show the first version of the set concerned. An illustration was probably commissioned when the set was first issued and was then reused in every subsequent catalogue (ICP), regardless of the changes made to individual figures in the set. Thus page 3 shows sets 102 and 53, both of which contain a row of Grenadier Guards firing. Set 53, brought out in 1896, is illustrated with a bemedalled officer, while set 102, which dates from 1899, is illustrated with a wasp-waisted officer; for both there are illustrations of the old volley-firing Guardsman rather than the improved figure substituted in about 1901.

This supposition is not totally consistent, however. For instance, the illustration on page 7 of set 3, the 5th Dragoon Guards, shows the head-up trotting horse dated 12.12.1902, and the Black Watch, set 11, is shown with the 1903 figure. Yet set 22, which also contained a row of Black Watch, is shown as it appeared originally in 1894, complete with germanic Horse Guards and cross-legged Lancers. It is much more likely that Britains used old illustrations rather than making up some display sets of early figures. Occasionally there were genuine mistakes: for example, the illustration of set 84 of the '1915' catalogue purports to contain 2nd Life Guards, whereas it clearly shows Hussars. All in all, the point to remember is that nothing should be taken for granted when you look at a catalogue.

Illustrations from the 1915 catalogue, showing some of the inconsistencies mentioned in the text above. These illustrations are typical of the toy catalogues of the day. The top two are to be found on page 3 of the 1915 catalogue, the third on page 7 and the fourth on page 3 again.

Chapter 6
Figure design and set presentation

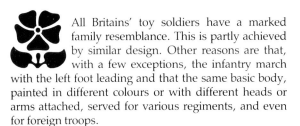

All Britains' toy soldiers have a marked family resemblance. This is partly achieved by similar design. Other reasons are that, with a few exceptions, the infantry march with the left foot leading and that the same basic body, painted in different colours or with different heads or arms attached, served for various regiments, and even for foreign troops.

This was simple commercial common sense. Reusing a few basic figures saved an enormous amount of design time. Even so, Britains did not do this to anything like the same extent as Heyde of Dresden, the most prolific German exporter of toy soldiers, whose catalogue stated:

The soldiers in size 2 can be supplied in the uniforms of all regiments of whatever military organized nation of the world. This does, however, by no means exclude that we are able, by means of our well stocked assortment of various forms and moulds, to satisfy any justified requirements of our customers, as regards soldiers manufactured in all other sizes.

Britains' portrayal of troops of different nationalities, by contrast, was much more conscientious, and it was quite ready, for instance, to change the style of rifles or horse furniture to make the figures look right. Naturally, in achieving an overall Britains 'look' it helped a great deal that William Britain carried out all the design work, or at least supervised it. The end result was a consistent output that enables collectors then and now to recognize the Britains' style at a glance

As has been noted, Britains made a great virtue of the fact that all its troops were produced in a standard scale (54mm), and it regularly pushed this fact in its publicity. This was indeed the case, and the exceptions, mainly the B and W series, made up only a small proportion of total production.

The chief basic figures on which the different sets were based are listed in the Figure Type and Sequence Glossary (pages 169–78).

Methods of presentation

In presenting its sets, Britains normally followed a number of 'rules', and it is useful to bear these in mind when examining sets. The following 'rules' apply to standard-size first-grade sets.

Number of pieces Britains was very methodical about this and by 1900 had established a set pattern. There were five cavalry, eight movable-arm infantry or ten fixed-arm

infantry to a single-row box. The extra labour involved in assembling movable arms was compensated by including two fewer figures. Since the vast majority of infantry did in fact have movable arms, the usual number in a single-row box was eight.

Make-up Sets normally had seven identical figures and an officer. If an officer required a brand-new casting, eight identical infantrymen were sometimes used, eg set 212 Royal Scots and set 213 Highland Light Infantry. Sometimes there were variations – a pioneer or a musician might be included. If including extras was simple, because castings already existed or only simple arm changes were required, then Britains often took the opportunity to offer special value. Thus before the First World War Indian Infantry sets 67 and 68 and set 76, the Middlesex Regiment, included a pioneer. Sets of fixed-arm figures were well supplied with extras, some of which had movable arms. Set 16 Buffs on Guard, for instance, boasted officer, drummer and bugler.

Cavalry sets These normally had four identical figures and an officer. Often the officer was the same casting

with different paint and a different arm; or a trumpeter would be used if an officer required a different casting. To vary the make-up of cavalry sets, troopers' horses were frequently painted different colours in pairs: eg sets 12 and 13, 11th and 3rd Hussars. Naturally this could not be done when regimental horses were in reality all one matched colour, as with the Household Cavalry (black) or the 2nd Dragoon Guards (bay). Occasionally, the horses that carried two pairs of troopers were on different castings; this happened with the early Middlesex Yeomanry, set 83.

SET 83, MIDDLESEX YEOMANRY, FIRST VERSION
Until c.1928, the first-version set had a mixture of troopers' horses, here three donkey horses and one rocking horse. Normally there would have been two of each. The britches have a carefully painted double red stripe. This is the highest set number I know of issued without the set number printed on the label. (Phillips, London)

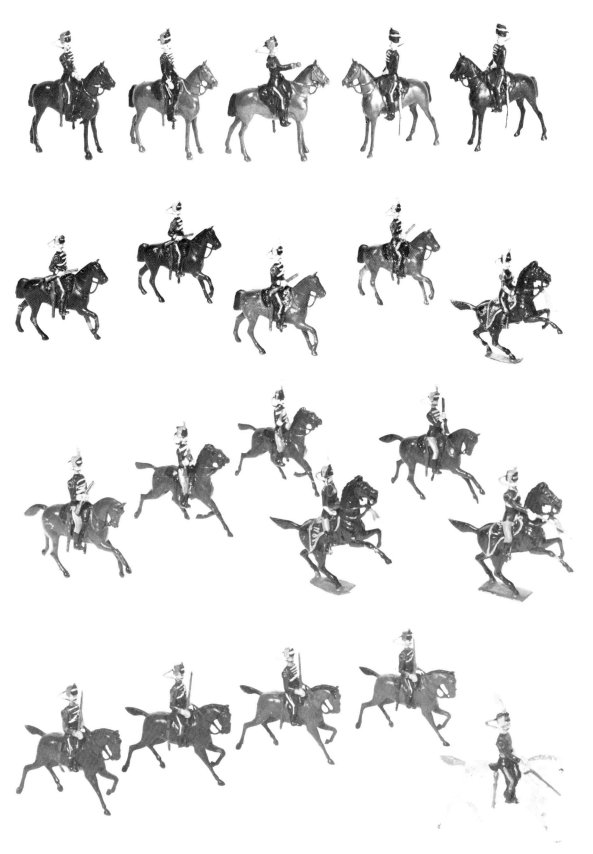

Large sets Known as display sets in the catalogue listings, these were usually two- or three-row boxes made up of a combination of single-row sets. There were mixed displays (eg set 55, which contained sets 13, 32 and 33) and multiples of the same set (eg set 60, which consisted of three rows of set 66). In the multiple display sets there was often some variation in each row; thus set 60 contained an officer and a trumpeter. Much larger sets had more variations or extra quantities of the same figure. Rows of seven cavalry or fourteen infantry were the most common (see pages 96–7 for set 73).

Variations in set size During the 1930s, the ten-man fixed-arm infantry sets were reduced to nine and then to eight men, presumably to increase profits, or at least maintain them in the face of increasing production costs. In many cases, the rows of fourteen in the large display cases were reduced to twelve at about the same time.

'Sets' of nine or eight fixed-arm figures that seem for other reasons to date from before 1933 are probably missing one or more figures.

The B series smaller-size sets, which also have best-quality paint, are made up with the same consistency. The standard box contained four cavalry or seven infantry, a formula that apparently enabled Britains to sell them at exactly half the price of the standard-size sets. The few display sets in the range were also multiples of the single-row sets.

In the A, W and other second-grade series, set size was not nearly so rigid. In the early X series, six cavalry or twelve infantry seem to have been normal. In the A series, boxes usually consisted of six cavalry or nine infantry, in the W series four cavalry or six infantry. During the late 1920s, however, so many new sizes were tried out that in the second grade a basic box size could hardly be said to exist any longer. In the best quality, by contrast, basic sizes still predominated.

SETS OF HUSSARS (See also Chapter 18.)
Top row: Set 315, 10th Hussars, c.1935. This set was at the halt, and was first produced in 1929. All the troopers had empty hands, painted flesh colour, but the officer had brown gloves.
Second row: Set 13, 3rd Hussars, c.1903. This set normally had troopers mounted on the donkey horse, the first version, or on the cantering horse dated 12.2.1903, the second version. This variation finds them mounted on the Scots Grey horse dated 1.11.1902. Another variation is on pony horses.
Third row: Set 12, 11th Hussars. Front right are two prancing-horse officers: the first version, and then the second, which is a remodelling of the first version to include a movable arm and a square base. Both have throat plumes. The second version is rare as it was only issued with the set c.1906-10. Second and third from the left are first-version troopers on donkey horses, but the paint style is so similar to the second-version troopers shown first and fourth that this might be an unusual example of a set c.1903 containing a mixture.
Bottom row: Set 99, 13th Hussars, first version on pony horses. Note how the troopers' horses have a moulded prick ear, which is absent from the officer's horse. This version is rare, only being issued from 1899 to 1903. (All Phillips, London)

Chapter 7
Identification markings underneath figures

 While Britains was establishing its new line of toy soldiers, it was too busy to worry about identifying their origin. Soon, however, like all successful businesses, Britains attracted plenty of competition. Ex-employees who had learnt the technique of hollowcasting set up in back rooms all around east London. Rather than make new models, many of these small new concerns copied or adapted Britains' own.

Under existing copyright law, Britains could bring an action for piracy against a competitor so long as each of their own models was signed and dated. From 1900 onwards, therefore, each figure bore the name Wm Britain Jnr and showed the date on which the master figure had been made.

The first dated figure, dated 1.6.1900, was set 105, the Imperial Yeomanry. When, inevitably, this figure was copied, Britains brought test cases against several manufacturers (see page 27), winning easily. Britains' style of mould was thus effectively protected, and competitors had to start from scratch.

TABLE OF DATED FIGURES

Date	Type of figure: Example	Illustration on page:row:figure
1.6.1900	* City Imperial Volunteer on guard	121
1.6.1900	* City Imperial Volunteer, officer with sword and pistol	121
1.6.1900	Imperial Yeomanry, fixed-arm, trot	120
1.1.1901	4th Hussar, one-eared full-stretch horse at gallop	33:3:2
20.1.1901	* Slade Wallace equipment figure, Dublin Fusilier	117:2:8
20.1.1901	* Box-pack Highlander marching, Gordon Highlander	77:1:11
20.1.1901	* Attention figure, Grenadier Guard	69:2:1
1.2.1901	* Small-size Edward VII, gilt (paper label only)	64
1.2.1901	* Miniature Life Guard (paper label only)	61:1:1
1.2.1901	* Small-size running infantry, Grenadier Guard	69:1:14
1.7.1901	* Standing firing, Coldstream Guard	69:1:6
1.7.1901	* Lying firing, Coldstream Guard	69:1:9
1.7.1901	* Highlanders firing, Gordon Highlanders	77:3:13
1.7.1901	* Officers with Binoculars, standing, Black Watch	77:2:1
1.7.1901	Officer with Binoculars, kneeling, Gordon	77:3:9
1.7.1901	* Standing firing with puttees, Gloucestershire Regiment	117:3:8
1.8.1901	Bust of King Edward VII	64
1.11.1901	Small-size Artillery Team Horse	116
1.2.1902	Bust of Queen Alexandra	64
4.7.1902	Miniature Hussar officer	61:3:2
4.7.1902	Miniature Lancer officer	61:4:1

Date	Type of figure: Example	Illustration on page:row:figure
1.11.1902	'Scots Grey' walking horse	52:2:3
12.12.1902	Head-up trotting horse, 5th Dragoon Guards	49:2:4
12.2.1903	Cantering horse, 11th Hussar	53:3:3
18.8.1903	Horse at the halt, 5th Irish Lancer	57:2:1
17.12.1903	Charging Highlander, Black Watch	77:4:5
16.1.1904	* Charging Japanese	124:4:1
16.1.1904	* Russian Infantry	124:2:1
26.4.1904	Small-size head-up walking horse, 1st Dragoon Guard	49:1:7
9.5.1904	Small-size galloping horse, Scots Grey	52:4:7
4.7.1904	Small-size Hussar at halt, 11th	33:4:1
25.7.1904	Small-size trotting horse, Life Guard	44:1:8
11.8.1904	Small-size walking horse, tail down, 1st Dragoon Guard	49:1:4
26.8.1904	Small-size Lancer at Walk, 17th	57:1:7
7.9.1904	Footballers	149
7.9.1904	Russian Cossack	124:3:3
20.3.1905	Royal Army Medical Corps (various types)	112
20.3.1905	* French Matelots (paper label only)	132:2:4
9.5.1905	Fixed-arm French Officer	128
9.5.1905	French Infantérie, full-trouser or gaitered	128
9.5.1905	French Zouave charging	132:2:7
9.5.1905	Second date on French Cavalry, French Cuirassier	132:3:2

Date	Type of figure: Example	Illustration on page:row:figure
1.8.1905	Box-pack Infantry marching at the slope, Fusilier	84
16.11.1905	Gaitered officer marching, Fusilier	84
14.3.1906	Team horse walking, collar harness, Royal Field Artillery	89
26.3.1906	Bust of General Booth	—
3.5.1906	Salvation Army (various types)	148
23.5.1906	Zulu (this was the last original figure issued with an oval base)	105
15.6.1906	US Style on guard, Boer	117:1:6
15.6.1906	US Style shoulder arms, Boer	117:1:7
7.5.1907	Alfred Britain's Hussar at halt	64
13.6.1907	Alfred Britain's Hussar at walk	64
1.7.1907	Alfred Britain's riderless horse	64
12.11.1907	North American Indian on foot, on guard	157
12.11.1907	North American Indian Chief with tomahawk	157
12.11.1907	Royal Naval Volunteer Reserve, shoulder arms	88:4:9
12.11.1907	Petty Officer, walking, movable arm	88:4:12
6.2.1908	North American Indian, mounted full gallop	157
16.2.1908	Prussian Infantry, rectangular base	133
16.2.1908	Prussian Officer, rectangular base	133
16.2.1908	Second date on Prussian Hussar	133
15.6.1908	Railway staff, porters, guard etc	—
1.8.1908	Railway staff, engine driver, stoker	149
19.8.1908	Chauffeur	—
1.10.1908	Civilians and Policeman, arms behind back	148
8.12.1908	Movable-arm Bass-Drummer	72
18.3.1909	French Officer with blanket roll	128
20.7.1909	Boy Scout, on patrol	149

Date	Type of figure: Example	Illustration on page:row:figure
19.8.1909	Scoutmaster	148
19.10.1909	Officer on Prancing Horse, new model, Life Guard	44:4:3
17.1.1910	Standing on-guard Infantry, Royal West Surrey Regiment	81:1:12
24.2.1910	'1910' marching figure without pack, Royal Sussex Regiment	81:3:4
9.5.1910	Head-level spindly horse officer	—
9.5.1910	Head-up spindly horse officer	—
1.6.1910	Paris office 'Infantérie de Ligne à Grande Tenue'	128
1.8.1910	Kneeling Boy Scout	148
1.12.1910	Tree and gate to go with Scouts	149
20.2.1911	Boy Scout signaller	149
23.3.1911	Fixed-arm Boy Scout, later numbered 29c	148
1.5.1911	Movable-arm infantry bandsman, Coldstream Guards	72
17.7.1911	Mounted Arab	109
6.3.1912	Highland Piper, Seaforth Highlander	77:1:2
8.4.1912	Small-size Highlander in full dress, Cameron Highlander	77:2:8
18.4.1912	Improved small-size marching sailor	88:3:4
1.7.1912	Small-size French Infantry at the trail	132:1:9
1.7.1912	Small-size 'German' Infantry at the slope	132:1:3
27.7.1912	Bersaglieri	133
9.9.1912	Small-size French infantry in kepi, slope	132:1:6

* These figures were also issued with paper labels bearing the same date.

The table above and opposite lists all the dates that appeared under Britains' figures, in so far as I have been able to discover them. The date is listed in the first column, followed in the second by the figure first issued with that date. The third column indicates where the figure is illustrated. Only one example of each basic figure is given with each date. The other figures made from the same type are listed in the Figure Type and Sequence Glossary (pages 169–78).

Figures were normally dated with raised lettering under the belly of the horse on mounted figures or under the base of foot figures. In order, presumably, to gain rapid copyright protection, paper labels were stuck on the bases of a number of figures, although most of these models were later produced with embossed bases. Both paper labels and embossing carried one date for each style of figure, and this date remained the same no matter how many different heads or arms were used. Curiously,

paper labels used the style of dating '1st Feb 1901', while the embossed equivalent read '1.2.1901'. On some foreign cavalry figures, whose horses were remodelled to show continental equipment, both the date of the original model and the date of the modification were shown.

Dating of figures continued until the Copyright Act of 1911 came into effect, after which it was sufficient only to name models to prove origin. From 1913 onwards, no

new models were dated by Britains, but of course until new moulds were made production figures continued to show dates, frequently until well into the 1920s. One double-dated figure was even used for a new Life Guard officer in about 1954, and the dates 12.2.1903 and 9.5.1905 on the belly of the horse indicate that this figure was modified for the French market in 1905.

From the collector's point of view, it is sad that dating was discontinued, since it gives us a point of origin for each new model. Dated figures are an interesting sub-group of figures to collect. It must be remembered, however, that:

1 Models created before 1900 but still in production between 1900 and 1925 (eg Lancer officer turned in the saddle) were never dated.

2 Dated figures were only used as they were introduced.

3 Therefore only a proportion of the production in any given year is dated.

4 New models introduced from 1913 onwards were not dated.

5 New moulds made after 1912 for previously dated figures were not dated.

6 A dated figure could have been produced at any time from the date itself until about 1925.

7 It is not known what time elapsed between the date on the figure and the actual arrival of the figure in the shops. A rough idea can be formed from the fact that all the figures dated May 1906 appear in Gamages' 1906 catalogue. It would seem likely that figures dated later than July in a year would be made in preparation for the next year's trade fair season in January.

As the glue dried out, paper labels dropped off easily. Sometimes the clean circular patch they left behind on the base of the figures can be seen. There are no set dates between which paper labels were used. Most likely (ICP), they appeared only on figures for which there was considerable demand and for which insufficient engraved dated moulds were available. This tended to happen most often between 1900 and 1905, although I do possess some standing firing square-base figures with paper labels. The latest figure to bear a paper label was the Matelot, set 143.

Other base stamps

Before dating began, Britains' figures had no stamp at all. After the First World War, normally all the company's figures were marked 'Britains Proprietors Copyright'. Models for export were also stamped 'Made in Great Britain' at first, later 'Made in England'. The export stamp was sometimes the reverse way up from the rest of the lettering. Some of the stamps, the one under the oval-base Highlander for instance, are very elegant.

Kneeling figures without bases always caused problems. After our period, little metal 'Made in England' tags were cast on these and some other figures in the mould to make them comply with US import requirements. The tags could then be broken off before the toys were played with. Experiments were also made with embossing the word 'England' up the inside forearm.

Models either made in Britains' Paris works, or made in England for export to France, had the word *déposé* embossed on the base or on the horse's belly. When the Paris Office closed in 1923, many of the moulds must have returned to London to produce *déposé* embossed bases for many more years. In fact figures made in France can be identified more easily from their style of paintwork. (See also pages 162–3.)

The zinc alloy models made after the Second World War had no lettering on their bases, although they were otherwise the same as the standard lead figures.

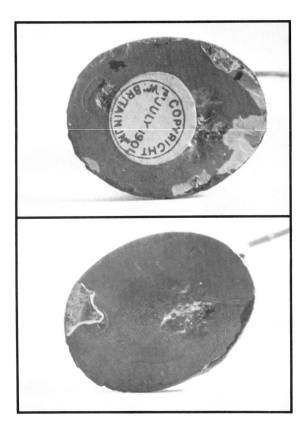

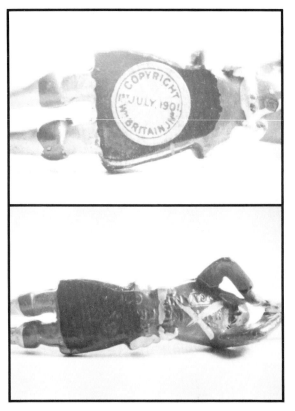

Top Left: Underneath of an oval base, showing the paper label with the date '1st July 1901'. Curiously, paper labels used this style, while the embossed equivalent always read '1.7.1901'. Bottom left: A similar oval base showing a faint impression where a paper label was once stuck. These faint impressions establish which sets were issued with labels on them.

Top centre: Underside of a lying firing Gordon Highlander showing the paper label identical with that stuck on the oval base top left. There was so little room to stick a paper label on the kneeling figures that they rarely have them, or else they all fell off much more easily. Bottom centre: The same version as at the top, but from an engraved mould.

Top right: Underside of a square base. Most so-called square bases are rectangular, but for simplicity most collectors call them square, as they have squared-off corners. Early square bases often had embossing in an oval pattern. Below right: 'Made in England' has been added to the embossing for this square base, the other way up from the rest of the lettering.

Chapter 8
Heads and arms

Heads

Britains quite often took advantage of the fact that the three-part mould made it easy to put different heads on the same body. Differences in heads fall into two distinct categories: there can be different heads on figures meant to represent the same model; and different heads on the same body, intended to turn one model into another.

Many different head shapes can be discovered on identical body shapes from the early, experimental, period of production. Early Foot Guards, Life Guards, Infantry of the Line and Highlanders in foreign-service dress are examples. Some of these heads are flatter than others, some smaller, some more pointed.

Foot Guards heads are probably the most varied type. Some have plumes moulded on the left of the bearskin, others on the right; still others have no plumes at all. Theoretically, those with the plume on the left should be Grenadiers or Welsh Guards, whereas those with the plume on the right should be Coldstreams or Irish Guards and those with none at all Scots Guards. However, Guards with heads moulded with a plume on the right are quite often found with a white plume painted in on the left, thus representing a Grenadier. The shape of the bearskin also alters quite markedly between the marching and firing figures.

Infantry of the Line produced before the First World War fall into three distinct types: the very early 'flat' head, the small pointed head and the medium-sized standard head. At about the time of the First World War, Infantry of the Line heads appear to have been made larger, like those of Hussars and Sailors. When the box-pack figure was introduced in 1905, Fusilier heads became larger. So the general rule is: the smaller the head, the earlier the figure. The increase in head size matches the increase from the early 52mm models to the standard 54mm.

Highlanders in foreign-service dress wear the foreign-service dress helmet with a pugaree wound round it, giving the hat a three-tiered appearance. This was also worn by the officer of the West India Regiment (set 19), the Royal Lancasters (set 148), the Mountain Artillery (set 28) and the Boer War Infantry sets of Dublin Fusiliers (set 109), the Devonshire Regiment (set 110) and the Gloucestershire Regiment (set 119). However, early sets of Camerons (set 114), Dublins (set 109) and Devons (set 110) appeared first in smooth foreign-service helmets, that is without the pugaree, as did early officers for the sets of Highlanders firing.

Movable arms

Arms that could be moved to different positions on the mould seem to have been another Britains' innovation – at least as far as mass-produced figures are concerned. Early experiments included plug-shoulder figures of cavalry: Lancers (see pages 40 and 56) and Scots Greys (see page 38). In these figures a plug attached to the arm to be moved was inserted into a hole that went right through the shoulders. As this method is more suited to solid than hollowcast figures, it probably originated in Germany.

The plug hand was another early experiment: hands holding different weapons and mounted on plugs could be inserted into holes in the cuffs of arms. This method was used for the early large-size Fusiliers and for the first Highlander figures (both page 40). The Highlanders had rifles, the officers swords. Once again, this method seems typically German.

Britains probably introduced its standard method in 1896 as an improvement over fixed-arm figures, which simply had both arms incorporated into the mould and were therefore immobile. Movable arms were cast separately from the figures to which they were to be attached. They were cast with a loop at the shoulder end that slipped over a stud-like projection from the appropriate shoulder of the main figure. The metal of the stud was flattened with a hot tool so that its end spread outwards to grip the shoulder loop of the arm.

Although this innovation was widely welcomed, as it resulted in more play value, the fixing method was never entirely satisfactory and often led, after some play, to 'loose arms' (a term meaning that an arm comes off a figure easily). Britains tried various experiments to rectify this fault, and on the cavalry figures the fixing became quite good; a wide lip held the arm in place, and a tool with a centre punching action was used to spread the lip in a circular fashion. Thus early cavalry figures (those

INFANTRY OF THE LINE BANDSMEN WITH DIFFERENT-SHAPED HEADS
On the left is probably the earliest shape of head, c.1895, a rather flattish shape without very much detail. On the right is the next type of head, rather small, probably in use c.1897-1903. Next, centre left, comes a much better shape of head, this one dating from c.1910, followed finally by the slightly larger standard head, c.1920, centre right. Infantry of the Line bands certainly look best if made up of figures all with the same type of head, although genuine mixtures have been known to leave Britains' factory.

dating from before about 1900) have a different style of shoulder, the projection being finished off with a tool that left a striped effect on the metal. (The two different methods are quite well seen in the 17th Lancers from box 73, page 97.)

Infantry figures changed very little, the stud-like projection becoming a little more generous. The arms often had a groove under the loop so that it could be tightened with small padded pliers. Sometimes the arms were put on before the paint, and so on mint models the arm is often fixed in place by the paint.

As well as the models to which they were fixed, arms were also often changed, and establishing which arm is on a particular model can be another clue about when that model was made. Normally, only one type of arm was used for a particular set at a particular time, although there were sometimes inconsistencies.

Normally a set is not considered matched unless all the figures have the same arm. The only exceptions I know, apart from when the composition of the set calls for a mixture, are during the changeover from the 1930s to the 1950s pattern arm at the slope. Some sets produced at this time have been observed mint in their original boxes with figures having some of each type of arm. This happened during 1948–9.

In some cases, particularly foreign infantry, sets have been completely fitted with abnormal arms. There are also some sets – eg Russian, Spanish, Bulgarian and Montenegrin Infantry – in which slope or trail arms, or a mixture of the two, might be used. However, I cannot recall any cavalry set in which the four troopers have not had the same arms.

All in all, any mixture of arms should give pause for thought.

Opposite: **Armology**
To describe arms, collectors use a group of shortened expressions whereby the arms are defined by the weapon they carry. For example, an arm with a hand carrying a rifle is called a 'rifle arm', a pair of arms carrying a musical instrument is called 'instrument arms', and an arm where the hand is empty is called an 'empty arm'.

'Armology' is very useful in dating and matching figures. Remember, however, that new arms only came into use gradually, and sets that one might expect to be equipped with later arms can still possess arms of an earlier style.

A *Left to right are shown: cavalry trumpet arm; arm for base drummer; ramrod arm, as used on gunners in sets 148 and 149; arm with tomahawk; arm with an empty hand; arm with pistol from cowboy figure.*

After the Second World War, Britains allowed Hamleys, the celebrated London toyshop, to stock spare unpainted arms, and from the 1930s Britains had also supplied them to anyone who wrote requesting them. In consequence there exist quite a large number of arms that are genuine but have never been used on a figure. All these date from after our period.

B *Top is shown the later 'trail arm' with the rifle at the trail, and, beneath it, the earlier type, in which the magazine is in front of the trigger guard. The change occurred c.1912.*

C *The rifle arm on the left belongs to a US figure. The arm in the centre, with its baggy sleeve, comes from the Evzone figure. The gun on the right, shorn of its arm, belongs to the early at-attention figure and can claim to be the most attractive model rifle produced by Britains.*

D *The first four arms on the left show the normal sequence of rifle arms 'at the slope' with bayonets fixed. Left to right: early 'loose-sling' rifle arm; 'tight-sling' arm c.1920; standard 1930s rifle flat to the shoulder, in contrast with the first two, which are*

edge-on; late pattern rifle used from c.1952 until production ceased. In this last view little change is evident, but seen from the front the bayonet sticks out to the side. This sequence can be seen from a front view in the illustration of a 'company' of Fusiliers on pages 84–5.

The last two arms in this group show the early and late rifle types without bayonet, with loose and then tight sling. This was the only change made to rifle arms without bayonets fixed through the whole course of Britains' production, and took place c.1920. All the arms in this group were initially designed to be used with British Army models, although they were used on many other models as well.

E *Sword arms. The furthest left is the early type, with a thick blade. Above it and to the right is shown the normal type produced after the First World War. The sword arm to the extreme right was used for the French Cuirassiers and for some other foreign cavalry. Below it is the 'outstretched' sword arm. This one was for infantry officers; the cavalry type had a different wrist position, illustrated for instance on page 140, 3rd row, figs 1 and 4. The centre arm in the bottom row is a 'long-carbine' arm with the top of the shoulder loop missing, a common fault in 'second-hand' arms; the long carbine was introduced for cavalry*

figures c.1912. Above it is an arm with the rifle shouldered; this is outside our period and was only introduced with set 1858. The position of the rifle is known as 'slung' and should not be confused with the drill position of shouldered arms, in which the rifle is carried tucked into the side (see page 117, top row, fig 7) or at the slope, as in group D.

F *Lance arms. The two on the left are for Lancers at the canter, the three on the right for Lancers at the halt. The difference is in the pennon, which flies at the canter and droops at the halt. For some reason Britains always cut its lances at the halt a little shorter than those made for moving lancers.*

The lance is made in three pieces: the arm, which has a hole through the hand; the wire lance shaft; and the head and pennon, which is a separate casting fixed to the end of the wire. A separate lance head can be seen on the far right. Lance arms for lancers on the move were produced in two main types. The first, as shown here, was somewhat crude, with a thinner, flatter and longer head to the lance than the later type. The wire of the lance ran right up the arm and emerged at the elbow. In the later type, introduced with set 128 in 1903, the hand has a gauntlet, the forearm is at a different angle, and the wire emerges through the cuff of the gauntlet.

Close-up of a curious 17th Lancer in 'Ulundi' foreign-service dress from set 81. It seems as though part of the helmet has not been properly moulded. Rather than being rejected at that stage, the casting has been sent to the paint shop and been painted up as normal, except that, since half the helmet is missing, the **inside** *of the hollowcast head has been painted white, which to the casual glance makes it seem as though the model is intact. It is just possible that this is not original Britains' paint, but close examination has not revealed any overpainting. A fault on this scale is very unusual to find, as Britains' quality control was usually excellent.*

A

B

C

D

E

F

21

Chapter 9
Painting

An examination of the paintwork will reveal to within a few years the date when a Britains figure was manufactured. The illustrations in this book show the variety of paint styles used during the first 40 years of Britains' toy soldiers, plus, by way of contrast, a few later examples.

Throughout the period covered by this book, Britains prepared its own paint from pigments and varnishes, and its staff painted all the figures on the premises. Only after the Second World War was ready-mixed paint obtained from outside suppliers; it was not until then, too, that the company started to employ outworkers to paint its models.

Best-quality paintwork was of a high standard right from the start. Faces were fully painted in flesh colour, and eyes, moustache and cheeks were painted on top; hair was painted at the base of the helmet. Eyebrows were also often painted in, although only full-dress Highlanders and the Royal Navy could be certain of receiving them. Very early paint seems to have contained less varnish than later, or possibly coarser pigment. The result was a rather matt finish, accentuated by age if the paint has faded through over-exposure to light or to the sun.

To begin with, rifle butts were painted brown and the rest of the weapon left as bare metal, but this practice ceased in about 1902. (See for example the two Welch Fusiliers on the left of the 3rd row of set 73, page 96.) Thereafter rifles and carbines were painted metallic brown all over. Bayonets and swords were never silvered during our period, but were left as bare metal, which means that later repainting or embellishment is very easy to detect.

Britains appears not to have used undercoat, but the successive layers of paint built up at the collars, for instance, and the generally fairly liberal coatings of paint mean that the figures seem not to be as detailed as they in fact are. Normally the flesh colour was painted on first, then the main coat and hat colours on top. Speed was of the essence, and it may be that the confidence speed required led to the painting of such straight crossbelt lines: each line simply required one swift stroke with a well-loaded brush.

Best-quality painting always included stripes down trousers as applicable; 'facings' on collars and cuffs; gold buttons and belt buckle; belt and crossbelt as applicable; and different coloured boots, if necessary. In the early days, even more detail was applied – white piping to the cuffs and coat tails of the Foot Guards, for instance, and sometimes a gold chinstrap.

When production was booming, more painters were probably taken on, and the overall standard of painting dropped in consequence (ICP). How else can one explain the often rather ugly paintings of the early to mid-1920s? When lay-offs took place during the depression, only the best painters remained, and so standards went up. In my judgement the most attractively painted models date from before 1914 or after 1930.

Little special painting was done until the mid- and late 1930s. Work was needed then, and the Drum and Fife Band of the Royal Welch Fusiliers (page 73) and the Black Watch at the slope (page 77) both date from this time.

The small-size B series was also painted to best quality, in so far as this was possible on smaller working surfaces. All other small-size series (see page 166) had a second-grade painting. During the early years, this still included green bases and black eyes, even a belt, but by the early 1930s the cheap P series was being introduced, with an absolute minimum of colours, and this 'third-grade' painting rapidly became the norm. The gilt figures were 'fourth grade'; they were cheapest of all and were simply dipped in gold paint. Often castings that did not quite pass inspection were sold as gilts rather than being remelted.

If the castings were painted straight after being cast, the metal underneath the paint would stay bright. But if there was any delay, the metal would go dull. Both conditions can be observed in Britains figures.

Paris Office figures (see pages 162) can be identified by their rather pale grey faces and by the liberal use of brown for accessories. In addition they lacked the detail

Left: Britains' painters working their way through masses of castings. The lady nearest the camera is painting set 460, Colour Party of the Grenadier Guards. The nearest two blocks of figures are colour sergeants, and the next two blocks are officers. She is half way through adding some detail to the officers. This picture confirms that, at least at this time, a single painter would complete all three different types of figures in this set, thus giving a matching style of paint to the whole set. (Britains Ltd)
Opposite top: *Set 143, French Matelots. Contrast this c.1930 set in glossy finish, with the earlier set,* ***Opposite centre,*** *where the light does not reflect from the c.1905 paint as much. This is due to the different amount of varnish in the paint.*
Opposite bottom: *Examples of Egyptian infantry, left to right, c.1906, c.1901 with dark blue uniform, c.1904, c.1956 officer and c.1930. (Phillips, London)*

of the British models and some of the figures do not fit into the list of British set numbers.

Unless regimental tradition dictated otherwise, Britains included two each of two different coloured horses in each set of five cavalry, the fifth being an officer or trumpeter. The two colours were usually black and a rich mid-brown with plenty of red in it, though sometimes a darker mid-brown. The trumpeters usually rode grey horses, the officers black or brown. In very early sets, the officer sometimes rode a light brown horse with a lot of yellow in it; this may have been meant to represent sorrel.

Curiously, Britains very rarely painted reins and harnesses in, except on the Household Cavalry, horse teams and a few special sets such as the General Staff. Painted reins in other figures indicate repainting or embellishment.

Chapter 10
Boxes

Although most collectors enjoy lining up toy soldiers on parade, another pleasure is to see them 'as new' – as if on display in the toy shop window. Still tied into their boxes, toy soldiers evoke the longings of childhood, now fulfilled as a treasured possession, yet still untouchable, lest the undoing of the string should break the spell.

There is no doubt that for many collectors the original box considerably enhances the quality of a set of soldiers. The existence of a box is usually a reassurance that the set of soldiers it contains is correct. But since many collectors assemble sets in boxes even when pieces are missing this is no guarantee. Boxes are also yet another clue to the age of a set – so long as you are convinced that the set is in its original box in the first place!

From about 1900 to the mid-1930s, the normal Britains' box consisted of a shallow tray about 1 inch (3 cm) deep and a separate lid made out of a slightly larger tray. Both were made of brown strawboard and covered in paper, usually red. Various types of packing material were used to immobilize the toys, most often a white-faced insert card with holes punched at appropriate intervals and stamped with Britains' trademark. Thin black string was then threaded through the holes and round the models to hold them firm. A label was stuck on top of the lid and usually over one end as well so that box numbers could be noted when the boxes were stored end on.

To punch out the insert cards, Britains used an ingenious machine with numerous rows of holes and loose punching pegs that could be placed in any position. This explains the wonderful variety of hole patterns in the cards, which could thus be adjusted to take mixed cavalry and infantry sets or awkward shapes such as gunners or mules. Another machine helped the girls on the production line to thread the soldiers on to the cards. The thread was fed round a series of pulleys so that there were two rows of thread for each single row of soldiers. With a weight holding the thread taut, the insert card and the soldiers were placed on top of the thread, which was exactly in line with the upper and lower holes of each row. With a crochet hook, the packer then pulled the thread through each hole and over the head or feet of the soldier.

This method made packing operations deft and rapid. It also gives a good indication of whether a set has been retied in its box, since if the string pattern underneath the card does not follow the original holes, the set has probably been retied. Only boxes in which the string is continuous throughout and runs in row by row

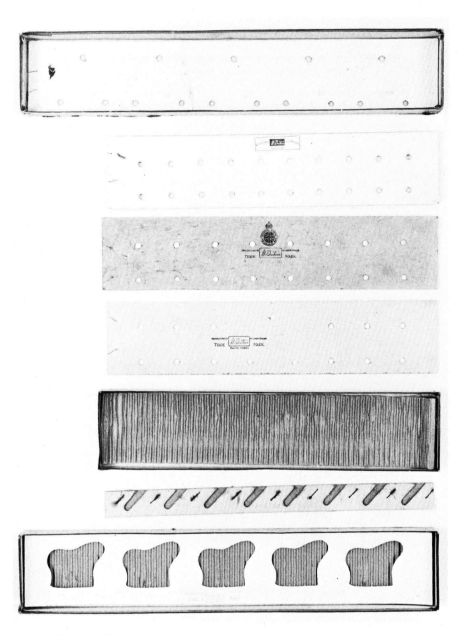

OPPOSITE:
THREADING MACHINE
The girl is tying set 59 on to the appropriate insert card, which has been punched with 30 holes in alternate rows of five and ten. (Britains Ltd)

PACKING INSERTS
Top to bottom: 1 The tray and insert of a cavalry box, showing the three holes for each of five figures. The holes allowed the thread to come up in a loop from the other side of the card, and pass round the rider's head and two legs of each horse. 2 An early insert for a set of ten infantry, c.1910. If this card were found in a box for a set of eight figures, it would obviously be incorrect. 3 An insert for a set of eight figures, c.1922, with a 'National Scheme for Disabled Men' stamp. 4 Insert for a set of six men and a mounted officer. 5 New style of packaging, c.1935-9, possibly deriving from the Parade Series idea (see pages 188-9). The bases of eight Infantry fit into the slotted strip of folded card, which is held together with staples. The whole row then fits into the box tray against a strip of coloured paper. 6 The equivalent packaging for cavalry sets. Two legs of each horse fit through the cut-outs in the insert, thus anchoring the figure.

of holes can accurately be described as 'Mint, still tied in original box'.

Before card inserts were introduced, which was probably in about 1900, the bases of infantry were fitted into slots actually cut into the lower side of the box tray itself. A piece of paper backing was put under the figures, and the box was then filled with pleated brown tissue paper to prevent the soldiers moving out of their slots. Before the First World War, many boxes were stapled at the corners to strengthen them, although once the staples had rusted they made getting the lid on and off more difficult. In cavalry boxes, card divisions covered in stiff paper were used to form five compartments that held the mounted figures.

In the mid- and late 1930s, infantry were slotted into

a patent base strip and cavalry were put into a card cut-out. The sets were backed with coloured corrugated paper. After the Second World War card inserts and thread were used again.

Pleated tissue paper was always packed on top of the soldiers to stop them being damaged. None the less, the various packing methods all resulted in rub marks of one sort or another: neck and ankles of infantry strung on to a card insert, for instance.

Box sizes

Most early single-row boxes were the same size – about 14¾ inches long, 3½ inches front to back and 1 inch deep

(38 x 9 x 2.6 cm). Quite soon, however, Britains started to make cavalry boxes larger than infantry ones, and the standard size of the cavalry boxes became 18¼ x 3½ inches (46 x 9 cm) overall.

Some boxes for cavalry at the halt with lances were 16 x 4⅜ inches (41 x 11 cm), while boxes for some other cavalry types were also widened to 4⅜ inches (11 cm), maintaining the original 18¼ (46 cm) length. For some curious reason, set 99, 13th Hussars, was never packed in the wider boxes, which would have accommodated the officer's plume, and in consequence this is broken, bent or missing in nearly all the examples I have seen.

Two-row boxes usually measured 18 x 6¾ inches (46 x 17 cm); three-row 18 x 10½ inches (46 x 26.5 cm); and four-row 18 x 13 inches (46 x 33 cm). Most early examples of these multiple-row box sizes were rather smaller.

Labels

Britains always made a point of using attractive, well-designed labels on its boxes, since these helped to catch the customer's attention and increased sales. At first, one of the family drew up the lettering required for the lid, and the printer executed it in type and decorative motifs. Soon, however, illustrations were used. The label on set 19, the West India Regiment (see page 99), is a good example; so too is the 5th Irish Lancers.

Catalogue numbers were first shown on box labels in 1898. Existing labels for previously un-numbered boxes simply had the number added to the label in an appropriate place, and the label was also extended round the end of the box.

Shortly before the First World War, Britains started to commission the artist Fred Whisstock to design most of the new labels for new sets; he also did new designs for most of the earlier boxes. He signed himself Fred Whisstock, or, as on box 200, just after the end of the war, L/C (Lance-Corporal) Fred Whisstock. To my knowledge, the latest catalogue number set for which he designed a label was set 400, Life Guards with cloaks, produced in 1930, which means that he was working for Britains for at least 17 years from about 1913. But many of his distinctive designs continued to be used until some time after the Second World War.

Only the single-row boxes had individual labels. The labels found on larger boxes and display boxes could be used for a number of different sets. Since demand for these larger boxes was unpredictable, it was presumably uneconomic to produce specific labels for them. This explains why the various 'universal' labels – *Armies of the World*, *Types of the British Army* – evolved. During the 1920s and 1930s they were often simply rubber stamped with the number of the set contained in the box. This was occasionally done with single-row sets too; for instance on my US Machine Gunners box the label is for set 198 and is overprinted.

From the 1930s onwards, the trend was towards fewer labels to suit more boxes. After 1949 a few different

*Before Frederick Whisstock's
time (see page 25), the normal
procedure at Britains appears
to have been to write out all
the copy that was to appear on
a label and send it down to the
printer for him to make it up
and print a quantity. Some of
the resulting designs are most
ornate and interesting, and all
have a wonderful period feel to
them. As a new batch was
required, so any additions
(such as new battle honours or
a set number) would be added,
sometimes causing a very
minor change to a design. On
the other hand, the printer
might have broken up the type
and need to start again, so
that there would be several
similar but different labels for
the same set. In the early
period, the label just covered
the top of the box, but later, as
can be seen in the third box
from the bottom, the title and
set number were printed on
the end of the label, which was
then bent over the edge of the
lid. This one has not been
positioned quite correctly. The
titles of the sets are self-
evident, but the set numbers
are not so plain. From top to
bottom they are 11, 118, 112,
36, 76, 121, 9 and 119. These
particular boxes all date from
about 1909. (Phillips,
London)*

Regiments of All Nations designs in full colour covered the whole range.

Until 1949, Britains' labels were printed, with very few exceptions, in just one colour, usually black on a light shade of yellow, green, blue or white. Other background colours sometimes used were cream, pink and orange. The labels made the boxes look colourful and were quite cheap to produce. Particular sets were not allocated a specific colour, and often the same label was printed on half a dozen different backgrounds.

Labels for large or expensive boxes were often printed in gold on a dark solid colour, commonly black. Although very striking originally, the gold has tended to fade, and on some of the first boxes, such as the 12th Lancers (page 56), has almost entirely vanished.

Above: *Top to bottom: 1 This box, numbered 100, contained copies of Britains' Life Guards. While not a direct copy of a Britains' box, the style is so similar that the intention is clear. 2-7. Attractive examples of typographical label design with 'printers' hearts and flowers' from 1900 onwards. The Chinese Infantry box dates from the 1920s. 8 One of the more ornate of Whisstock's designs, for set 152, for which earlier type-set designs also exist. (Phillips, London)*

Chapter 11
Britains' competitors

 Like all successful commercial ventures, Britains soon attracted plenty of competitors who tried to emulate its achievements. Since the hollowcasting process was such a crucial factor in Britains' success, many of them were former employees who knew how it was done. German and French firms, presumably alarmed at decreasing exports to the United Kingdom, tried the method too.

Little is known about Britains' competitors, and our chief interest is to distinguish their copies of Britains' models from the real thing. The term 'Britains Copy' has gone into the collector's vocabulary, and some of the copies themselves are shown on pages 28 and 60.

Of all the surviving non-Britains figures made before 1914, about half are copies, subtle, or unsubtle, of Britains' originals, and the remainder are totally different. Many of the latter figures were in much livelier action poses, in contrast with Britains' rather disciplined

ANTI-PIRACY NOTICE
Britains tried to prevent competitors pirating its figures by dating them (see page 16). These are two of the four results of High Court actions, which Britains included in the 1915 catalogue (and presumably also in earlier ones) to deter would-be pirates. The names cited, Hanks Brothers and Company and James Renvoize, are those of quite well-known competitors of Britains, who in common with other firms went on to produce toy soldiers of their own design with their own copyright dates. Prior to the court ruling, however, Hanks in particular had engaged in a considerable amount of piracy. A figure by Renvoize, possibly the one cited in the action, is shown on page 65. Some copies by Hanks are shown on page 60. Two other cases were also mentioned in the 1915 catalogue, the defendants being Davies and Company and David Mudie, both of whom had copied the bust of Edward VII illustrated on page 64.

CAUTION.

Britains' Copyright Models of Soldiers and Horses.

The attention of the Trade generally (Wholesale and Retail) is called to the following actions:—

In the High Court of Justice
King's Bench Division.   1901. B. No. 3341.

BETWEEN

BRITAIN AND OTHERS—*Plaintiffs.*

v.

HANKS BROTHERS AND COMPANY—*Defendants.*

This case which came before Mr. Justice Wright on the 18th April, 1902, in the King's Bench Division of the High Court of Justice, was an action brought by the Plaintiffs (who carry on business as toy manufacturers, and who make, among other things, metal casts of soldiers and horses), to restrain the Defendant Company, their servants or agents, from making, selling, or exposing for sale, or otherwise disposing of any pirated copies or casts of certain metal casts or models which have been put forth and published by the Plaintiffs and for other relief.

Evidence having been taken and the case having been argued ; Mr. Bousfield, K.C., and Mr. Bonner appearing for the Plaintiffs, and Mr. T. E. Scrutton, K.C., and Mr. H. M. Giveen for the Defendants, His Lordship, Mr. Justice Wright, ordered that judgment should be entered for the Plaintiffs (and such judgment was accordingly entered) for **an injunction restraining the Defendants, their servants and agents, and each and every of them, from infringing the Plaintiff's Copyright** dated 1st June 1900, and known as the "Imperial Yeoman." And His Lordship also ordered that **an enquiry and account should be taken** by one of the Masters of the Supreme Court **as to the damages sustained by the Plaintiffs, by reason of the Defendants infringement of the said copyright.** And that the Defendants should deliver up to the Plaintiffs or destroy all pirated copies or casts of the said copyright of the said Imperial Yeoman. **And that the Plaintiffs should recover against the Defendants their costs of action up to and including judgment and their costs of the said enquiry and account,** such costs to be taxed as between Solicitor and client. And that the Plaintiffs were to be at liberty to apply in chambers as to payment of the damages when so assessed as aforesaid.

In the High Court of Justice
Chancery Division.   1902. P. No. 469.

BETWEEN

BRITAIN AND OTHERS—*Plaintiffs.*

v.

JAMES RENVOIZE—*Defendant.*

The Plaintiffs are toy manufacturers, and the articles manufactured by them include metal casts of horses and soldiers. The above action was brought by them to restrain the Defendant, his servants and agents, from making, selling, or exposing for sale, or otherwise disposing of any pirated copies or casts of certain metal casts or models which had been put forth and published by the Plaintiffs, and other relief.

The case came before Mr. Justice Kekewich on the 12th May, 1902, when counsel (Mr. Warrington, K.C., who, with Mr. J. M. Stone, appeared for the Plaintiffs) intimated that it would not be necessary to trouble the Court with hearing the case as the Defendant **had admitted** to the infringement and consented to the Order following. Counsel (Mr. R. J. Parker) appeared for the Defendant. The Court thereupon ordered and adjudged that the Defendant, James Renvoize, his servants and agents, and each and every of them should be **perpetually restrained from infringing the Plaintiffs' Copyright** dated 1st June, 1900, and known as the "Imperial Yeoman" and being the exhibit marked W.B. 1 in the Statement of Claim in the action. **And it was ordered that the Defendant, James Renvoize, should pay damages, deliver up to the Plaintiffs all pirated copies or casts together with the mould or moulds of the said Copyright of the said "Imperial Yeoman." And it was ordered that the Defendant, James Renvoize, should pay to the Plaintiffs the costs of the action as between Solicitor and client.**

Above: The Foot Guard on the left is the Britains' volley-firing Grenadier, the first version of set 34. On the right is a copy of this figure, probably by Hanks or Reka. The metal of which the copy is made is much brighter and more brittle, and the actual casting itself is thinner and therefore feels lighter. (Phillips, London)

Top right: These Hussars, which are hollowcast and are mounted on a very good copy of a Britains rocking horse, were made in Germany by Gebrüder Heinrich. For a picture of a similar set of Horse Guards in their original box, see page 59. The possibility exists that in the very early days William Britain Senior had Georg Heinrich turn out some designs for him, which would explain the germanic figures (see Chapter 14). Maybe the rocking horse figure should be added to the germanic group. (Phillips, London)

Centre right: At a time when Britains almost always printed its labels in one colour only, this competitor's label was in full colour. This is the only known reference for Faudel Phillips & Son. The box lid is extremely attractive. The figure on top, a rather poor copy of a Britains' soldier on guard, presumably belongs inside the box. He has yellow facings, but, since the Royal Warwickshires have blue facings, this is either a manufacturer's error, or the wrong figure. (Phillips, London)

Bottom right: Copies or near copies of Britains' Infantry of the Line. The three marching on the right are similar to Britains only in style, since the movable arm is on the opposite shoulder to the one normally used by Britains, and the modelling of the packs and belts is distinctively different. By contrast the drummer, bugler, foot and mounted officer, and the two versions of figures kneeling on guard, are extremely similar to Britains. The figure on the extreme left marching at the slope is rather too thin to be mistaken for a Britains' product. The closest copy in this group is probably the bemedalled officer third from the left at the back, which one could pardonably believe from this photograph to be by Britains. Although not shown here, the most widely copied of all the early Britains figures was probably the Infantryman of the Line standing on guard. The inferior quality of the paint on these figures is fairly apparent, particularly on the close copies of Britains, which competed directly with Britains' X series. (Phillips, London)

C.E.T. & CO.
This is from a catalogue c.1919 showing sets marketed by C.E.T. & Co. as the 'Charterhouse' series. Although these competed with Britains, Britains supplied many of the contents! Of the sets here, the St John's Ambulance, Sandbag Fort, Tank Warfare and Trench Warfare all show Britains figures on the label, although for the latter they are only four Highlanders. The claim 'our own design' top left cannot be true unless it refers only to the packaging, since all the contents are by various toy manufacturers. The 'Battlefield' includes sandbags, Rivolet (S.R.) guns and limbers with B.M.C. teams and Cavalry and Fry Infantry. 'Tank Warfare' contains French-made Renault tanks and miniature aircraft by Rivolet. Two of the other three sets are photographed in Chapter 37. (Ed Ruby)

style. But if these figures are put out on parade, their overall impression is nevertheless chaotic, in contrast with the steady ranks of Britains.

Simply because of the number and variety of its piracies from Britains, Hanks Brothers must have been one of the earliest competitors. The metal it used has a different consistency. Its figures were a lot shinier and did not take paint so well; nowadays they look 'flakey', and bright metal shows underneath.

Other competitors were James Renvoize, Reka, B.M.C. and John Hill. Renvoize took Britains' action for piracy to heart, abandoned his copies and went on to produce some very nice figures of his own, painted in best quality. The surviving models suggest that Reka produced a very large range before the First World War and again after it until the moulds were redistributed among their competitors in about 1930, perhaps as a result of a bankruptcy sale. Reka models were often marked C.W. Baker, in the same way that Britains was marked Wm Britain Jr. Reka concentrated on the cheap end of the market, where Britains was most open to attack, and was its chief rival here from about 1905 to 1930. Although it made some good-quality items, many of its models were very poor quality and produced in inconsistent scales, and designs were frequently changed.

The initials B.M.C. stand for Britannia Model Company, but Hill had registered the Britannia trademark previously, so that B.M.C. was never allowed to use its name in full. The style of its figures was pleasantly original; some were rather larger than Britains', others a little smaller. Its armies of foreign countries were particularly fine. John Wood, an ex-Britains' employee, produced one figure, of a Life Guard, bearing the name J. Wood, before he and his brothers decided to name their company John Hill, with the 'Johillco' trademark. Not a great deal was made before the First World War, but during the war and after it business increased, and by the early 1930s Johillco was probably Britains' chief rival.

These were by no means all Britains' competitors, since before the First World War in particular the market for toy soldiers was very large. The successful conclusion of the Boer War, the arms race with Germany and the spread of war-gaming, especially through the Boy Scout movement, all helped. The Scouts had their own publication – *War Games for Boy Scouts, Played with Model Soldiers* – which may well pre-date H.G. Wells' more famous *Little Wars*, published in 1913. Britains was not slow to cash in on this trend and in 1908 published its own war-gaming booklet.

In this atmosphere many firms thrived, often small or even 'one-man' concerns, but Britains met their challenge with small-size and second-grade models, and even unmarked and unbranded wholesale lines for the cheapest end of the market. After the First World War Britains again left its competitors standing when it unveiled its 'Home Farm' series, and by 1925 it was prosecuting Pixyland Toys for pirating farm animals. The struggle against piracy has gone on to this day, with a higher incidence of copying occurring in the 1950s even than in the early days. Pirates from Hong Kong have been even harder to catch. Competition in the toy trade was never-ending, and continually motivated Britains to experiment and produce new lines.

Chapter 12
Collecting terminology

Like their fellow-collectors in every field, collectors of toy soldiers have evolved a shorthand jargon to describe items and define their condition.

Paintwork

One the rare occasions when sets turn up that have never been unpacked from their original boxes, they are described as **mint**. Boxed sets that have been damaged without having been unpacked are nevertheless described as mint, although the damage should also be mentioned as part of their true description.

Individual toy soldiers which on superficial examination appear to have intact paintwork are described as **excellent.** Figures with obvious evidence of damage to the paintwork are categorized **good** (only a few chips or scratches), **fair** (presentable, although with a number of scratches), and **poor** (so much damage that the model is no longer pleasant to look at).

Taking the illustrations of cavalry on page 33 as an example, only the first figure of the top row and the five figures in the 3rd row qualify as excellent. Most of the rest are in good condition. There are four exceptions. The second figure in the top row, which has a little dent in the neck between the two reins, the first in the 2nd row and the first in the 4th row are all fair. The sole poor figure is the 13th Hussar, 4th row, fig 3, which has a badly bent plume and is missing most of its sword. This is an example of a figure that is so rare that only poor examples are available to be collected. Most poor figures from sets in more plentiful supply are refurbished by collectors to delight the eye as repainted or converted figures.

Normally the initial letter of each term is used – **M, E, G, F, P.** Gradings such as **G to E** or **G–E** are also used. This denotes that the item is not quite E but towards that end of the G spectrum, as for instance the second figure of 2nd row, page 33.

Damage

Damage is described separately from the condition of the paintwork, since an otherwise perfect (E) figure may be missing, say, a leg, and it would be difficult to establish a grading scale that takes both factors into account.

Occasionally imperfect castings left Britains' factory fully painted. Some faults are not especially noticeable. For instance, the tip of the sword scabbard on the kneeling officer with binoculars is occasionally missing, either because of a casting error or because it has been broken off subsequently. An original casting flaw may spoil a figure's appearance slightly, but generally collectors accept that it does not detract from an original set, and it is not considered 'damage' as such. The term **damage** is used to describe accidents after the item has left the factory.

Lead figures are quite easily broken, especially if dropped on to a hard floor. The traditional method of restoring a broken head by carving a matchstick to fit tightly into the hole in the neck is best, as no adhesive foreign matter is introduced. Parts that are bent but not broken can often be bent back into shape. But take care to do this very slowly. The metal can be made less brittle by warming it, preferably in front of the fire, since the surface of the metal should be warmer than the interior. Once a crack has appeared in the metal, it will not normally bend back.

Good permanent repairs to broken figures are best done with solder or epoxy resins, and epoxy putty can be used to fill dents and mould missing parts. Cyanoacrylate glue (often known as super or instant glue) should not be used as it does not bond well with lead alloy.

Lead rot or **lead disease** – the oxydization of the lead alloy with a number of atmospheric pollutants into various compounds that make the metal turn a powdery grey – can be avoided by correct storage. In my experience, models are best stored in cardboard boxes lined with tissue paper (ie much the same materials as were used originally) and kept in a dry, well-ventilated area. Cotton wool, oak furniture and any kind of plastic wrappings should be avoided. Luckily lead rot is not contagious, and if storage conditions are improved the deterioration will cease.

Repainting

There has always been an urge to improve the work of the toymaker and add extra detail to figures, or, after much hard service with younger children, to give favourite troops a fresh uniform from a tin of paint: I certainly did both when I was young. Sometimes the extra detail is barely obvious, and the colour illustrations in this book will help readers to detect what is original and what has been added.

The term **repainting** is used for a figure that has been re-done from top to toe. **Partially repainted** speaks for itself. Additional detail is known as **embellishment**, which may be **neat** or **messy**. Neat embellishment may not detract much from the original figure's appearance, but it will affect its value considerably. Where chipping or scratching has been filled in with fresh paint, it is referred to as **retouching**. **Restoration** is the term used for a successful re-creation of the Britains' factory finish.

In my opinion, any figure that is fair or better than fair is best left alone. If you do want to try to do up a figure in poor condition, the best way is to strip off all the remaining paint and start again from bare metal.

Figure Nicknames

Descriptions of these figures and information on their place in version sequences will be found on the page numbers listed:

List of special terms

Explanations of the following terms will be found on the pages shown:

PART THREE
THE BRITISH ARMY IN FULL DRESS

As might be expected, a very large part of Britains' production has been devoted to depicting the British Army in its most colourful uniforms. 'Full dress' simply means the complete regulation uniform with all the trimmings and accessories: the best dress that the soldier possesses. The Dress Regulations set out what was full dress for each regiment. These evolved continuously, and in practice regiments did not always keep strictly to them, so that even students of military uniform sometimes differ as to what was worn.

When Britains started to produce toy soldiers, full dress was already reserved for ceremonial occasions; as opposed to 'service dress', issued as necessary for active service, and 'undress', the term used for everyday working clothes. Britains did not concern itself with 'undress', since the soldiers beloved of the public always appeared in full dress. Parts Four and Six show how Britains depicted the British Army at war, in 'service dress'.

Britains did not go into the very intricate detail of full dress. But it did put in sufficient to make the various regiments identifiable, unless their uniforms were nearly identical in real life. Some differences in dress – headgear, kilts and so on – could be shown in the modelling. Others had to be differentiated by different coloured paint: the jacket and trousers, plumes, busby bags, facings (ie collar and cuffs), kilt tartans and stripes down the trousers, all of which Britains faithfully reproduced, though of course in a stylized fashion suitable for quick application by painters.

The first three colour illustrations in this Part show an example of each of the regiments of the British Army that Britains made during our production period, as a reference to the stylized uniform used by Britains. The illustration on page 33 shows the cavalry regiments (although the 5th Lancer was unaccountably absent without leave); the infantry regiments are on page 37.

Chapter 13
The organization of the British Army

Cavalry regiments

The cavalry regiments of the British Army were armed and equipped as the various traditional types which had endured in the armies of Europe over the centuries. In 1914 there were 31 regiments, 22 of which Britains made as toy soldiers. In 1922 many regiments were amalgamated in the interests of economy, but this had no immediate impact on Britains. Even when, ten years later, this event did reach the toy soldier world, the only result was the loss of set 23, the 5th Lancers (could this be why they are not represented overleaf?), and the appropriate retitling of some other sets.

Taken in order of seniority, the types of the British Army cavalry are as follows:
Household Cavalry, Chapter 15, pages 41–6
Dragoon Guards, Chapter 16, pages 47–50
Dragoons, Chapter 17, pages 51–2
Hussars, Chapter 18, pages 53–4
Lancers, Chapter 19, pages 55–8.
The Household Cavalry and Dragoon Guards comprise the heavy cavalry, and are numbered separately. The Dragoons, Hussars and Lancers comprise the light cavalry, and are numbered in one sequence according to the seniority of the regiment.

The Household Cavalry

The Life Guards, named in 1660, and the Royal Horse Guards, which date from 1661, form the Household Cavalry, the cavalry component of the Household or Guards Division. From 1788 to 1922 there were two regiments of Life Guards, the 1st and 2nd, and Britains made models of both. Examples are shown as figs 1 and 2 of the top row overleaf, both wearing the distinctive red coat and white plume. The difference between the regiments is that the 2nd Life Guards used a white sheepskin saddlecloth, a detail which Britains were careful to paint in. Although the two regiments were amalgamated in 1922, Britains continued to produce 2nd Life Guards until 1941. The Royal Horse Guards, represented by fig 3 of the top row, have blue coats with a red plume. All the Household Cavalry wear the 'Cuirass' (ie breast- and back-plates), the last survival of medieval body armour and the mark of the 'Cuirassier' style of European cavalry widely popular until the First World War. Household Cavalry horses were invariably black except for those ridden by musicians. The ceremonial duties of the Household Cavalry include mounting guard at Whitehall and providing the escort to the royal carriages and the state coach.

Dragoon Guards

The first six of these regiments were raised in 1685, the seventh in 1688. Originally termed 'Regiments of Horse', ie heavy cavalry, they underwent various reorganizations before emerging as the 1st to the 7th Dragoon Guards in 1746. Britains made models of five, leaving out the 3rd and the 4th. The distinctive uniform detail of the Dragoon Guards is the brass helmet with horsehair plume. The 1st Dragoon Guards are represented by a small-size figure (top row, fig 4) showing the red coat with blue facings and the red plume. The 2nd Dragoon Guard at the end of the row wears yellow facings and a black plume. The 5th Dragoon Guard (2nd row, fig 1) has a white-over-red plume and green facings, since this regiment has Irish connections. The 6th Dragoon Guards (2nd row, fig 2) have blue coats and a white plume and facings, and the 7th red coats, blue facings and a black-over-white plume.

Dragoons

Originally, these were mounted infantry equipped with a heavy musket, known as a 'dragon', for use both on horseback and dismounted. Seven regiments had been formed by 1689, but shortly thereafter the term 'dragoon' came to mean heavy cavalry. The 'regiments of horse' were named Dragoon Guards, and three of the lighter 'dragon' regiments became 'Dragoons', which were also heavy cavalry armed with sabres and carbines. These three were the 1st, 2nd and 6th regiments, the Royals, the Scots Greys and the Inniskillings – the English, Scottish and Irish regiments that together formed the 'Union Brigade' at Waterloo. The other 'dragon' regiments became 'Light Dragoons', which then over the years became Hussars and Lancers. By 1914, the Dragoons wore white metal helmets like those of the Household Cavalry, except for the Scots Greys, the 2nd Dragoons (2nd row, fig 4), who wore their distinctive bearskin cap. The 1st Dragoons had red coats, blue facings and a black plume (2nd row, fig 5); the 6th were never done by Britains in full dress and so are represented in Boer War service dress (3rd row, fig 3).

Hussars

During the Napoleonic Wars, the term Hussar came into general use for light cavalry armed with sabres. The 3rd, 4th, 7th, 8th, 10th, 11th, 13th, 14th, 15th, 18th, 19th and 20th Regiments of Light Dragoons became Hussars. Head-dress was the busby with busby bag, the plume being at the front. Shown here are the 3rd (3rd row, fig 1), 4th (3rd row, fig 2), 10th (3rd row, fig 5), 11th (4th row, fig 1) and 13th (4th row, fig 3). Because of the way the Hussars are facing in this illustration, the different colours of the busby cannot be seen. They are: 3rd, light blue; 4th, yellow; 10th, red; 11th, crimson; 13th, buff. All wear blue coats and trousers, except for the 11th, who have the crimson trousers that gave rise to their nickname, the Cherrypickers. Of the seven regiments not shown here, none except the 7th Hussars, produced after the Second World War, was ever made by Britains other than as special orders for collectors.

Lancers

The remaining regiments which were designated 'Light Dragoons' became 'Lancers', in imitation of Napoleon's Polish Lancer regiments. Head-dress was the Polish Lancer cap with a coloured plume. By 1900 there were six Lancer regiments, the 5th, 9th, 12th, 16th, 17th and 21st. They all had blue coats, except for the 16th, which had red, and were otherwise distinguished by the colour of their plumes and their plastron, the coloured piece of cloth covering the chest. The 5th Lancers, not represented here but shown on page 57, have a green plume and a red plastron, the 9th a black and white plume and red plastron (3rd row, fig 4), the 12th a red plume and red plastron (4th row, fig 2), the 16th a black plume and blue plastron (4th row, fig 4), the 17th a white plume and white plastron (4th row, fig 5) and the 21st a white plume and light blue plastron (4th row, fig 6). The Lancers were the most recent innovation in the cavalry regiments; indeed the 21st (Empress of India's) Lancers was designated a Lancer regiment as recently as 1897.

Types of cavalry figure

Besides showing one of each cavalry regiment Britains made during our period (with the exception of the 5th Lancers), the illustration opposite also depicts a good variety of the different types of mounted models done by Britains. So that readers can become familiar with them, they are described briefly in the table below. The order of the list is by rows from top to bottom, working from left to right.

Regiment	Type of figure	Date type of figure first made	Set number from which figure comes
1st Life Guards	second-grade spindly head-level horse	c. 1900	—
2nd Life Guards	full-gallop two-eared horse	c. 1924	43
Royal Horse Guards	second-grade spindly head-down horse	c. 1894	—
1st Dragoon Guards	small-size first version head-up horse	c. 1898	57
2nd Dragoon Guards	rocking horse	1896	44
5th Dragoon Guards	Scots Grey walking horse	dated 1.11.1902	3
6th Dragoon Guards	RHA Officer horse	1895	106
7th Dragoon Guards	head-up trotting horse	dated 12.12.1902	127
2nd Dragoons	tin-sword Dragoon horse	1895	32
1st Dragoons	second-grade spindly head-up horse	c. 1900	4X
3rd Hussars	donkey horse	1893	13
4th Hussars	one-eared full-gallop horse	dated 1.1.1901	8
6th Dragoons	fixed-arm Imperial Yeomanry horse	dated 1.6.1900	108
9th Lancers	officer turned in saddle	1894	24
10th Hussars	at-halt horse	dated 18.8.1903	315
11th Hussars	small-size at-halt horse	dated 4.7.1904	10b
12th Lancers	cantering horse	dated 12.2.1903	128
13th Hussars	small-size first-version trotting horse	c. 1896	87
16th Lancers	plug-shoulder Lancer horse	1893	—
17th Lancers	small-size Lancer at walk	dated 26.8.1904	13b
21st Lancers	pony horse	1899	100

Examples of British Cavalry described opposite.

Infantry regiments

Page 37 shows examples of each of the British Army infantry regiments made by Britains during our period. Originally, these regiments were numbered like the cavalry, but in 1881 most regiments were given a new county title, and the numbering was officially abolished. For purposes of seniority, however, the regiments maintained the same order, and so it is still useful to record their numerical sequence.

Many of the figures listed are not illustrated elsewhere in the book, and reference is often made to them elsewhere.

Between 1893 and 1932, Britains made models of 34 regiments of the 74 in existence in real life. In 1937, Britains produced a series of 47 regiments marching at the slope which depicted many of those not made during our period, but these 'Famous Regiments of the British Army' fall outside the scope of this book.

Like the cavalry, the infantry fall into various types according to their traditions, equipment and uniforms. These are:

The Foot Guards, Chapter 22, pages 66–70
Highlanders, Chapter 24, pages 75–8
Lowlanders, also in Chapter 24, illustrated page 37
Infantry of the Line, Chapter 25, pages 79–84
Fusiliers, Chapter 26, pages 85–6
Rifle regiments, Chapter 26, pages 86 and 88.

Foot Guards

Together, the five regiments of Foot Guards form the Brigade of Guards, the infantry component of the Household Division. The most famous of their duties are carried out in full dress: guard-mounting at Buckingham Palace and Windsor Castle, the ceremony of the Keys at the Tower of London, and the Queen's Birthday Parade, the Trooping the Colour. Although they were originally numbered as three regiments, in a separate sequence from the Regiments of the Line, by 1893 the numbering had been abandoned – and indeed two of the regiments had not even been formed then.

The five regiments are shown as the first five figures on the left of the top row on page 37. The Foot Guards all wear a bearskin Grenadier cap, red coat and blue facings. Blue facings are worn by all British Army regiments with official royal connections, and these of course include the Guards. Four of the regiments have a plume set in the side of the bearskin. The Grenadier Guards, named in 1660, wear a white plume on the left of the bearskin. The Coldstream Guards, also named in 1660, wear a red plume on the right. The Scots Guards, named as the 3rd Foot Guards in 1685, wear no plume. The Irish Guards, formed in 1900, wear a blue plume on the right, although Britains often painted it more green than blue (the example on page 37 is a very dark green). The Welsh Guards, formed in 1915, wear a white-over-green-over-white plume on the left, which Britains represented by a white plume with a green horizontal stripe through it.

Opposite: Top to bottom: 1 Double-row box with a nice label that could be used for any set containing types of the British Army. 2 A similar box with a Whisstock-designed label to do the same job. The space in the centre could be overprinted either with a specific set title, or, as here, with a general title, after which the set number was added with a rubber stamp. This box contained 16 British Infantry in gasmasks, marching at the trail. 3 A box to take nine or ten infantry, or sets including a tent. The set number is overprinted in the circle to the right. This box contained Scots Greys and Scots Guards with a Bell Tent.

Right: Early black labels for large boxes, overprinted in gold ink. These were similar to the labels used by German manufacturers and were supposed to impart a luxury feel to the expensive sets.

The groupings of buttons on their tunics also differentiate the Foot Guards, but Britains did not include this detail in the painting.

Highland regiments

Highland regiments usually wear tartan kilts in full dress, and are associated with various clans or areas of the Scottish Highlands. In 1914 there were five Highland regiments, all of which were modelled by Britains. Examples of each are shown on page 37. The Black Watch are the senior Highland regiment, formed just before the rebellion led by Bonnie Prince Charlie in 1745; they wear a red hackle in their feather bonnet and a dark green kilt with black stripes (3rd row, fig 6). The Seaforth Highlanders have a white hackle, and their kilt is dark green with vertical white and horizontal red lines (4th

bonnet, red doublet and green trews with yellow stripes (page 37, top row, fig 6). The Highland Light Infantry wear a shako and tartan trews with a white vertical and red horizontal stripe (4th row, fig 2). These are the only Lowland regiments depicted by Britains during our period. Of the other Lowland infantry, Britains did produce models later of the King's Own Scottish Borderers and the Cameronians, although not the Royal Scots Fusiliers.

Infantry of the Line

At the beginning of our period, normal full dress for regular infantry was red coat, blue trousers and a spiked helmet, and this is how the majority of regiments were shown by Britains, the exceptions being those in some form of service dress. All Infantry of the Line are standard county or city regiments. The only difference in their uniforms is the colour of the facings or helmet, the facings being the contrasting colour worn at the collar and cuffs. Regiments designated as Light Infantry often had green facings; the facings of royal regiments were blue, the other regiments had colours traditionally associated with them.

On page 37 the following regiments are shown:
Top row, fig 7: the Royal West Surrey Regiment; blue helmet, blue facings.
Top row, fig 8: the Buffs, the East Kent Regiment; blue helmet, yellow facings.
2nd row, fig 1: the Royal Lancaster Regiment; in foreign-service helmet holding a ramrod (see pages 105, 106 and 136).
2nd row, fig 2: The Royal Warwickshire Regiment; blue helmet and blue facings.
2nd row, fig 5: the Devonshire Regiment; in Boer War service dress (see pages 117 and 118).
2nd row, fig 6: the Somerset Light Infantry; dark green helmet and blue facings.
2nd row, fig 7: the East Yorkshire Regiment; blue helmet and white facings.
2nd row, fig 8: the Royal Irish Regiment; blue helmet and blue facings.
2nd row, fig 9: the Green Howards, the Yorkshire Regiment; blue helmet and green facings (the officer shown has gold cuff decoration).
3rd row, fig 3: the Gloucestershire Regiment; in Boer War service dress (see pages 117 and 118).
3rd row, fig 4: the Worcestershire Regiment; white helmet and white facings. (Britains used white-painted helmets to depict the white cloth cover some regiments occasionally put over normal blue helmets.)
3rd row, fig 5: the Royal Sussex Regiment; white helmet and blue facings.
3rd row, fig 7: the Middlesex Regiment; blue helmet and usually yellow facings. Very early models, like the one shown, have white facings.
3rd row, fig 9: the Manchester Regiment; blue helmet, white facings.
4th row, fig 1: the York and Lancaster Regiment; blue

row, fig 3). The Gordon Highlanders have a white hackle, and a dark green kilt with yellow stripes (4th row, fig 4). The Cameron Highlanders' hackle is white, the kilt dark blue with yellow vertical and red horizontal stripes (4th row, fig 5). Finally, the Argyll and Sutherland Highlanders have a white hackle, and their kilt is green with light green stripes (4th row, fig 6). All Highland regiments when wearing kilts also wore sporrans, fur decorated pouches. The decorations consist of two rows

of tassels or one row of tails, which are longer. Britains usually took care to represent these details.

Lowland regiments

The senior Regiment in the British Army after the Foot Guards, the Royal Scots are also the senior Lowland regiment. Their uniform comprises a Kilmarnock helmet and white facings.

Fusiliers

The Royal Fusiliers, the City of London Regiment, formed in 1685, was the earliest Fusilier regiment. The original purpose of 'fusiliers' was to act as an escort to artillery. For this purpose they were provided with flintlock 'fusils' which did not need lighted matches, unlike the matchlock muskets of the ordinary infantry. This was obviously an advantage when open barrels of gunpowder were nearby. In the late 19th century, the eight Fusilier regiments, five of which were made by Britains during our period, wore a racoon or seal-skin Fusilier cap.

Page 37 shows the Northumberland Fusiliers (2nd row, fig 2) with a foreign-service helmet, the Royal Fusiliers (2nd row, fig 4), the Lancashire Fusiliers (top row, fig 1), the Royal Welch Fusiliers (3rd row, fig 2), and the Dublin Fusiliers (4th row, fig 7).

Rifle regiments

A further development of Light Infantry, the rifle regiments were formed in 1797 in imitation of the Austrian Jaegers. They had rifled muskets which, although slow in operation, were accurate for skirmishing. The rifle regiments' green uniforms are the earliest example of camouflage uniforms in the British Army. Their distinctive full-dress headgear is a rifle busby with the plume at the front. In 1914 there were four rifle regiments in the infantry. One, the Cameronians, has already been mentioned as a Lowland regiment, while another, the Royal Irish Rifles, was never done by Britains. The other two are the King's Royal Rifle Corps (page 37, 3rd row, fig 8), shown here with the early spiked helmet rather than the more common busby to which Britains soon changed; and the Rifle Brigade (page 37, 4th row, fig 8).

Completing the British Army in full dress are the artillery (chapter 28, pages 91–4); the general staff (chapter 21, pages 63–4); the Corps of Engineers, whose pontoon wagons appear in chapter 31, pages 113 and 114; and the Departmental Corps, the Army Service Corps and Royal Army Medical Corps, who also appear on those pages. There are no representatives of the Ordnance, Veterinary, Military Police or Pay Corps.

The illustrations of infantry on page 37 provide a useful introduction to many of the different types and positions of model figures Britains used. Together these illustrations represent all the British Army regiments made as toys by Britains until 1932. In the table, right, they are set out in order of the 1914 Army List. The list is by rows from top to bottom and left to right. Since full regimental titles have already been given, abbreviations are used here.

Regiment	Regimental number	Type of figure	Date when figure first made	Set number from which figure comes
Grenadier Guards		early volley-firing figure	1895	34
Coldstream Guards		kneeling firing	1.7.1901	120
Scots Guards		standing officer with binoculars	1.7.1901	130
Welsh Guards		1910 marching figure	24.2.1910	253
(NB The Irish Guards are senior to the Welsh, and are thus shown here in the wrong order.)				
Irish Guards		box-pack marching figure	1.8.1905	107
Royal Scots	1	special figure made for this regiment	1924	212
West Surrey	2	1910 marching figure	24.2.1910	29
East Kent	3	second-version standing on guard	17.1.1910	16
Lancaster	4	standing at attention	20.1.1901	148
Northumberland Fusiliers	5	small-size marching at trail	1898	21b
Warwickshires	6	early figure at present arms	1923	206
Royal Fusiliers	7	box-pack marching figure	1.8.1905	7
Devonshire	11	Slade Wallace marching figure	20.1.1901	110
Somerset Light Infantry	13	kneeling on-guard figure, second version	17.1.1910	17
East Yorks	15	second-version attention figure	c.1926	113
Royal Irish	18	kneeling firing	1.7.1901	156
Green Howards	19	officer with standard, full trouser	1934	255
Lancashire Fusiliers	20	small-size marching at trail	1898	17b
Royal Welch Fusiliers	23	bemedalled officer	1894	74
Gloucestershire	28	standing firing figure in puttees	1.7.1901	119
Worcestershire	29	second-version drummer boy	c.1900	18
Sussex	35	fixed-arm valise-pack marching figure	1895	36
Black Watch	42	plug-handed Highlander running	1893	11
Middlesex	57	wasp-waisted marching at trail	1897	76
King's Royal Rifle Corps	60	early pigeon-chested running at trail	1899	98
Manchester	63	small-size marching at the slope	1898	206
York and Lancaster	65	closed-elbow running at trail	c.1926	96
Highland Light Infantry	71	special figure made for this regiment	1924	213
Seaforths	72	box-pack Highlander marching	20.1.1901	112
Gordons	75	standard marching Highlander	c.1913	77
Camerons	79	marching officer in full dress	1932	—
Argylls	91	standard charging Highlander	17.12.1903	15
Dublin Fusiliers	102	small-size running at trail	1.2.1901	19b
Rifle Brigade	unnumbered	valise-pack marching figure	1897	9

RECOGNIZING REGIMENTS

Most British Army regiments in full dress wear red coats and blue trousers. The Guards are distinguishable by their black bearskin, or large roundish fur cap. The Fusilier regiments have a similar cap made from raccoon or sealskin which is markedly smaller. Most Highland regiments wear the kilt, and recognizing them is just a matter of remembering how Britains represented that particular tartan (see text). Both Lowland regiments made by Britains during our period, the Royal Scots and the Highland Light Infantry, are modelled wearing tartan trews. Rifle regiments wear green uniforms and usually have a busby with a short plume. The Rifle Brigade has black facings while the King's Royal Rifle Corps has a red Austrian knot on each cuff. Fifteen of the figures illustrated here represent 'county' Infantry of the Line regiments, whose normal full-dress uniform includes a spiked helmet. Clues to identity are that Light Infantry have green helmets and regiments with royal in their title have blue facings. Britains also tended to distribute the various different poses possible for the troops among different named regiments, so that, for instance, all present-arms Line Infantry with green bases are Warwickshires and all Line Infantry at attention are East Yorkshires. Further experience in regiment recognition can be gleaned from reading Chapter 25.

Chapter 14
Germanic figures

This chapter deals with Britains' earliest toy soldiers, all of which were models of the British Army. This group of figures is known as the 'germanic' group, since they look like contemporary German-made toy soldiers. The group comprises the following figures: germanic Life Guard; plug-shoulder Scots Grey; plug-handed Fusilier; plug-handed Highlander; plug-shoulder Lancer.

Some of these appear as the first version of sets described in the ensuing chapters, while others were produced for such a short time that numbered sets of them never appeared. The latter are detailed below as 'un-numbered', and an explanation of how they may have fitted chronologically into Britains' production is given on page 178.

Set 1, 1st Life Guards, five germanic Life Guards, one painted with a gold sash to represent the officer. The germanic Life Guard is a fixed-arm cavalryman, rather smaller than standard size, with continental-type horse furniture and a wide-bladed tin sword. It is agreed to be Britains' very first figure. Some time after the prancing-horse officer was first made, it was substituted for the fifth germanic Life Guard.

Set 2, Royal Horse Guards, five germanic Life Guards. This set was exactly the same as set 1, apart from the differently painted uniform. The same remarks about the officer also apply. The germanic Life Guard was used in sets 1 and 2 from 1893 to 1897.

Set 3, 5th Dragoon Guards, five germanic Life Guards. Once more, this set was composed exactly as set 1, with a new uniform. Although the Royal Horse Guards were an obvious choice for set 2, the reason why set 3 should be the 5th Dragoon Guards is not clear. As in the former two sets, the prancing-horse officer was introduced *c*.1895. The germanic Life Guard was used in set 3 until *c*.1903.

Un-numbered, Scots Greys, six plug-shoulder Scots Greys, four with a sword arm at the carry, one with a trumpet, and the officer with the sword arm outstretched. The plug-shoulder Scots Grey is a largish figure (60mm scale) with a movable arm attached to a plug that goes right through the shoulders to the other side of the torso.

Un-numbered, Royal Fusiliers, eight infantry and a mounted officer represented by a plug-shoulder Scots Grey. The plug-handed Fusilier is in the same scale as the Scots Grey. The hand with the rifle plugs into the wrist so that the rifle is at the slope. Unlike most Britains figures, the right leg is forward.

Un-numbered, 12th Lancers
Un-numbered, 16th Lancers
Un-numbered, 17th Lancers
Each of these sets comprised nine plug-shoulder Lancers, one of which was an officer and another a trumpeter, provided with appropriate different arms. These arms were made on the same principle as the plug-shoulder Scots Grey above. The plug-shoulder Lancer is a smaller than standard-size cavalryman at the full gallop, with the four legs of the horse outstretched. There were two versions of the mould, the earlier without a capline. In the earlier sets, the Lancer caps were painted silver, the officer's gold. These Lancers were sold in a box measuring 12 x 9⅛ inches (30.5 x 23.2 cm).

PLUG-SHOULDER SCOTS GREYS
One of the highlights of the Richards collection was this set of germanic Scots Greys. The only defect is a bent front leg on two figures. Note the trumpeter at the front and the officer at the rear, whose arms are different from the rest. (Phillips, London)

**PLUG-HANDED
FUSILIERS**
*This superb boxed set was a
highlight of the Hanington
collection, and may well be a
true first version of set 7,
although set numbering on
the box had not been
introduced by the time this
version was withdrawn.
The size and style of label and
packing shown here are
exactly similar to the earliest
sets of Life Guards (see page
40). Unfortunately the box
has not been preserved in as
good condition as the figures.
Still, this is the only known
example of this box, and as
such fetched £3800 in summer
1984 at auction at Phillips,
London. (Photo, Phillips,
London)*

Set 11, Black Watch, seven plug-handed Highlanders, one with a sword being the officer. The plug-handed Highlander is a kilted scotsman running at the trail wearing a full bonnet. He has a plug hand grasping a rifle or a sword. Early sets of the Black Watch had all ranks painted with gold tops to their sporrans, and the set I have has gold shoulder straps. In a later set, all sporrans have black tops except the officer's, which is gold. In addition, the officer has a red sash over his left shoulder.

Set 15, Argyll and Sutherland Highlanders, seven plug-handed Highlanders, one being an officer. Early sets had painted black kilts with white stripes and black sporrans with five white tassels. In my set the officer is only distinguished by the plug sword. Later sets have dark green kilts with light green stripes, and white sporrans with five black tassels and a yellow top.

Set 77, Gordon Highlanders, five plug-handed Highlanders, one of which was an officer and two pipers. These were done in standard Gordon painting: gold facings for the officer, red sash, white sporran with five gold tassels, white belt with gold buckles.

Set 88, Seaforth Highlanders, twelve plug-handed Highlanders, one being an officer, and two pipers. This was a two-row set in standard Seaforth painting: gold facings for the officer, red sash, white sporran with five gold tassels, yellow belt without buckle. I have seen a full set of Seaforths painted with both straps and shoulder cross belts, whereas the other three sets have only one cross belt over the right shoulder. The Black Watch

plug-handed Highlander also appeared in display set 22 until 1904, and the Gordon plug-handed Highlander in display set 73 until 1901.

The plug-handed Highlander was obviously popular, and remained in production for ten years until it was replaced by the charging Highlander dated 17.12.1903.

Comparison of Britains' germanic figures and figures made in Germany shows how much Britains' first models were influenced by Germany. I have even suggested that Britains directly copied figures produced by Heinrich or painted their figures in London.

Germanic figures: descriptions

Top row This shows the interior of the earliest Britains' box I have, the Germanic 1st Life Guards, resting on a straw-backed backing paper in exact imitation of the Heinrich sets shipped from Germany. The box label is very simple. At the top right are examples of hollowcasts probably made in Germany. Below is a solid German-made personality figure, probably by Heyde, either Lord Kitchener or King Edward VII. Its quality shows what Britains had to compete with, although it cost two shillings, while a whole box in Gamages' 1902 catalogue of Britains figures was only tenpence halfpenny.

2nd row Fig 1 is the Germanic Royal Horse Guard, figs 2–4 are three assorted copies, look-alikes or predecessors. Figs 5–7 are 5th Dragoon Guards. Fig 5 is the officer with gold sash, fig 6 the early trooper with

wide tin sword, and fig 7 the somewhat later trooper with a narrower tin sword.

3rd row Fig 1 is the trumpeter from a plug-shoulder Scots Grey set. Note that the head looks more like a Fusilier than a Scots Grey, so maybe the figure originated as the officer for the Fusiliers. Fig 2 is the real Britains plug-handed Fusilier; this example has no base. The German look-alike next to it has light blue facings, a common German mistake in painting British Army figures. Figs 4 and 5 are first-version plug-shoulder 17th Lancers, showing the silver Lancer cap and the officer's gold cap. (For the set of 12th Lancers in the second version, see page 56. For an example of the 16th Lancer, see the front jacket.) Fig 6 is a copy of a Britains plug-shoulder Lancer, but with a normal-style protruding stud to take the movable arm instead of a plug. Fig 7 is a German-made Lancer based on a figure like the germanic Life Guard.

4th row Plug-handed Highlanders: figs 1 and 2 are from the Black Watch. Fig 1 has a light green kilt, fig 2 the later dark green painting. Fig 3 is a copy by Renvoize. Fig 4 is an Argyll officer in a curious black kilt with white stripes that appears to have been an early painting; I have never seen an Argyll officer with a proper sash. Fig 5 is a private, figs 6 and 7 show an officer and private of the Seaforths, figs 8 and 9 the Gordons private and officer. Note that the rifle of the Seaforths private has all-metallic painting, indicating that this style of rifle painting was introduced before 1903. Fig 10 is another copy, possibly by Reka.

Examples of germanic figures, described on page 39.

Chapter 15
The Household Cavalry

The Household Cavalry was composed of three regiments, the 1st and 2nd Life Guards and the Royal Horse Guards. Throughout the 73 years it produced hollowcast toy soldiers, Britains made more different figures of these regiments than of any other, including set 51 Life Guards and set 38 Horse Guards in the first-grade standard size alone. For our period, however, only ten basic types in first-grade sets of standard and smaller sizes need be examined. Household Cavalry were also included in 26 display sets during the period, and two of these will be discussed in detail, since their types are different from those in the basic sets.

Set 1, 1st Life Guards, four troopers and an officer. This set – Britains' first – was produced from 1893 to 1966. (The first germanic version of this set is discussed on page 39.) Set 1 endured to the end of production, four other versions apart from the germanic being made. The illustration here shows the second, third and fourth; the fifth was made in 1953, after our period.

At the top is the 1897 fixed-arm version with tin sword, with the first-version officer on prancing horse. Note the compartmented box, with the paper backing tinged slightly brown.

In the next box below is the first version with movable arms. The troopers are wearing aiguillettes as in the fixed-arm version. The officer on the prancing horse now has a movable arm as well which dates this set to about 1907. The backing paper on this set is not original, since at this date the set should have an insert card (see page 25).

Third is the same version, but with the aiguillettes gone, and the new model officer on prancing horse dated 19.10.1909. The aiguillettes were removed c.1909, probably because they gave the impression that all the troops were non-commissioned officers.

Fourth is the 'standard' set of the Life Guards, with two fully moulded ears as opposed to the one-eared styling of all previous versions.

The fifth set is the same as the fourth, but the collars are painted blue instead of red. For some reason Britains painted the wrong (red) colour on the collars, or maybe just thought they were letting the red of the jacket show. At any rate, in about 1930 the correct blue facings were painted on the collar. When set 400, the Life Guards in Cloaks, was made, Britains may have realized that a blue collar was needed and corrected all the Life Guards.

The fourth and fifth sets are held in the card cut-outs used for cavalry sets between 1934 and 1938. Only the third set has the normal card insert.

Set 2, Royal Horse Guards, four troopers and an officer. During our period this set was exactly the same as set 1, the 1st Life Guards, except for the paint. The Horse Guards were painted with blue collars until c.1930, after which they changed to the correct red.

Set 43, 2nd Life Guards, four troopers and a trumpeter.

At first all the figures in this set were on the rocking-horse cavalry figure. The first changed was to the one-eared full-stretch gallop horse dated 1.1.1901; then the trumpeter was quickly altered to the head-up trotting horse dated 12.12.1902. Finally, in the mid-1920s, the troopers changed to the reworked two-eared standard full-stretch galloping horse.

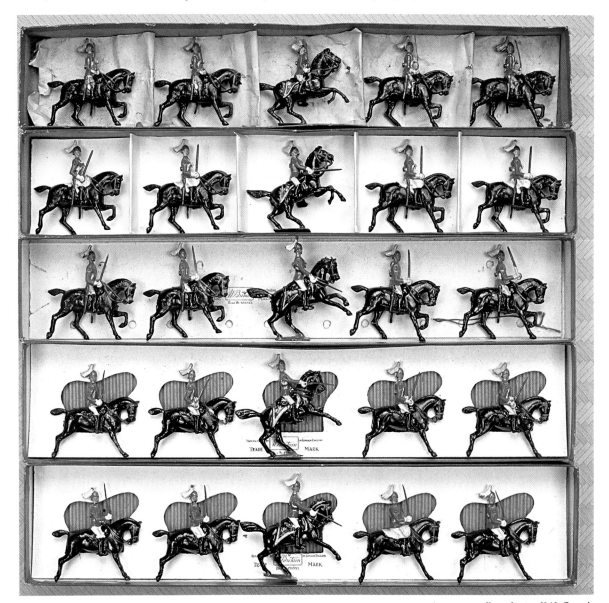

A sequence of boxed sets of Life Guards.

Set 72, Life Guards 1837-1897, 12 figures, two being officers on prancing horses. This most interesting box was produced as a souvenir for Queen Victoria's Diamond Jubilee. Half the set was the same as set 1; but the other half had different heads depicting the helmet with the large fur crest current at Queen Victoria's accession in 1837. The figures were second-version with tin swords, which confirms that this version was current in 1897. It is possible that this version of the Life Guards was created for this set and was afterwards used to replace the germanic figure then current in set 1.

Set 72 was so popular that after the Jubilee the label was altered to 'Life Guards Past and Present', and sets continued to be issued in the movable-arm version, both with and without aiguillettes. In its 1915 catalogue Britains referred to the set as 'Waterloo Life Guards', a term that has been popular among collectors. But the uniform is not correct for 1815, since the helmet depicted was only introduced for the Life Guards in 1817.

Display set 93, contained a lower layer of Horse Guards, comprising officer on prancing horse, two trumpeters and six troopers with lances on full-gallop rocking horses and 15 normal troopers with tin swords. Within this set, all these figures followed the normal sequences of later versions, except that the trumpeters remained at the full gallop when they might have changed to the head-up trotting horse, as happened in sets 43 and 44.

Sets 101 and 103, Household Cavalry Bands. These are described on page 45.

Display set 129, contained two rows of 2nd Life Guards, comprising a trumpeter and 13 troopers (illustrated on page 48). This set was identical to set 43, except that the front rank of four troopers carried lances. The lance-carrying troops in this set and set 93 have sometimes confused collectors, who believe they are a basic set of five, but all those that I have seen have been traced to the large boxes.

Set 400, Life Guards in Winter Dress, contained Life Guards in red cloaks, four troopers with swords, and an officer. The officer was the same figure but given a different movable arm, with an empty white-gloved hand.

Small-size sets

Set 1b, 1st Life Guards, small-size, three troopers with swords and officer or trumpeter

Display set 84, contained one row of 2nd Life Guards. They carried carbines and were given the distinctive white sheepskin saddlecloth of their regiment.

Display set 58, contained one row of Royal Horse Guards. Richards gives the 2nd Life Guards a number, 7b in the B series, and the Royal Horse Guards 2b. This may

*Right: Boxes for set 1 and 1B. Top to bottom: 1 Set 1B small-size, **c.**1900. 2 Set 1B small-size, **c.**1905. 3 Set 1 **c.**1895. 4 Set 1, **c.**1896. 5 Set 1 **c.**1897. 6 Set 1, Whisstock design, **c.**1913. 7 Set 1, 1930s pictorial box.*
*Opposite: Boxes for Household Cavalry. Top to bottom: 1 Early A series box, **c.**1926. 2 Later A series box, **c.**1935. 3 Whisstock label for set 2, 1920. 4 Earlier label for set 2, 1897. 5 Early design for set 43, 1897. 6 Whisstock label for set 43, 1920. 7 Whisstock label for set 400, 1930. The later boxes all show the words 'TRADE MARK REGD. No. 459993'.*

well be correct, since these numbers are missing, presumed withdrawn, from all the listings I have examined. On the other hand, I have never seen any evidence that they actually were issued.

Small-size Life Guards in second-grade paint were also made both before the First World War and in the W series after it. Horse Guards were not nearly so common.

Both Life Guards and Horse Guards appeared in the X and A series of second-grade paint sets. Since I have never seen one, it is unlikely that the germanic figure was ever used in the second grade, the various spindly-legged horses being preferred. Early versions were given the head produced for the first officer on the prancing horse, but later versions had a different head, like that of the standard first-grade trooper.

2nd row Figs 1–3 are small-size Horse Guards from set 56. Fig 1 is a trooper on the small trotting horse, and fig 2 is the officer. Fig 3 shows the Horse Guard painting of the trooper dated 25.7.1904. Fig 4 is a standard-size Horse Guard trumpeter on the standard two-eared full-gallop grey horse from set 93. Figs 5 and 6 are A series Horse Guard and Life Guard types, two more different varieties of which are shown on page 33.

3rd row Figs 1–3 are 2nd Life Guards from set 43. Fig 1 is the trumpeter on the rocking horse, fig 2 is the equivalent trooper. Fig 3 is a trooper on the one-eared horse dated 1.1.1901, but as he carries a long carbine rather than the short type carried by fig 2 he must date from after c.1908. Fig 4, Life Guard officer on a prancing horse, is an interesting curiosity. Someone seems to have forgotten to clip off the throat plume, unless a 1st Dragoons officer was painted as a Life Guard by mistake! Fig 5 shows the normal first-version Horse Guard officer on the prancing horse. Fig 6 is the same figure with the fur-crested helmet and uniform of the Life Guards in 1837, from set 72.

4th row Fig 1 is a copy Life Guard; the horse's head is higher than in the Britains' figure. Fig 2 is a second-version tin-sword Horse Guard from set 2. Fig 3 is another copy of a Britains Life Guard, almost identical except for the girth moulded on to the belly of the horse. Fig 4 is a Horse Guard on a pony horse and carrying a carbine. I have no explanation for this figure; perhaps it featured in set 93 at some period. Figs 5 and 6 are the trooper and officer of the Life Guards in Winter Cloaks, set 400, c.1930.

Further examples of Household Cavalry are to be found elsewhere in the book. Page 33 shows a 2nd Life Guard with a lance, from set 129. These types, of course, feature prominently in the picture of this set on page 48. Another large box, set 73 shown on page 96, has some interesting types of the 2nd Life Guards. Small-size Life Guards in second-grade paint were included in some of the Encampment sets shown in the 1914 catalogue, and samples of these are at the top of page 85.

Inevitably, the Household Cavalry were among the most copied of Britains figures. There are some further examples of these copies on page 60 and also on page 40, where copies of first-version Household Cavalry figures are shown.

Household Cavalry are also featured in the miniature troops, illustrated on page 61, and on page 64 King Edward VII appears in miniature with his escort of Life Guards. Since many cavalry regiments contributed to the British Camel Corps on campaign in the Sudan in 1898, the Camel Corps figures shown on page 108 may well have been Life Guards. Finally, a further curiosity, a French Cuirassier apparently painted originally as a Horse Guard is shown on page 132.

The Household Cavalry: descriptions

Top row Figs 1–4 are small-size Life Guards. Fig 1 is the first-version fixed-arm officer, followed by a copy of him by another manufacturer. Fig 3 is a first-version small trotting horse. Since this trooper is equipped with a carbine, he is probably from set 84. Fig 4 is a first-version head-down cantering horse. Note the sword arm on this figure as opposed to the later sword arm on fig 8. Fig 5 is a W series Horse Guard, a fixed-arm model derived from fig 4. Fig 6 is a first-version head-up cantering horse, again with a carbine and so probably from set 84. Figs 7 and 8 show Life Guards on the second-version horse dated 25.7.1904; fig 7 is gilt.

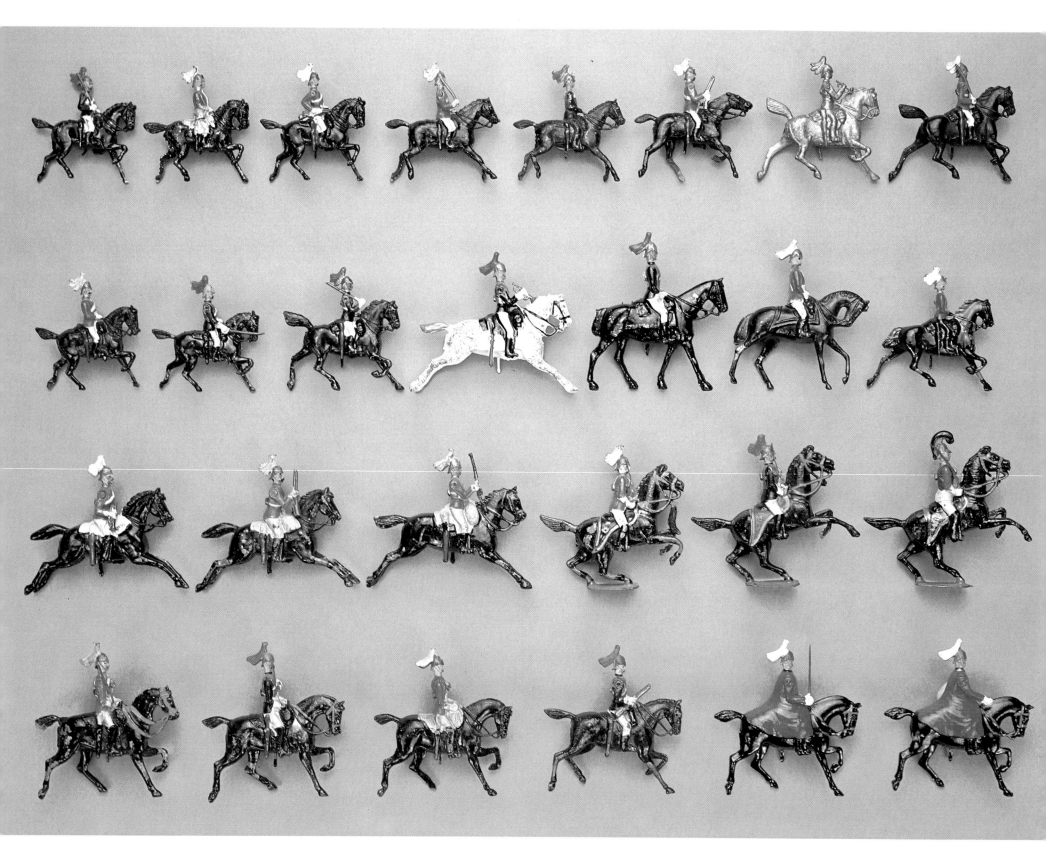

Examples of Household Cavalry, described on page 43.

The mounted bands of the Household Cavalry

The mounted Band of the Life Guards – or, as Britains termed the set in the catalogue, 'No 101 Full Band of the 1st Life Guards. Modelled and painted in the very best style. Price 5/6' – was certainly a distinctive and spectacular set of toy soldiers. The illustration above shows the four different styles of mounted band during our period. From left to right, they are:

Blue band with slotted arms, c.1905
Red band with slotted arms, c.1905
Blue Band with movable arms, c.1912
Standard band with movable arms, c. 1930.

The individual mounted bandsmen are based on the ordinary fixed-arm one-eared Household Cavalry trooper of 1898, built up to represent the state dress of the band. (State dress is the gold uniform worn by the band only in the presence of the sovereign.) Interestingly, in contrast with nearly all the other cavalry horses, the Household Cavalry bandsman was never changed to a two-eared horse, although the sword in its scabbard was removed after the Second World War.

The first two bands shown are of the slotted-arm version. Slotted arms is the term used to describe

Above: Four Britains' Bands of the Household Cavalry (see text on left).

Left: Detail from the display above, showing a good view both of the 'blue' band and particularly of the bandsman playing the bombardon. This instrument, much like a Sousaphone in shape, was included in Britains' sets 37, 73, 101, 103, 131 (two) and 132. No movable-arm model of the instrument was made, a bass horn being substituted, so the bombardon was only included in Britains' bands from 1895 to 1911.

Britains' early method of assembling bandsmen with their arms and instruments, by which all bandsmen produced before mid-1911 were made. The figure was moulded with two grooves or slots in the shoulder, and the arms and instrument were cast separately with flanges that fitted into the slots. A light touch of solder kept the assembly together. The disadvantage of this method was that the instrument arms could not be moved up and down. On the new band figures, dated in the foot models 1.5.1911, both arms end in a shoulder loop rather narrower than the normal single-arm loops and fix over two studs, one protruding from each shoulder. This arrangement enabled the instrument arms to move up and down, giving the option for the band to be playing or not, as the occasion demanded.

The blue slotted-arm band is so designated because the gold state dress is dominated by the blue undercoat, as opposed to the red variation next in line. Neither uniform is really representative of real life, and why Britains persisted in these colorations is a mystery, although I expect, as usual with Britains, that there was a good explanation. Len Richards believed that set 101 was the red band and that the blue band was set 103, the Band of the Royal Horse Guards. I have seen so many blue bands in original boxes 101, however, that I would argue that the reverse is true. In fact, I have never found any evidence for the existence of set 103, since it does not appear in any catalogue and I have never seen a box so designated. If, however, Britains were asked to produce a different band to represent the Royal Horse Guards, this is how it might have gone about it, and thus on ICP this is a good explanation for the red band. If only a few were to be produced Britains might not even have gone to the trouble of doing a different label for the box.

The instrumentation of the slotted-arm bands was as follows: one kettle-drummer; one cymbalist; two trombonists; two trumpeters (short cornet type); one euphonium-player; one bombardon-player; one piccolo-player; two clarinet-players; one bassoon-player.

The instrumentation remained the same when the movable-arm figure was introduced, except that the bombardon (the instrument shown at the front left corner of the blue and red bands) was replaced with a bass horn.

Shown as the third band across on the previous page is the blue band in a movable-arm version c.1911, another reason for thinking that this was the standard set 101 at the time, since I have never seen a movable-arm red band. The standard and more correct painting of set 101, produced between 1920 and 1941, is shown on the right of the line.

SET 101, BAND OF THE 1ST LIFE GUARDS

This is known to have been the original box for this good set of slotted-arm bandsmen in blue and gold coats. Such original boxes as have been found for the red- and gold-coated variation have also been for set 101, so the question of whether either was ever issued as set 103, Band of the Royal Horse Guards, remains unresolved at the time of writing. (Phillips, London)

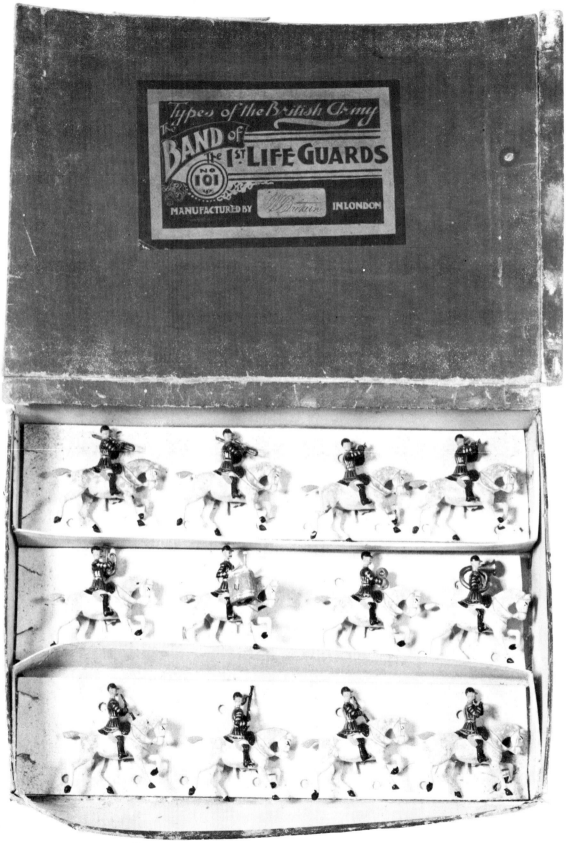

Chapter 16
The Dragoon Guards

Of the seven Dragoon Guard regiments in the British Army, Britains did not make models of the 3rd or 4th, although, on amalgamation, the 7th became the 4th/7th.

Set 3, 5th Dragoon Guards, four troopers and an officer. This was the third set ever made by Britains, although why this should be so is not clear. The early version was germanic, with gold sash officer (see page 40), then for a short period, presumably *c*.1901, the tin-sword Household Cavalry figure was used. The troopers then changed to the trotting figure dated 12.12.1902, while the officer remained on a prancing horse, which never had a throat plume in this set.

Set 44, 2nd Dragoon Guards, the Queen's Bays, four troopers with lances and a trumpeter, all at the full gallop. The first version was on the rocking horse. When the 12.12.1902 trotting horse became available, the trumpeter was changed to that, and a little later the colour of the trumpeter's horse changed from grey to bay.

Set 57, 1st Dragoon Guards, small size, officer, trumpeter and five each of troopers with carbines and troopers with swords. For some reason Britains painted the 1st Dragoon Guards in set 129 with yellow facings, although those in set 57 had the correct blue. No satisfactory explanation of this has yet been suggested.

Display Set 85, contained a row of four small-size 5th Dragoon Guards. These were shown in the 1915 catalogue to be in active-service order with lances, thus explaining this figure, which is rare.

Set 106, 6th Dragoon Guards, the Carabiniers, officer and four troopers with carbines. Distinctively, the uniform is all blue, and early troopers had the correct double white stripes down the breeches. The set first appeared using the one-eared galloping horse dated 1.1.1901, the officer being the same as the RHA officer but with a Dragoon Guard helmet and the horse painted grey.

Set 127, 7th Dragoon Guards, Princess Charlotte's, contained officer and four troopers with slung lances. The officer was on the one-eared galloping horse, and the troopers on the trotting horse dated 12.12.1902.

Display set 129, contained a double row of 14 1st King's Own Dragoon Guards depicted on the head-up trotting horse dated 12.12.1902, with the officer on the one-eared

galloping horse dated 1.1.1901. All carried swords.

Few Dragoon Guards appeared in second grade, the only ones I know of being the 6th, in set 8X. The pony-horse 6th Dragoon Guard attributed to Britains by Len Richards is actually a copy (see page 60, row 3, fig 2). In my opinion, this version never existed.

BOXES FOR DRAGOON GUARDS

Top to bottom: 1 Very early un-numbered box for set 44, 1896. 2 Later box for set 44, 1902. Note the reference to Copyright models by Wm Britain Jnr, which appeared on boxes as Britains put copyright dates on their figures. 3 Plain gold-on-black label with box for set 57, this being the size of box to take twelve small-size cavalry. Those in this set were the 1st King's Dragoon Guards. 4 and 5 Labels for set 3, the only difference being the addition of Boer War battle honours to 5, just underneath the horse's head on the right. Because of the reference to copyright models, 4 is probably 1903 and 5 c.1905 after the battle honours had been awarded. It is difficult to know why the trooper illustrated is carrying a carbine, since the Britains models normally carried swords.

SET 129

When it introduced very large boxes in 1906, Britains produced a representative box of the cavalry of the British Army. This became set 129 and comprised 14 each of the 2nd Life Guards, the 1st Dragoon Guards, the 2nd Dragoons, the 11th Hussars and the 12th Lancers – a 'squadron' of each different type of cavalry in the British Army.

This illustration shows what the 70-piece set looked like. I say this, because I have had to make the group up of a number of odds and ends rather than present a complete original set. As a result there are some anachronisms and deviations from the normal make-up in the group of figures on view.

The 2nd Life Guards should provide four figures with lances in the front rank, and these are on parade, but, as in most of the other contingents, figures dated from before and after the First World War are both included. In the 2nd Life Guards, the latecomers carry the long carbines.

During our period the 1st Dragoon Guards appear only in this set in standard size, although set 2074 was produced with them in 1953. Here they appear on the head-up trotting horse dated 12.12.1902, with an officer on the galloping horse dated

1.1.1901. The earlier figures have thick swords in contrast with the thin swords of later models.

The Second Dragoons, the Royal Scots Greys, contribute a perfectly normal squadron, an officer and 13 men on the normal horse. Nor do the 11th Hussars attempt anything unusual, just the normal figures with the officer on the prancing horse from set 12.

The 12th Lancers offer a little variety, in that half the troop hold their lances and the other half carry them in the slung position. In the basic set of 12th Lancers, number 128 (see page 55), the lances were usually slung only at this period. Those in our picture are all slung, which is wrong. A 12th Lancer at the carry is shown on page 33.

In spite of these shortcomings the mass of cavalry represented by a complete set 129 is so magnificent that I thought it only right to reproduce it as well as I might here. The chances of an original set surviving intact in good condition seem to be rather remote, although a number of badly damaged sets do appear, and these make good subjects for collectors skilled at restoring and repainting.

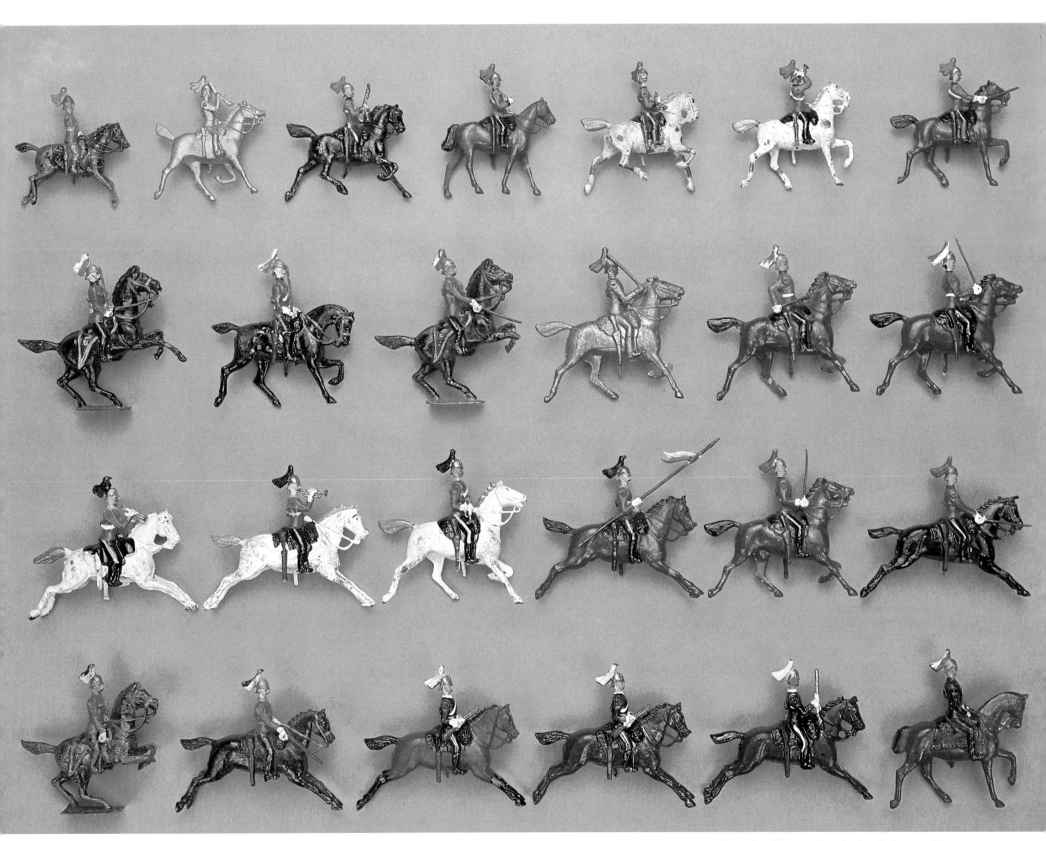

Examples of Dragoon Guards, described on page 50.

The Dragoon Guards: descriptions

Top row Small-size 1st Dragoon Guards, all from the 12-piece set 57 except for the gilt model. Early versions of this set are very hard to find. A first-version trooper on the head-down horse is shown, arm missing, and a trooper with carbine on the head-up horse is the 1st Dragoon Guard on page 38. Next in line is a gilt figure of the first-version, tail-up horse, with the trooper carrying a carbine. The second version of this set also had a variety of horse types. Figs 3 to 7 show two troopers with carbine and sword, two different trumpeters, the first with a matchstick mended head, and an officer. Figs 3 and 5 are on the horse dated 25.7.1904; fig 4 is dated 11.8.1904 and figs 6 and 7 are dated 26.4.1904.

2nd row This row shows types of set 3, the 5th Dragoon Guards. (For the germanic first version of this set, see page 33.) Fig 1 is the first prancing-horse officer with tin sword, followed by the very rare second version, also with tin sword. Although this one is probably a contemporary repaint, I have seen a few genuine originals. Another rare variant is the 5th Dragoon Guard, on page 33, with a 1902 Scots Grey horse. The scarcity of the second version suggests that the first, germanic model was used for a longish period, but after the 12.12.1902 horse became available plenty of set 3 were produced with it. Fig 3 is the movable-arm prancing-horse officer, derived from fig 1. Fig 4 is a gilt example of the early trooper dated 12.12.1902, showing the arm with the thick sword. Fig 5 is the similar undated trooper, *c*.1925, with a thin sword, while fig 6, by way of comparison, is paint style *c*.1935. Note that the correct white-over-red plume coloration has been reversed by mistake in the last two figures.

3rd row Figs 1–4 are types of the 2nd Dragoon Guards. The first figure is the trumpeter on the rocking horse, *c*.1898, the equivalent trooper being the 2nd Dragoon Guard on the jacket. Figs 2 and 3 are also trumpeters, a one-eared figure dated 1.1.1901 and a rare grey figure dated 12.12.1902. Soon after the trumpeter's horse is painted bay, the same colour as the troopers' horses. Fig 4 is a trooper dated 1.1.1901. Figs 5 and 6 show a trooper and officer of the 1st Dragoon Guards *c*.1935. The officer on the one-eared horse and the trooper dated 12.12.1902 trooper from this set are shown in front of set 129 (page 48).

4th row Fig 1 is an unusual prancing-horse officer of the 7th Dragoon Guards which may have been used *c*.1908. His condition is poor, the sword is missing from the arm and a leg is broken from the horse. Like all Dragoon Guards officers on prancing horses, he has no throat plume. The normal officer for this set on the one-eared horse dated 1.1.1901 is fig 2. The trooper dated 12.12.1902 is the 7th Dragoon Guard on page 33. The 6th

Dragoon Guard early troopers dated 1.1.1901 are figs 3 and 4 of this row. Notice that the horse of fig 3 is a bay with black points; sets had two of each colour, but probably only one with black points painted on the legs. These two have the short carbine. The officer for this set is on the same horse as the RHA officer, but with a Dragoon Guard head, and is shown as the 6th Dragoon Guard on page 33, *c*.1905. Another, *c*.1925, is shown as a Britains' copy on page 60, 3rd row, fig 6. Fig 5 is a later trooper, *c*.1930, with a long carbine, and fig 6 is an X series, set 8X, on the level-headed horse.

BOXES FOR 6TH DRAGOON GUARDS

Top to bottom: 1 Typographical label for the first version of set 106, 1901. 2 Whisstock label design for the same set, 1914. 3 and 4 The 6th Dragoon Guards were used in the X series, and, as with the labels for the best-quality figures, the designs changed from time to time. 4 has the label bent over the right-hand end of the box, and the reference number 8X appears there. It is extremely rare to find second-grade boxes from the early period, and even rarer to find any with a catalogue number. The normal number of figures included in these X series cavalry boxes is six, in contrast with five in the best-quality boxes. As sometimes happens, 4 has had its label rather spoilt by someone doing ink doodles over it. Since it is the only example I have ever seen, however, one cannot be choosy.

Chapter 17
The Dragoons

Britains made models of all three Dragoon regiments on the Army List in 1914.

Set 31, the 1st Dragoons, the Royals, officer and four troopers, all on the same horse. This set was made in 1895 with a new and rather large fixed-arm tin sword figure. The troopers have a distinctive head with the horsehair plume falling straight down the helmet rather than flowing out behind as in the Household Cavalry and Dragoon Guards. The 1st Dragoons in the X and A series are shown similarly. The officer of set 31, on the other hand, was on the prancing horse, exactly the same model as in the Household Cavalry but with the addition of a throat plume. Indeed, it may be that the prancing-horse figure with this head was made for set 31 in the first place, and that later someone had the bright idea of clipping the throat plume off to make a Household Cavalry officer, since for some time there was no different figure for the officer in sets 1, 2 and 3, just a trooper with a gold sash (see page 40).

Set 32, the 2nd Dragoons, the Royal Scots Greys, officer and four troopers, all on the same horse. Because of their unusual uniform, which was like the Foot Guards, the Scots Greys sold very well, second only to the Household Cavalry. Britains produced a very large scale germanic set of six with plug shoulders, which never received a set number (see page 38). This set, which is extremely rare, was probably replaced in 1895 with what became set 32, using the same horse as the 1st Dragoons. In an interesting variation, some early sets were given a Foot Guard style round bearskin. Only later did the correct tall bearskin with the long white hackle become standard. In set 32, the Scots Grey officer, by contrast with the 1st Dragoons, was the same figure as the trooper with a gold sash and, when separate arms were provided, an arm with an outstretched sword.

Of the first 500 main-series sets, Scots Greys appear in 12, set 59 being a double row, an honour never accorded to any other British Cavalry regiment. In addition, Scots Greys were used extensively for X, A, B and W series sets. There are 24 separate different models shown in this book, probably the highest total for any mounted regiment. Their popularity has meant that many have survived, and fortunately their price is relatively low.

X series box for 1st Dragoons. Britains seems not to have been too proud of the X series, as the company's trademark does not appear. The reference on this box on the end is 4X.

Britains only depicted the 6th Dragoons, the Inniskillings, in Boer War Service dress (see page 117 and also an example on page 33).

The Dragoons: descriptions

Top row The 1st Dragoons: figs 1–4 are from set 31. Fig 1 is the officer on prancing horse with throat plume, fig 2 the first-version trooper with fixed arm and tin sword. Figs 3 and 4 show troopers on the Scots Grey horse. Fig 3 is the earlier one dated 1.11.1902, and fig 4 the later one with a shorter rein, in a paint style *c*.1935. Fig 5 is an X series model on a fixed-arm pony horse, and fig 6 is an officer for the A series, unusually on a grey horse. The trooper for the A series, *c*.1930, is shown on page 33.

The figures in the next three rows are all of the 2nd Dragoons, Royal Scots Greys.

2nd row Figs 1–4 are the main sequence of figures in set 32. Fig 1 is the fixed-arm model with the Foot Guard head. Note the sword scabbard painted in gold rather than silver. Fig 2 is the same as fig 1 but with the correct Scots Grey head. On page 33 the officer for this set is shown with a gold sash. Fig 3 is the long-rein movable-arm figure dated 1.11.1902 and fig 4 the short-rein trooper. Note that the sword on the later figure is thinner and that the painting of the grey horse is done with black stipple brushwork, as opposed to the earlier all-over cream. Fig 5 is the Scots Grey pony-horse fixed-arm figure from the X series. Fig 6 is an A series Scots Grey on a thinner version of the head-up spindly horse used for the 1st Dragoon above.

3rd row This small-size Scots Grey figure was used for fig 1, a mounted Foot Guards officer on a black horse, and for fig 2, a W series Scots Grey. Fig 3, an early X series

figure on a head-down spindly horse, has a Foot Guard head like the first variation of the first-grade figure (2nd row, fig 1). Fig 4 is similar to fig 3 but dated *c*.1932, when this figure was given a base between the two hind legs so that it could slot into 'Parade' baseboards (see page 188). These figures with bases are extremely rare, and this example is badly damaged. Fig 5 is also something of a rarity, of the interesting rather than the valuable kind, being an ordinary first-grade trooper in a second-grade paint finish. I have no explanation for this; all I know is that it is very uncommon. Fig 6 is a small-size figure, probably number 13d from the bulk-packed figures. Fig 7 is a head-level spindly horse from the 1920s A series.

4th row Fig 1 is another W series figure, *c*.1932. Note that it is basically the same horse as the figure above, but that the tail has been remodelled into the main casting, perhaps to make it less easily broken. Fig 2 is a gilt first-version small-size figure, and fig 3 is a matching fixed-arm officer from set 6b. Fig 4 is another figure of the same type, but with a movable arm carrying a lance rather than the normal sword. The arm appears to be genuine, although it could possibly have been swopped from a 16th Lancer. Fig 5 shows the normal trooper with sword from an early set 6b. Fig 6 is a small-size trooper on a head-up cantering horse from set 6b, and fig 7 is the second-version galloping figure dated 9.5.1904, this one being an officer with the outstretched sword arm. Note that, like the standard-size Scots Grey officers, he has a gold sash.

Other illustrations of Dragoons:

Page 48: the Scots Greys, part of box 129.
Page 60: several interesting copies of Britains' models.
Page 64: the honorary Colonel in Chief of the 1st Dragoons, HIH Wilhelm II, 'Kaiser Bill'.
Page 97: a rather battered group of first-version Scots Greys, part of box 73.

Examples of Dragoons, described on page 51.

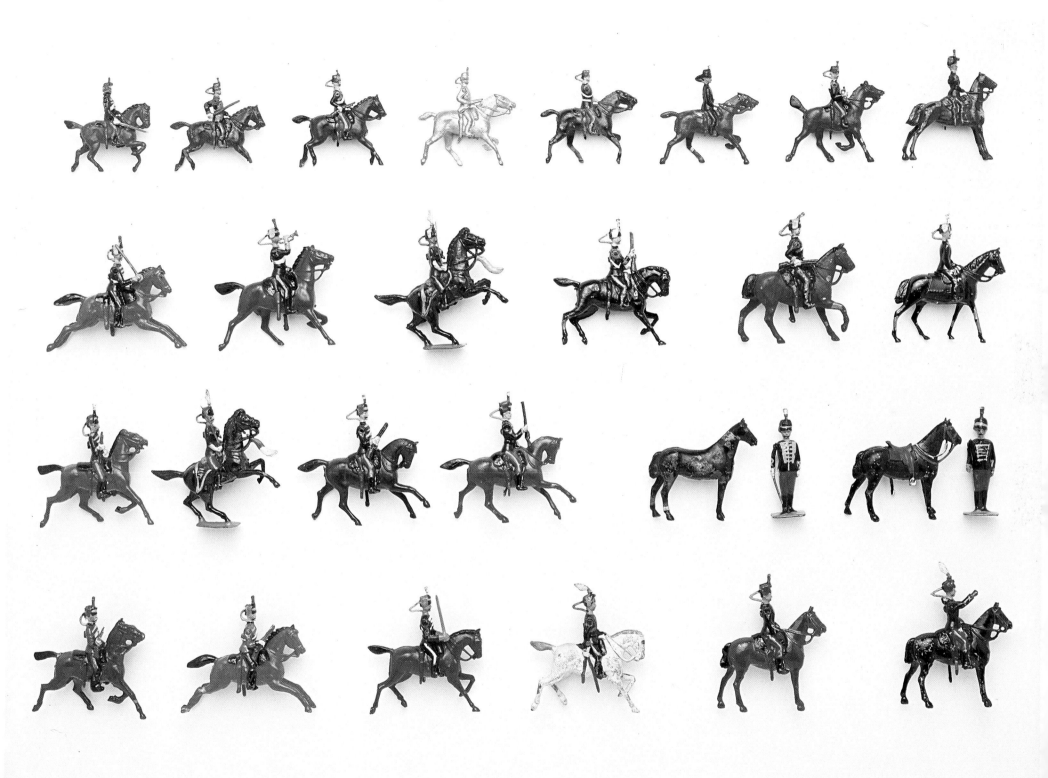

Examples of Hussars, described on page 54.

Chapter 18
The Hussars

Set 8, 4th Hussars, four troopers and a trumpeter on rocking horse. The troopers normally carried swords. All the figures changed to the one-eared galloping horse dated 1.1.1901, and the trumpeter changed again to the head-up trotting horse dated 12.12.1902.

Sets 12 and 13, 11th and 3rd Hussars, each four troopers on horses and an officer on prancing horse with tin sword and throat plume. Issued in 1893, these were chronologically (as opposed to numerically in the listing) the first of Britains' Hussars. The donkey-horse fixed-arm figure with carbine was a little under-size. Occasionally these two sets varied to the pony horse or Scots Grey horse. Both sets changed to the cantering horse dated 12.2.1903 when this became available. The officer followed the usual sequence for the prancing-horse figure.

Set 83, Middlesex Yeomanry, normally containing two donkey-horse troopers and two on the rocking horse with an officer on the prancing horse. These are included among the Hussars because of their Hussar-style uniform. This was a mixed set, and combinations of three and one were not unknown. When figure dating began, the cantering horse dated 12.2.1903 and the galloping horse dated 1.1.1901 were used, but c.1928 the galloping horses were dropped, and sets appeared with all cantering figures. The officer remained on the appropriate prancing horse.

Set 87, double row of small-size 13th Hussars, six troopers, one trumpeter, one officer. This set is very rare.

Set 99, 13th Hussars, four troopers and an officer. These sword-carrying figures were first produced on the pony horse; the officer had a tall plume and outstretched sword arm. Soon after it was issued, the figures all changed to the 12.2.1903 cantering horse. For some reason Britains packed this set in a box too narrow to accommodate the officer's tall plume, which is therefore nearly always broken or missing in the surviving sets.

Set 182, 11th Hussars, is an interestingly different set, brought out in 1913, containing four riderless saddled horses at the halt, with three troopers and an officer dismounted to stand beside them.

Set 270. This display set combined dismounted 11th Hussars (set 182) with a mounted set on the horse at the halt, including matching officer. These figures all had empty hands.

Set 315, 10th Hussars, is a similar five-piece set, using exactly the same mounted figures at the halt, one of which is illustrated on page 33.

Britains' favourite Hussar regiment in the first grade was obviously the 11th, with their Cherrypicker red trousers. They appeared in six display boxes before 1932 and in more later. It is worth noting that the Royal Horse Artillery in full dress has a Hussar-style uniform, so mounted gunners and officers should not be confused with any Hussar regiment.

For X and A series figures, Britains generally specified 3rd Hussars as the regiment used, the figures being various spindly-legged horses with Hussar heads. In the small size, in addition to set 87, set 10b was the 11th Hussars. The second version of this contained a unique mounted figure at the halt dated 4.7.1904, the set comprising three troopers and a trumpeter. A fixed-arm version of this figure at the halt was used as an M series Hussar. In small-size second grade, sets 8w and 30w contain four and eight Hussars respectively, with a fixed-arm figure derived from the early B series. There were also 'mini' gilt Hussars in set 14w, which contained six figures for the same price as the normal painted set with four figures.

The Hussars: descriptions

Top row Figs 1 and 2 are small-size 13th Hussars from set 87. Fig 1 is an officer on a small trotting horse; condition is F–P, and his sword has been soldered. Fig 2 is a trooper on the head-down cantering horse, condition F, with two legs missing from the horse. These figures are so rare that they are desirable in any condition. Figs 3–8 are 11th Hussars. Fig 3, the 11th Hussar equivalent of fig 2, is from set 10b and carried a carbine. Fig 4 is a Hussar in gilt on a cantering head-up horse of the same period. Fig 5 is the same figure fully painted, from set 10b; the arm on this figure is missing. Fig 6 is a W series Hussar based on the same figure but reworked with a fixed arm. Fig 7 is a first-version trumpeter on the early tail-up walking horse from set 10b. Finally, fig 8 shows the later fixed-arm Hussar designated 5m. The second-version B series Hussar from which this is derived, dated 4.7.1904, is on the jacket.

2nd row Figs 1 and 2 are 4th Hussars from set 8. Fig 1 is the first-version rocking-horse figure and fig 2 shows the trumpeter on the head-up trotting horse dated 12.12.1902. The full-gallop trooper dated 1.1.1901 is shown on the jacket. Figs 3–6 are 3rd Hussars from set 13. Fig 3 is the first-version officer on prancing horse with throat plume, the matching donkey-horse trooper being on the jacket. Fig 4 is the unusual pony-horse trooper, and fig 5 the unusual Scots Grey horse trooper. Fig 6 is the A series 3rd Hussar on the head-up spindly horse.

3rd row 11th Hussars: figs 1–4 show types from set 12. Fig 1 is the first-version fixed-arm donkey horse with carbine, fig 2 the matching officer on prancing horse. Fig 3 shows a trooper of c.1908 on the cantering horse dated 12.2.1903. Note the early small head; the metallic paint on the short carbine shows that the figure was not produced right at the start date. Fig 4 shows a trooper c.1935 by way of contrast. The horse is the same, though there is now no date underneath. The trooper's head is larger, and his carbine longer. Figs 6–8 come from set 182, but fig 5 is a puzzle, being a riderless and saddleless horse. It is dated 18.8.1903, which shows that it is derived from the Lancer at the halt of that date, as is the saddled horse of set 182 (fig 7). Fig 6 is the early standing officer with sword and white gloves; note the very thick painting of the frogging across the chest. Fig 8 is the late trooper of set 182, c.1930. Like all the troopers in this set, his arm has an empty hand.

4th row Figs 1 and 2 are Middlesex Yeomanry from the first version of set 83; fig 1 is on the donkey horse, fig 2 on the rocking horse. Note the double red stripe down the breeches, one of the features of very early Britains' painting for sets depicting cavalry who wore double stripes in real life. The matching officer on prancing horse is shown on page 65. Figs 3 and 4 shown 13th Hussars from set 99. Fig 3 is the early trooper on pony horse, fig 4 the matching officer. Note that his plume has become bent because the box was too narrow. Figs 5 and 6 show 11th Hussars at the halt from set 270. Fig 5 is c.1932, and by way of contrast fig 6 shows the paint style of an officer c.1940; he is rather neater, his moustache has gone, and his gloves are white rather than brown.

Other illustrations of Hussars:
Page 48: the 11th Hussars, part of box 129; in the forefront is a good view of the later officer.
Page 60: interesting copies of Britains Hussars.
Page 61: 'Mini' Hussars.
Page 64: the special group of Hussars designed by Alfred Britain and dated 7.5.1907.

Chapter 19
The Lancers

Un-numbered plug-shoulder Lancer sets were produced of:

12th Lancers
16th Lancers
17th Lancers.

Each of these sets comprised seven troopers, officer and trumpeter.

The lance heads and pennons of the plug-shoulder Lancer are loose on the lance, and can be twisted so that the pennon flows back when the lance is in the upright position or droops below the lance when the lance is lowered for the charge. For further discussion of this germanic figure, see page 38. An example of the 16th Lancer is shown on page 33, and the 17th Lancers appear on page 40.

Cross-legged Lancer sets are:
Set 23, 5th Royal Irish Lancers
Set 24, 9th Queen's Royal Lancers
Set 33, 16th The Queen's Lancers.

Each of these sets (illustrated with their box lids overleaf) contained four troopers of the cross-legged Lancer type at the halt and a turned-in-the-saddle officer. The cross-legged Lancer is beautifully moulded with separated reins, and the standing horse is portrayed a little restless, scratching the back of one fetlock with the other hoof. The officer, copied from a Simkin print, is Britains' longest-lived figure, since it was produced from 1894 to 1966, tin sword and all. For many collectors, this magnificent model is the epitome of Britains, and its appearance so early was a happy augury.

After ten years of production, the cross-legged Lancer in all three sets was replaced by the new cavalryman at the halt dated 18.8.1903. The new figure had a movable arm, normally a short lance at the carry, although I have seen some sets of the 16th with slung lances. After the First World War, the wording underneath the figure was changed and the date removed, but the figure itself was not modified.

Right at the end of our period, Britains recognized the 1922 amalgamation of the 16th and 5th Lancers, and discontinued set 23, retitling set 33 as the 16th/5th Lancers.

Display set 73, normally contained a row of the same figures that appeared in set 81 (see below). Occasionally it included 17th Lancers in full dress, which was an uncommon variation.

Set 81, 17th Lancers, active-service order. These figures are referred to as wearing Ulundi foreign-service dress,

and are described on page 106.

Set 94, 21st Lancers, active-service order. This set, referred to as wearing Omdurman foreign-service dress, is described on page 107. The same set was later changed to represent Lancers of the First World War in steel helmets, and these are described on page 139.

Set 100, 21st Lancers, full dress, four troopers and a trumpeter. There was a great deal of interest in the 21st Lancers, since the regiment was re-formed in 1897 and equipped for the first time as Lancers, then went on the following year to distinguish itself at Omdurman. This set was first produced using the pony-horse figure, which was changed to the cantering horse dated 12.2.1903 when this was available.

Set 128, 12th Lancers, four troopers and an officer. This set was produced using the cantering horse dated 12.2.1903. The officer was normally on the head-up trotting horse dated 12.12.1902, but sometimes on the same horse as the troopers. The arms provided for this set were usually of the slung-lance type, but, when 14 of the same figures appeared as part of the large cavalry display set 129, half were given lance arms at the carry (see page 48). Set 128 was the last new single best-quality set of Lancers to be produced during our period.

X and A series second-grade Lancers tended to be

BOXES FOR SET 12B, SMALL-SIZE 16TH LANCERS
This was an extremely attractive set. In the first version the regiment appeared in red jackets with white foreign-service helmets. The box at the top is an early pictorial small-size box, c.1899. Note the number 12 with a lower-case b, whereas later the b became upper case. The box has round metal corner reinforcements. Below is the slightly larger box to take the khaki second version, with a Whisstock label, c.1914.

models of the 9th at the halt, although the 5th were also used. The figure was the same as the 18.8.1903 dated Lancer at the halt, with either a lance at the carry or an outstretched sword arm and with varying degrees of second- or third-grade paint. All three types of spindly horse were used for walking sets, painted once more as 9th.

In the small size, Lancers were well represented by set 13b, 17th Lancers in full dress, and 12b, 16th Lancers in foreign-service order. In the first version the 16th had red coats, then changing to all-khaki (for the latter, see page 116). A mini-lancer officer dated 4.7.1902 was used for a long time in the W series painted gilt (see page 61).

All the cavalry regiments in the British army except the Hussars practised with the lance, and on parade their front ranks were often equipped with lances – which explains why Britains gave lances to many models that were not Lancer regiments.

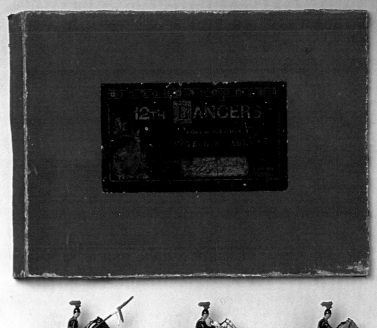

Above: A complete set of plug-shoulder 12th Lancers, *c.*1894. The officer was on a pale brownish-ochre coloured horse, the trumpeter on a grey; four troopers were on black horses and three on brown. The box lid is also shown, but the original bright gilt printing on the black label has almost faded out. This lid was once in the collection of Len Richards and probably led him to conclude that the set contained 12 pieces. Since then, however, a complete box has been seen, with partitioning which confirmed that nine is the correct number. For further consideration of plug-shoulder Lancers, see Chapter 14.

Left: Complete sets of cross-legged Lancers in their boxes. Top to bottom: 5th Royal Irish Lancers, 9th Queen's Royal Lancers and 16th The Queen's Lancers. The boxes for these Lancer sets brought out the best of Britains' early efforts, and the labels must be contenders for the most attractive Britains' labels ever.

Examples of Lancers, described on page 58.

The Lancers: descriptions

Top row These are all small-size figures from the B series. Figs 1, 2 and 5–7 are 17th Lancers from set 13b, and the two in red coats, figs 3 and 4, are 16th Lancers from set 12b. Fig 1 is the first-version fixed-arm officer, followed by a matching trooper. Fig 3 is a movable-arm officer, followed by a head-up horse with a trooper. The 16th Lancers only wore this uniform with red coat and white foreign-service helmet in the first version, changing in the second version, issued in about 1904, to the khaki foreign-service dress of the Boer War. (A set of these is shown on page 116.) Figs 5 and 6 are head-down and head-up first-version cantering horses with troopers; the lance-head of fig 5 is missing. Fig 7 is the second-version officer, on the horse dated 26.8.1904. The matching trooper, illustrated on page 33, carried the new lance. The lances on the early small-size figures were cast all in one, whereas the later ones are made up of an arm and lance-head with pennon cast separately and joined together with a wire lance-shaft.

2nd row This row shows various types of Lancers at the halt, on the horse originally dated 18.8.1903. Fig 1 is a trooper of the 5th Royal Irish Lancers with the distinctive green plume, and fig 2 is a second-grade painting of the same figure. Fig 3 is a second-grade 9th Lancer. Figs 4 and 5 are troopers of the 16th Lancers, c.1905 and 1928. Note that the earlier figure carries the lance slung, which is unusual, and that his face is painted very pale. Finally, fig 6 is a 16th Lancer in second-grade paint.

3rd row Figs 1 and 2 are unusual figures of the 5th Irish Lancers. Fig 1 is at the halt but is fitted with the head normally used for figures on moving horses. It is painted in second-grade style like the figure above it. Fig 2 is an officer on a head-up trotting horse with an outstretched sword arm, similar in style to the officer of the 12th Lancers (fig 4) but not belonging to any catalogued set I know. This may have been a special order. Figs 3–5 are 12th Lancers from set 128, fig 3 the trooper with normal arm with slung lance. On page 33 is a trooper with lance at the carry that sometimes appeared in this set but was normally part of set 129 (see page 48). Fig 4 is the set's normal officer, although occasionally the officer was on the same horse as the troopers. Fig 6 shows an A series 9th Lancer on a head-level spindly horse.

4th row Figs 1–3 are 21st Lancers in full dress from set 100, the first two being on the pony horse. Fig 3 is the trumpeter on the cantering horse c.1930. Fig 4 is an example in colour of the unusual 17th Lancers in full dress illustrated at the top of this page. Figs 5 and 6 are further examples of second-grade 9th Lancers. These are probably earlier X series figures, as the horses are rather thicker and the paint more matt than on the A series example in the row above. Fig 6 is the officer on the spindly horse, painted grey following the colouring of the officer's horse in the first-grade set.

Other illustrations of Lancers:
Page 97, picture of set 73: assortment of types from set 81, the 17th in foreign-service order.
Page 133: 9th Lancers officer turned in the saddle; second-version germanic plug-shoulder trooper from 16th Lancers; 21st Lancers pony-horse trooper in contrasting colour from the one on page 57.

Top: 17th Lancers in full dress. These are unusual figures, in that Britains did not produce a regular catalogued set containing this regiment in full dress. The single-row set containing 17th Lancers was set 81, in which they wore 'Ulundi' foreign-service helmets. Possibly those shown here were issued as part of set 129, or they may have been a special order. They are in ordinary best-quality paintwork rather than a special standard. The fourth figure from the right has had an incorrect arm press on to its shoulder stud. The second figure from the right is shown in colour on page 57, 4th row, fig 4. (Phillips, London)

Above: Lancer boxes, top to bottom: 1 Whisstock design for set 128. 2 Early typographical box for set 33. 3 The Whisstock design for set 33. Note that the boxes for Lancers at the halt are shorter than for the Lancers at the canter.

Chapter 20
Copies of Britains

The number of people who set up in competition naturally worried Britains. Even worse was when they copied Britains' own designs. Chapter 11 (pages 27-9) has briefly discussed some of the people concerned. This chapter examines some of the pirate products themselves.

A glance at the next page explains why Britains often repeated phrases such as 'when buying Britains soldiers, see that they are Britains' and 'genuine only with this trademark' in their advertising. At first sight the illustration shows an interesting collection of Britains' cavalry figures. In reality, however, the only Britains items are: top row, fig 1; 3rd row, figs 1 and 6; and 4th row, figs 1 and 6. The figures shown include some models which I and Len Richards before me at one time believed were made by Britains but which I must now conclude were made by another company.

Top row Fig 1 is a Britains' rocking-horse 4th Hussar trumpeter c.1898, followed by copy rocking-horse figures depicting 3rd and 18th Hussars, Life Guards, Horse Guards, 6th Dragoon Guards and 2nd Dragoon Guards. Figs 2 and 4 have movable arms, while the other copies are fixed-arm. Fig 6 is shown in plate 54 in Richards' book, where it is attributed to the X series. For a long time I considered figs 5–7 to be Britains' second-grade figures, although this did not explain the Horse Guard, fig 5, on a brown horse, something never knowingly perpetrated by Britains. When I found a set 8X containing six 6th Dragoon Guards in a different model from fig 6, I changed my mind and now believe that these three figures are copies.

2nd row More examples of movable-arm copy rocking horses: two different Scots Greys, Indian Army Lancer, 16th Lancer trumpeter, and another two 2nd Dragoon Guards in exactly the same stance as those in Britains' set 44.

3rd row Fig 1 is a Britains pony-horse 17th Lancer trumpeter, followed by (figs 2–5) copies depicting 6th Dragoon Guards, 11th Hussars, 1st Dragoons and Scots Greys. The 6th Dragoon was illustrated as a Britains figure in the 3rd row, plate 28 of Len Richards' book. Fig 6 is a Britains 6th Dragoon Guard officer, based on the RHA officer, and fig 7 is a beautiful copy of it done as a Scots Grey.

4th row This starts with a Britains 1st Dragoon officer with movable arm, c.1907. Fig 2 is an early figure from the United States, made by a firm called Barclay, showing the influence there of the prancing-horse officers Britains exported to the USA under their arrangement with C W Beiser (see page 150). Fig 3 is a different copy in gilt; although the arm is movable, the base is wedge-shaped, like the earlier Britains fixed-arm figures. Fig 4 is rather different, and judging by the paint a later, fixed-arm cavalry officer sporting a totally incorrect uniform. Although much of the detail is different, Britains' influence is still clear. Fig 5 is a copy made in Argentina of a Britains Argentine Cavalry figure. Compare this with the set shown on page 160. Fig 6 is a Britains X series 1st Dragoon with a rather sloppy point job, and fig 7 is a gilt copy of it.

Apart from examining the lettering, there are a number of ways of deciding whether a particular model is a genuine Britains. Check whether a girth is moulded on the horse's belly: Britains showed a girth only on the early prancing-horse figure. The metal the model is made of is another good clue. If the metal shows through the paint brightly, and the paint flakes off easily, the model was probably made by Hanks or Reka, both of whom often used this type of alloy. Arms are another give-away, since, although the rest of the model may look like a Britains figure, arms are often cast in a different style. With cavalry, look at the inside of the horse's leg; a Britains model will be fully rounded, while copies often look flat and unmodelled. None of these clues is infallible, but some will often help.

The figures on page 60 not already identified are probably by Hanks or Reka, both of whose products are characterized by moulded girths. All in all, the jungle of unidentified figures from the early years of hollowcast toy soldiers remains a serious problem.

BEST METAL. BEST MAKE. Horse Guards. Made in Germany.

Left: Boxed set of Heinrich hollowcast Royal Horse Guards. These figures are extremely similar to the Britains' rocking horse, and inevitably beg the question of who was copying whom. The packing and style of box, too, are very like Britains' in 1893-4 (see page 40, top left). I have never seen a Britains' box from this very early date for the Royal Horse Guards, but since Britains entitled its first set 'Life Guards' rather than '1st Life Guards', as it did shortly afterwards, the second set might well have been called 'Horse Guards' rather than 'The Royal Horse Guards', as Heinrich has done here. Britains' rocking horse, the first cavalry figure with a movable arm, was introduced in 1896. Either this German figure was already being marketed, hollowcast and with the completely new loop-and-stud method of arm-fixing, or else this is a quick German copy of Britains' latest idea. It is possible that Heinrich and Britains had an arrangement to pool designs and ideas, but in that case why was Heinrich bringing out sets named in English to compete in Britains' home market? (Phillips, London)

Examples of copies of Britains' cavalry, described on page 59.

60

Chapter 21
Royals and unusuals

As a company alert to commercial opportunities, Britains did not limit itself rigidly to its standard ranges. This chapter includes unusual items, things which did not fit conveniently under another chapter heading and a few stop press discoveries.

Mini-cavalry

Britains produced a short series of very small-size cavalry figures in 1901-2, each about 45mm tall including the horse and thus in about 30mm scale. (The smallest B series figure is in 43mm scale.) These mini-cavalry are illustrated right, where 16 of them are shown in four rows. There are three basic types: a Household Cavalry figure on a walking horse; a Hussar officer at the halt; and a Lancer officer at the canter.

The Household Cavalry figure is probably the most common of the three, but is often not attributed to Britains, because there is no Britains' embossing on the belly of the horse or elsewhere. I have seen these figures with a paper label dated 1st Feb 1901, these being the quite well painted variety shown as fig 1, the Life Guard, and fig 2, the Horse Guard, in the top row. Other paint

Above: Two examples of territorial infantry in peak caps as seen at the coronation of George V in 1910. (Phillips, London)

Above: Mini-cavalry.

variations were as 1st Royal Dragoons, with different degrees of paint detail (top row, figs 3 and 4, 2nd row, figs 2 and 3), with a khaki coat (2nd row, fig 1) and in gilt or silver (2nd row, fig 4 and 3rd row, fig 4). The gilt variety was issued in an un-numbered box of twelve, also quoting the date 1st Feb 1901 on the box label.

After the First World War, this model, along with the other two types, found its way into the W series, where the Household Cavalry were in a set of six in gilt finish, designated set 13w, Life guards (Gilt). In the 1931 catalogue, this figure also appeared as bulk-sale item 1d painted, costing a penny halfpenny, and 15d gilt, at one penny.

The miniature Hussar and Lancer officers are both engraved with the same date, 4.7.1902, and thus followed the successful introduction of the Household Cavalry figure. Both are extremely detailed models. Fig 1 of the 4th row shows just how much detail was attempted, since this is one of the pewter master figures from which the production brass moulds were cast. Note that in contrast with fig 2, which is a production gilt, the master figure does not have a capline, which presumably was engraved into the brass mould direct. Nor does the master figure include the lettering on the belly of the horse that appears on the ordinary figures.

Figs 3 and 4 of the 4th row are a later version of the Lancer officer, with the tail moulded differently, presumably to make it less fragile. Of course there is no date underneath this later figure. The Lancer figures appeared in the 1931 catalogue as set 15w, comprising six figures, and singly as 3d painted and 17d gilt.

Figs 2 and 3 of the 3rd row show the Hussar figure. The earlier officer on the left has a tall plume and a throat plume on the horse, details missing in the later silver figure on the right, which is undated. In the 1931 catalogue, the set of six gilt Hussars was numbered 14w, the singles 2d painted and 16d gilt.

These small novelties had a great deal of competition and in many penny bazaars one could buy two in a box for a penny. Nevertheless, Britains strove to keep ahead on quality. Fig 1 of the 3rd row is one of the better-made competitors, a Hussar that looks like a cross between the Britains Life Guard and the Hussar at the halt. When collecting these miniature figures, be continually on the look-out for copies, some of which are remarkably similar to Britains.

Royals

Britains began to produce models of royalty soon after they started manufacturing hollow castings, and it may well be that not all are now known. Britains adopted the traditional portrait of sovereigns, the head and shoulders bust. At the top left-hand corner of page 64, busts of King Edward VII, dated 1.8.1901, and Queen Alexandra, dated 1.2.1902, are illustrated. Busts like these were usually given a gold or copper finish, and I have never seen a fully painted example. Similar busts are known to

have been made of Queen Victoria, William Booth, the founder of the Salvation Army, William Shakespeare and, later, Madame Tussaud. They are all hollow castings, made in exactly the same way as the soldiers.

In the row below these busts are a group of fixed-arm cavalry figures in the same scale as the B series. These show a second-grade painted Life Guard, a model of King Edward VII derived from the same figure but painted gilt and another Life Guard in gilt that matches the monarch. I have seen the figure of the king with a B series paper label dated 1st Feb 1901, although I have always wondered if this is correct. Queen Victoria died on 22 January, so a master figure dated 2nd February would involve fast work but could have been done. The bust, on the other hand, is dated 1.8.1901. The miniature figure of Edward VII is quite recognizable. He is presumably acknowledging the plaudits of his people by doffing his Field Marshal's hat. The hat and the hand holding it are a separate casting and plug into the wrist of the upraised arm – so here we have a plug-handed king.

It is noticeable that, although Britains made busts and other figures of Victoria, Edward VII, Edward VIII, George VI and Elizabeth II, none, at least so far as I know, depict George V.

On just one occasion, to my knowledge, Britains made a model of foreign royalty: William II, Emperor of Germany, otherwise known as 'Kaiser Bill', Queen Victoria's grandson and Edward VII's nephew. As 'one of the family' he received various British military honours, among them the Honorary Colonelcy of the 1st Royal Dragoons. The copper finish model of the Emperor is shown as fig 3 of the top row on page 64, next to the lid of the individual box for that figure. The figure is the normal casting used for the officer of the 1st Dragoons in set 31. Britains' 'copper' finish turned out more like a dull silver colour, almost gun-metal; details are picked out in gold paint. As sometimes happened with souvenir items, the box label is one of the few that does not bear Britains' trademark.

Alfred Britain's experimental Hussars

Some very interesting figures which Britains was kind enough to let me photograph appear in the bottom row of page 64. Fig 1 is an 11th Hussar at the halt with a movable arm with sword, in 60mm scale. By way of comparison, a normal-scale 11th Hussar from set 270 is shown immediately above. The large Hussar is marked 'Copyright A. Britain 7.5.1907', which means that in this case Alfred Britain rather than William Britain Junior created the master, and shows that talent for modelling was by no means confined to the older brother. To all appearances the figure is a normal production figure, but larger and with the extra paint details (reins, eyes and eyebrows on the horse) that one would expect Britains to include on higher-priced soldiers. Fig 2 next to it is a riderless horse in the same scale, dated 1.7.1907. For

another comparison of size, and to remind us that occasionally Britains did produce larger figures, fig 3 is a Racing Colours of Famous Owners' figure, in which the horse and rider are in an even larger scale. (See below for a separate discussion of Racing Colours.) Fig 4 is an unpainted casting of a Hussar at the walk, dated 13.6.1907. All three larger-scale horses are marked 'Copyright A. Britain'.

This group of figures was discovered in a drawer at the Britains' factory, together with the larger-size Dragoon and Hussar shown as figs 6 and 7 of the row above, with a normal 11th Hussar officer from set 182 next to them for scale comparison. The 1st Dragoon and 11th Hussar bodies are solid, and have the look and feel of German-made figures. Like German figures, they have sockets in the neck to take a separately cast head, but the heads are not the solid German-made ones but Britains' own hollowcast heads fitted on to the German bodies with a short piece of thick wire. The Hussar head is not the same as the heads on the figures in the row below, as one might have expected. The paintwork on these two figures on foot looks as though it was done by Britains and matches the cavalry below in style.

We shall probably never know for sure what exactly went on in this group of figures. They certainly never came on to the market. Perhaps Alfred Britain was experimenting with the idea of producing a larger-scale best-quality line to compete with the more expensive German toys produced by Heinrich or Haffner. Whatever the true situation was, these figures are fascinating evidence of the constant experimentation and development Britains devoted to improving its production.

Racing colours

This example from Britains' Racing Colours of Famous Owners series appears here mainly to compare the largest toy horse that Britains made with the large-size cavalry designed by Alfred Britain. It is, however, interesting to glance in passing at this separate little venture of Britains, started c.1925 as catalogue number 237. The idea was very simple: to produce a race horse with demountable jockey who could be painted in the colours of any owner. Britains produced a range of 12 of the most famous owners, all in individual boxes. Later, and also after the Second World War, many others were produced, including two series of American owners, all these being under new catalogue numbers.

The one shown here, dating from c.1937, is rather special, in that the Duchess of Norfolk included Mickey Mouse in her colours, and Britains had to obtain Walt Disney's permission to reproduce the colours on their model. The box label also includes a picture of Mickey Mouse and is thus unique in the Racing Colours series.

As might be expected, Britains would paint any racing colour to order, and many proud owners commissioned their own. The casting was also available unpainted, and as well as being used to reproduce existing colours proved an excellent aid to thinking about new designs.

Odds, ends and stop press

BRITAINS' MASTER FIGURE
Page 65 shows a mixture of interesting types, some of which come under the heading of 'stop press'. Fig 1 of the top row is a Britains' pewter master figure, which according to Britains must have been taken from the factory illicitly. As on the mini-Lancer officer on page 61, the detail is considerable. Comparing the master with the production model next to it shows how much original detail tends to get lost when the figure is painted.

The production figure is an example of an early Royal West Surrey Regiment firing from set 121. At this time, the base, like the master figure, was still oval-shaped, and the paper label dated 1st July 1901 can just be seen underneath the base. This model was manufactured sometime between late 1901 and *c*.1907.

SET 25, SOLDIERS TO SHOOT
Although this novelty appears as set 25 in Gamages' 1902 Christmas catalogue, it does not appear on the lists of toy soldiers issued by Britains in 1902 and 1904. Perhaps it was considered a novelty item and appeared in a separate catalogue of toys.

The figures included in this set are numbers 3 to 5 in the top row, page 65. There were four to a set, plus a bundle of wire ammunition, and at a shilling a box they were twice as expensive as the usual Britains' infantry. They were simple to operate. The thick rifle barrels were hollow, and a piece of ammunition was inserted at the breech, with a small part protruding. The spring just behind the kneeling figure was then flicked, and the ammunition 'fired' through the gun barrel. Like some of Britains' other departures from ordinary toy soldiers, these shooting soldiers do not seem to have been very popular and so are quite rare today.

ASSORTED NOVELTY LINES – THE D SERIES
Just below the soldiers is a pair of small-scale novelty items probably introduced in 1932. They are 26d, Gun (Mounted on Wheels), and 27d, Armoured Car, which sold for twopence and threepence respectively, less than the price of a single best-quality soldier. They are not easily identified as Britains, since they are similar to many other contemporary cheap toys, and the little gun does not even have the name Britains anywhere on it. They are also rather fragile, since the sides of the casting tend to be thin.

To the right again is the interesting small-scale Egyptian Camel Corps figure designated number 85c. Probably issued in 1934, and hence just outside our period, it is one of Britains' last smaller-scale figures. It never appeared with best-quality paintwork.

PRUSSIAN INFANTRY
On the extreme right of the top row of page 65 are two early Prussian Infantry figures, dated 16.2.1908. The officer, who is missing his sword arm, is on the left, the infantryman on the right. The infantryman's unique rifle arm was not used on any other model and was only used on this model before the First World War. It was much thinner than the standard type on both British and German post-war models. Compare the arm with the figures shown on page 133.

THE MIDDLESEX YEOMANRY
Fig 1 of the 2nd row on page 65 is a magnificent officer of the Middlesex Yeomanry, his horse decorated with a two-coloured throat plume. Because of its distinctive Hussar-type uniform, this figure should be matched with the troopers on page 53, all being from a set *c*.1899. The Middlesex Yeomanry were the only named Territorial or Yeomanry unit Britains ever depicted, although other models named simply Yeomanry (set 159) and Territorials (sets 160, 1537, 1538, 1540 and 1541) were produced.

BOER INFANTRY
Next in the 2nd row come two Boer Infantry, one at the slope with fixed bayonet, the other with a sword arm representing an officer. The unusual feature of these two is that, although they are the first version based on the valise-pack infantryman, they have slouch hats turned up at one side instead of the usual hat with a flat all-round brim. Compare these with the variations shown on pages 117 and 118.

RED-COATED INFANTRY WITH FUNNY HATS
The next group of figures (figs 4–7) on the 2nd row have always posed something of a mystery to collectors. The answer, as told to me by an elderly gentleman who had actually bought some as a boy from a department store in Cheltenham, is that they were offered as individual figures from counter packs at a penny halfpenny each. They were not the only figures so offered, as I have seen what I believe was such a counter pack containing four lying Gordons firing, four kneeling Coldstream Guards firing and four of the red-coated CIV figure shown here as fig 4. They were all in a small, brown, unlabelled box divided into 12 partitions, four to each row of three.

The figures shown here, however, are the types that were only sold like this and were not available in a standard set. Fig 4, as already mentioned, is the casting used for set 104, the City Imperial Volunteers, but painted in a full dress of red coat and blue trousers. Fig 5 is the similarly arrayed US Infantryman on Guard, dated 1905. Fig 6 is perhaps the oddest of all, being a normal 17.1.1910 figure with a head taken from a French Chasseur. The example shown does not have a date underneath, so it is probably a 1920s figure, from the period for which we are ill provided with catalogues. So far as I know, none of these figures has ever appeared in any catalogue. Fig 7 is the figure at the shoulder-arms position seen as a Boer or used in American Soldier

Company sets. This one is the odd one out of these four figures as it has a black rather than a brown hat.

Another figure that belongs in this group is the normal Infantry of the Line on-guard figure dated 1910 and painted with a brown helmet. Britains may have intended these figures to represent something in particular, but we do not know what. Since they appeared in these loose-assortment counter-display packs, however, in all likelihood they were simply intended to be something a little different to help sales along. Nevertheless, it was unusual for Britains to produce any soldier not modelled on a specific uniform, so in due course a more plausible explanation may emerge; or it may be established that these figures, though made by Britains, were distributed by another firm that did not care so much for accuracy.

A CASE OF PIRACY
The last two figures in the 2nd row are gilt Imperial Yeomanry, the first by Renvoize, the second by Britains. The influence of the Britains' figure can clearly be seen in the Renvoize model, and the court order restraining James Renvoize from infringing Britains' copyright is reproduced from the 1914 catalogue on page 27. The case was heard in 1902, so it remains open to conjecture whether the Renvoize Imperial Yeoman shown here is the one over which Britains took action or whether it was one produced later. It is sufficiently different – for instance, the rifle is held in the hand in a different way – to escape the charge of piracy.

SMALL-SIZE MOUNTED INFANTRY
The first four figures of the 3rd row on page 65 are mounted infantry in blue glengarries, red coats and beige riding breeches. They are from set 15b, and also appeared as a row in set 58 in the main series. This is the only small-size figure for which there is no equivalent standard-scale model. The only other Britains figure modelled with a glengarry cap is the piper in standard size.

Fig 1 is a first-version officer with a fixed arm, fig 2 a trooper with carbine from the same version but with a movable arm. Fig 3 shows a first-version head-up horse, and fig 4 is the second-version trooper, showing the horse dated 26.4.1904.

SMALL-SIZE FUSILIERS
Shown on the right of the 3rd row on page 65 are versions of small-size Fusiliers in addition to those on page 37. Fig 5 is a first-version officer, who, since he has a gold collar and cuffs, is indistinguishable between the 7th Royal or the Lancashire Fusiliers. The second-version figure at the trail, fig 6, has the white facings of the Lancashire Fusiliers, set 17b. It is not dated, suggesting that this figure did not originate before 1913. Figs 7 and 8 are the first and second versions of set 19b, the Royal Dublin Fusiliers. The first version is dated 1.2.1901, the second is undated, which also suggests that it originated in 1913. If the second version of these sets were only made from 1913 to 1916, their present scarcity would be explained.

Above and opposite: Examples of Royals and Unusuals, described on pages 62 and 63.

Fig 9 is the large-size second-grade paint Fusilier, designated 5h. The gilt version of this figure was numbered 2h.

General Staff

For the first 25 years of production, the only general Britains made to lead the troops was the one on the sway-backed horse. He must have been made in about 1897, since he appears in set 73 as well as in sets 130, 131 and 132. He is illustrated in the top right-hand corner of page 64, as well as in box 73 on page 97. He was also

available in gold paint as shown in the 2nd row, fig 5, page 64. Also featuring in the top row (fig 4) of page 64 is a flagrant Renvoize copy of Britains' general, although in my opinion the Renvoize is the nicer figure.

The special boxed set (number 201) of officers of the general staff that came out *c*.1920 was well worth waiting for. It contained three beautiful new figures: a general with binoculars: a general with an empty hand; and two examples of an aide-de-camp, one on a black horse, one on a grey. This set is illustrated left, complete with its splendid box label designed by Fred Whisstock. To compensate for the extra paint detail that went into these figures, the boxed set only contained four horsemen.

Chapter 22
The Foot Guards

 Britains produced 24 sets of Foot Guards in the main military series before 1933 containing different positions or regiments, and also repeated items in 14 other sets. The following sets came out before the First World War:

Set 34, Grenadier Guards, eight men standing firing with a boy drummer and officer. This was the earliest Foot Guards set, and it is surprising that Britains did not bring any out during the first two years of production. This one was first made in 1895. The standing firing man, known as the volley-firing type, was used only in this set apart from appearing in the X series, since, by the time more firing sets were introduced, the new range of firing figures dated 1.7.1901 had been created. At that time, the volley-firing figure was replaced by the new standing firing figure in this set.

Set 37, Full Band of the Coldstream Guards, 21 musicians
Set 69, Pipers of the Scots Guards, seven pipers
Both these musical sets are described in the chapter on Infantry bands, page 71.

Set 70, Scots Guards, running at the trail with mounted officer. This set, which is supposed to have contained six men with the officer, is a mystery, since there is no evidence for its existence other than Len Richards' assertion that the contents listed above were correct. The running at the trail figure only appeared in 1899, and the set did not appear in the first listing I have, dated 1902, or subsequently, so the possibility of its existence seems limited to three years only. I have never seen a box for it, and since the running figure was included in set 130 the existence of running Scots Guard figures is no proof either.

Set 75, The Scots Guards, six men marching at the slope, with officer and piper. This set, by contrast, was very popular and long lived.

Set 82, The Colours and Pioneers of the Scots Guards, seven pioneers and an officer carrying a flag rather than a sword. The flag was flat, as if it had been highly starched and was as stiff as a board. Only now, in 1897, were there sufficient sets of Foot Guards available to satisfy the strong demand for them.

Set 90, The Coldstream Guards, firing. This was a three-row display, containing one each of marching officer, officer kneeling with binoculars, bugler and

drummer, with seven standing, nine kneeling and ten lying firing men.

Display set 93. Various new figures of the Coldstream Guards were included in this large set, the lower tray of which contained Royal Horse Guards; the set is described on page 42. The top tray contained Coldstream Guards as follows: a 13-piece band, two buglers, four pioneers, two marching officers, an officer with colours, a mounted officer on a Scots Grey horse, 12 men running at the trail and 12 men marching at the slope without bayonets fixed.

Display set 102, containing the Grenadier, Coldstream, Scots and Irish Guards. This set contained one row of each of the the existing regiments of Foot Guards in 1901, which was the year after the Irish Guards were formed. The Grenadiers were exactly as in set 34; the Coldstream Guards were a row of eight at attention, one holding a flat flag; the Scots were exactly as in set 75; and the Irish were a row of six men running at the trail with an officer mounted on the one-eared full-gallop horse dated 1.1.1901.

Set 107, The Irish Guards, seven men at the slope with

BOXES FOR COLDSTREAM GUARDS
Top to bottom: 1 Early typographical design for set 120, c.1902. 2 Whisstock pictorial label for set 120. This set became one of Britains' most popular issues, and is very commonly found today. 3 Whisstock pictorial label for set 205. 4 Whisstock label for set 314. By the time sets 205 and 314 were issued, Whisstock was designing box labels to use from the start. Hence the Whisstock label is the only one ever found on the boxes for these sets. Notice how all his three different labels for the Coldstream Guards still have the linking device of the regimental badge. The badge of the regiment in the box was usually included in the design for the label by Whisstock.

66

an officer. This set was first made using the valise-pack figure. As in sets 75 and 82, the figure was changed to the box-pack type in 1905, and then to the marching figure without equipment in 1910 or soon after.

Set 111, The Grenadier Guards at attention. This set contained six men, and an officer mounted on the sway-backed horse.

Set 120, The Coldstream Guards, nine men kneeling firing with an officer kneeling with binoculars. This was always a very popular set, and many fine examples have survived.

Set 124, The Irish Guards, nine men lying firing, with a kneeling officer with binoculars. This set was not nearly so popular as set 120, and hence is considerably rarer today.

Display set 130, The Scots Guards. This was a massive 118-piece two-tier presentation box, and it is illustrated and described on page 68. This completed the tally of best-quality Foot Guards made before the First World War, apart from five repeats of previous sets in various display boxes.

After the First World War, the following new sets were listed before 1933.

Set 205, The Coldstream Guards at present, seven men with officer

Set 253, The Welsh Guards at the slope, seven men with mounted officer

Set 312, The Grenadier Guards in greatcoats, seven men with officer

Set 314, The Coldstream Guards at ease, eight men

Set 322, Fife and Drum Band of the Coldstream Guards, 17 musicians with eight rank and file (illustrated on page 73)

Set 329, Sentry box with sentry of the Grenadier Guards (later Scots Guards) (illustrated on page 68)

Set 429, The Scots Guards in greatcoats, seven men with officer, in a display with The Life Guards in cloaks

Set 438, The Grenadier Guards, Parade Series (see page 188)

Set 460, The Grenadier Guards Colour Party, two officers with drawn swords, two officers with colours and three colour-sergeants (illustrated on page 68). Later this set changed to the Scots Guards.

Foot Guards were very sparsely represented in the second-grade series – was it felt to be beneath their dignity? The early Grenadier standing firing was used for an X series set, but apart from that the earliest set in the A series was set 484A, produced in 1934.

In the small size, on the other hand, there is set 16b, the Coldstream Guards at the slope, and set 18b, the Grenadier Guards running at the slope. One of the Coldstream had gold collar and cuffs to represent an officer. Both boxes were produced in a second version c.1912, and these figures were adapted for the W series.

BOXES FOR GRENADIER GUARDS

Top to bottom: 1 Early box for set 34, c.1895. The set number does not appear on the box at this early date. 2 Whisstock pictorial label for set 34. 3 During the 1930s, after Whisstock had ceased to design labels for Britains, a number of replacements for his work were completed, although by no means all the sets were given new labels. This elaborate design was used for set 34 and other single-row sets of Grenadier Guards. 4 Early typographical box for set 111, c.1902. 5-6 Other similar box labels from much the same period, incorporating many of the same or similar elements from the type-setter's case. 7 Whisstock pictorial box label for set 111. 8 Whisstock label for set 312, one of his later designs. Note once more the regimental badge, a feature of all the Whisstock designs.

Whisstock universal label design, overprinted with title for set 460 (top) and an illustration (bottom). The lower label would be suitable for any large set of the British Army.

Above: Set 130 and other Guards

Most of the illustration above is taken up with figures from set 130, c.1928. The exceptions are set 329, Sentry in Sentry Box, and set 460, Colour Party of the Grenadier Guards.

The sentry and sentry box are extremely attractive. Britains made them in 1929 as a sixpenny line. To start with, as illustrated in the catalogue, the sentry was a Grenadier, the same figure as in set 314, the Coldstream Guards at Ease. This sentry is the only time a Grenadier at ease appears in the regular Britains' catalogues. As Britains never specified which regiment the sentry was until after the Second World War, they were at liberty to offer any figure. After a few years, the sentry was normally a Scots Guard, and this was standardized in catalogues issued after 1945.

The Colour Party of the Grenadier Guards changed as quickly as the sentry above to the Scots Guards, and this is confirmed by the rarity of boxes labelled Grenadier Guards. The set that came out in 1932, illustrated immediately to the right of the sentry box, comprised two officers with drawn swords held upright (a new position for infantry officers), three colour sergeants (the ordinary marching figure with a crimson sash painted in), and two bearers. This was a completely new figure that carried very nicely executed colours made of lithographed tin and joined to a wire pole.

The rest of the figures shown come from set 130, which Britains described as follows:

Containing a splendid collection of the Scots Guards, marching, running, standing at ease, standing, lying, and

kneeling firing, together with Pipers, Drum and Bugle Band, colours and Pioneers, mounted and unmounted Officers. Size of case 2 ft. 1 in. by 1 ft. 5 in. by 3 ins., with one inside tray, totalling 118 pieces of infantry.

This was the largest set of Foot Guards issued by Britains, indeed the largest set of any kind of infantry. All existing types of Foot Guards were included. The layout in the box was five rows of twelve figures in each tray; the two mounted figures replaced four infantry. This allowed for a row each of marching figures without and with fixed bayonets, seen at the rear left, a row each of pioneers, men running at the trail, standing at attention with the at-ease arm (later changed to the proper attention position), and each of the three firing positions, standing, kneeling and lying. Pipers, buglers and drummers made up the other two rows, including the Scots Guards mounted officer (not illustrated) and the mounted field officer, both of whom were on the sway-back horse. Some rows contained an officer, and among the band were a drum-major and bass-drummer. One unique feature was the standing officer with binoculars, the only time that a standing Foot Guard officer appeared in the regular catalogue apart from the very rare set 1909 in which there was a similar Coldstream Guards officer. Otherwise, all the figures in this set were available in other Foot Guard regiments elsewhere in the catalogue. The piper, colour, pioneer and marching at the slope figures were available in basic Scots Guards sets, but the other positions, if found painted as Scots Guards, can be identified as belonging to this set 130.

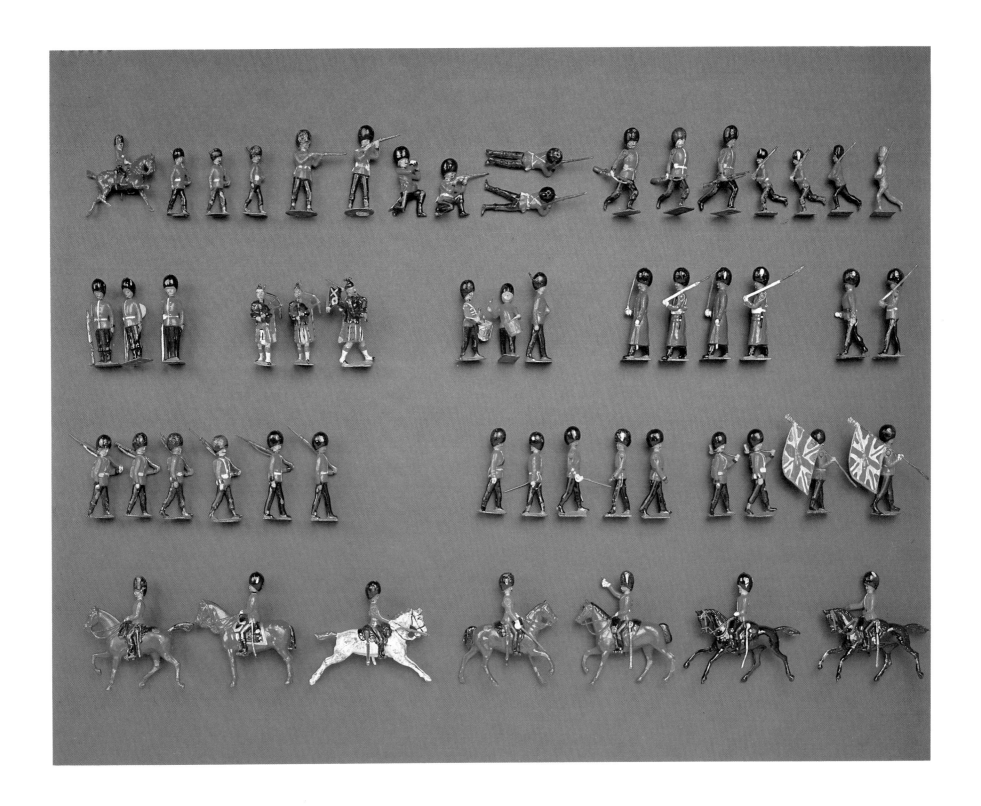

Examples of Foot Guards, described on page 70.

The Foot Guards: descriptions

The Foot Guards shown in the illustration on page 37 should all be turned in different directions in order to show their plumes. These are:

Grenadier Guards white on the left
Coldstream Guards red on the right
Scots Guards no plume
Irish Guards blue on the right
Welsh Guards white with a green centre

Top row Figs 1–4 and 14–17 are small-size. Figs 1 and 2 are early small-size second-grade Guards with no known set number. The foot figure appears in an illustration in the 1915 catalogue, ie British Army Encampment sets 01 and 02, but the mounted officer in these sets does not match the one shown here. Figs 3 and 4 are the first and second versions of set 16b, the Coldstream Guards.

Figs 5–10 show the models of the Guards in action firing; Britains never made models of Guards on guard. Fig 5 is an X series volley-firing Grenadier, although in second-grade paint he would not have been given a plume. The same figure in a first-grade paint was used for set 34. Figs 6, 8 and 9 are standing kneeling and lying firing Guards in gaiters from the Coldstream Guards, set 90. The oval base and paper label on fig 6 can just be seen. Figs 7 and 10 are from set 124, c.1932, when the lying firing Irish Guards were given a new feet-apart figure still with gaiters. A further change to full trousers took place in 1934, making examples like fig 10 rather rare. Fig 7 is the kneeling officer for the set; his plume, which is rather difficult to distinguish under the highlights, is a greenish blue. Irish Guards plumes varied from dark green to light blue according to when the model was made. Very early figures had greyish blue plumes (3rd row, fig 1). From 1905 to c.1930 the colour was dark green (top row, fig 13); thereafter a light blue was used (3rd row, figs 6 and 9). The plumes that Britains normally painted are quite small, although larger ones can sometimes be seen. They are always just a touch of the brush, so a carefully shaped plume might indicate subsequent repainting.

Figs 11–13 show Guards running at the trail, figs 11 and 12 being Coldstreams from the large box 93, both of the pigeon-chested type. Because fig 11 has an oval base, he dates from before 1910, and because he is holding a fully metallic painted rifle he was probably produced after 1904. Both figs 11 and 12 are in condition F, but fig 12 has a very chalky white face, which may have been caused by the bleaching effect of the sun. Fig 13 is a closed-elbow type, from set 102. Of the five small running at the slope types, figs 14 and 15 show two from set 18b, the Grenadier Guards, fig 15 having a very heavily painted plume. Fig 16 shows the larger second version, in this case painted as a W series figure. Fig 17 is the same figure in gilt.

2nd row Figs 1–3 show the three variations of the Grenadier Guards at attention from set 111, the officer for which is in the 4th row, fig 2. Fig 1 shows the early attention figure with the arm in more of an at-ease position. Early versions of this figure had a round base. Fig 2 is slightly tipped to the side so that the arm provided after the First World War can be seen clearly. In fig 3, a new figure with full trousers is present; this was introduced c.1934.

Figs 4–6 are the Pipers of the Scots Guards from set 69. Fig 4 is an early one from c.1900, with an oval base and very light green horizontal stripes to the tartan. The striping on figs 5 and 6 is the normal very dark green, the vertical stripes being white. Fig 5 is a rather unusual first version with a square base which must have been made after 1908 but before 1912 when the version dated 6.3.1912 and represented by fig 6 appeared.

Fig 7 is a pigeon-toed side-drummer of the Grenadier Guards, from set 34. Note the white piping painted in on the cuff at this early date (c.1897). Fig 8 is a full-trousered side-drummer, an individual figure in second-grade paint from the N series c.1938, and fig 9 the equivalent Guard marching at the slope. These two figures are quite common, particularly the marching type, and both were made after our period. Figs 10 and 11 are Scots Guards from set 429, and figs 12 and 13 the equivalent Grenadier Guards from set 312, the only difference being the white plume. The officers, figs 10 and 12, are a completely different casting from the men.

Fig 14 shows an officer of the Grenadiers with a very curious empty-handed arm rather than the usual arm with the outstretched drawn sword. Under most circumstances I would instantly suspect a replacement arm and retouching, but the paint and arm fitting do appear in this instance to be genuine. Fig 15 shows one of the Grenadier Guards at the slope from Parade set 438. This must have been one of the few sets that contained Guards marching at the slope without fixed bayonets.

3rd row Figs 1–6 show the evolution of the most common marching figure used by Britains. Figs 1 and 2 are Irish Guards of the valise-pack type, the first c.1901 with a brown-painted rifle and blue plume, the second with a metallic painted rifle. c.1905 and a green plume. Note that these and fig 4 have been painted with white gloves. Figs 3 and 4 are the oval-based box-pack figures dated 1.8.1905. Fig 3 has a rifle without a fixed bayonet, and is probably a Scots Guard from set 130. For some reason this figure has not had the crossbelts painted in. Fig 4 is also a Scots Guard, this time from set 75, and is a G–F example of the best paintwork including white piping at the cuff. Figs 5 and 6 show the 1910 marching figure, fig 5 being a Scots Guard with the old-style rifle with loose sling and fig 6 an Irish Guard with the 1920s arm.

Figs 7–11 show various types of officers. Fig 7 is the bemedalled officer from the same set of Irish Guards as fig 1 of this row, although it is hard to see the plume. The fact that this officer is still being used for set 107 makes us consider how long the movable-arm wasp-waisted officer (fig 8) was used. It must have been produced before mid-1900, or it would have had a date – yet set 107 cannot have been produced until the second half of 1900, since the Irish Guards themselves were not formed until

then. The answer is (ICP) that both types were in use, possibly interchangeably. Fig 8 shows a Grenadier Guard officer from set 34. Fig 9 is an Irish Guard officer of the type that was introduced in 1905 and was used until 1933. It comes from the same set as fig 6 in this row. Fig 10 shows a highly unusual officer of the Grenadiers based on the normal 1910 marching private, given an empty-handed arm and painted as an officer. Officers at this time were sometimes given brown gloves. A recently discovered group of figures has an officer of this variety leading seven Grenadier Guards at ease, in what appears to have been an alternative content for set 314. Fig 11 shows an officer of the Scots Guards of the type introduced in 1934 with full trousers to match the 1910 marching figure. In this example, a narrow blue cuff has been painted on, which is unusual in conjunction with the normal gold cuff and could be an embellishment.

Figs 12–15 show examples of the pioneers and colour-bearers from the Scots Guards set 82. The pioneers are based on the same figures as figs 1 and 4 in this row but have been given an arm with an axe. The officers are the same figures as figs 8 and 9 in this row but with an arm carrying a colour.

4th row. This row is devoted to mounted officers. Fig 1 is the mounted Coldstream officer from set 93. The plume is painted on the wrong side, since this figure is simply the tin sword Scots Grey painted up as a Guards officer on a brown horse, including a Scots Grey head with the plume moulded on the wrong side for a Coldstream Guard. Ironically, early sets of Scots Greys sometimes had Foot Guard heads (see page 52). Fig 2 is the officer of the Grenadiers which was part of set 111. The horse is the sway-backed type at the halt, and a crack in the neck where the head has been repaired can be seen. Fig 3 shows the officer of the Irish Guards from set 102 who led the six running figures, one of which is shown as fig 13 of the top row. Fig 4 is an inexplicable Guards officer on a 'Scots Grey' type horse, with a white plume on the wrong side for a Grenadier Guard. Fig 5 is similar, with a Scots Grey head and the plume painted to Scots Grey proportions, which still does not explain from which set it came. Maybe individual mounted Guards officers were produced as a souvenir line. Figs 6 and 7 are both mounted on the cantering horse, fig 6 being the officer for set 253, the Welsh Guards, very neatly painted, and fig 7 being yet another unexplained Grenadier.

One theory to explain all these Grenadier Guards mounted officers is that the composition of set 34 was sometimes seven firing, a drummer and a mounted officer rather than eight firing, a drummer and a foot officer. A set with these contents appeared at auction recently. Alternatively, set 438, the parade set of Grenadier Guards, could on occasion have contained a mounted officer. As a last resort in explanation, it is always possible that Britains sold these Grenadier Guard mounted officers on walking horses separately, in the same way that they undoubtedly sold their sway-backed horse General Officer. Trying to fit unexplained figures into the range is part of the fascination of collecting.

Chapter 23
Infantry bands

 Bands and military music are an essential part of the ceremonial side of army life, so no collection of toy soldiers could be complete without musicians. Within three years of starting production, Britains had provided three sets:

Set 27, the Band of the Line, including 12 musicians

Set 30, the Drums and Bugles of the Line, with eight musicians

Set 37, the Full Band of the Coldstream Guards, with a complement of 21

Apart from the mounted bands described in chapter 13 (page 45), Britains was content to offer these three sets, with the addition of a set of Scots Guard Pipers, number 69, until 1929, when the Drum and Fife bands illustrated on page 73 were introduced. No more were produced during our period, apart from the various bands included in the large sets, which were simply variations of the sets already mentioned. Later, especially after the Second World War, band production increased, and 20 other types of band, not counting large and small sets of the same type, were made.

The early infantry bandsmen were of the slotted-arm variety, their arms being fixed in exactly the same way as cavalry figures' (see page 45). The bandsmen had oval bases and the slotted-arm variety never was converted to a square base, even though it was in production until 1911, well after the introduction of square bases.

The first version of the new movable-arm bandsman, dated 1.5.1911, was still equipped with gaiters. But after a very short time the change to full trousers was made, the same date still appearing under the base. All dated bandsmen must have appeared between 1911 and 1916, since they are rarely discovered today. After the First World War, until c.1934, all bandsmen were full-trousered except for the drum-major, side- and bass-drummers, who retained their gaiters. After c.1934, these figures too changed to full trousers.

Set 27, The Brass Band of the Line, drum-major, two musicians with trombones, two with euphoniums, three trumpeters, one cymbalist, one side-drummer, one bass-drummer and one fifer. This was the set's title before 1914, although later it was catalogued simply as 'Band of the Line'. The instrumentation never altered. The collar and cuff facings were white. The bass-drummer can be distinguished by the colour of his drum, which during our period was blue, in contrast with the brown drum supplied with the Drums and Bugles of the Line, set 30. Before 1914, three distinct types of head with

spiked helmet – the 'flat', the 'small' and the 'standard' head – were used, which makes it easier to match up sets. After the First World War, the bands were issued with a variety of 'standard' heads which tended to be rather larger than the pre-war examples. These types are illustrated in chapter 8 (page 19). When these heads were produced is not yet certain, but it seems that flat heads came first, the change to small taking place c.1900 and then to standard c.1905. Alternatively, the small may have been used alongside or before the flat.

Set 30, The Drums and Bugles of the line, drum-major, four buglers, two side-drummers and one bass-drummer. This set was very good value, since it contained eight musicians for a shilling, whereas the twelve men in set 27 cost two shillings. All the figures were fixed-arm, but intricately cast and nicely painted. The four different figures in this set underwent a number

of changes during our period, and these are described below. The early drum-major was an oval-based figure with the baton grounded. The inside edge of the baton moulding was flat, and the top tended to break off. The figure was remoulded c.1913, and the new drum-major, although still a fixed-arm figure, had a wrist held forward with a spindle of wire embedded in it, around which the separate hand with baton could revolve, thereby simulating twirling or directional signals.

The bass-drummer was remodelled in 1908 and given two separate movable arms each holding a drumstick, one extended further than the other. This figure was put on a square base from the start. It was

dated 8.12.1908 and so cannot have been included in bands until the 1909 selling season.

At first the bugler was a figure of a boy, only 50mm tall. It was a lovely casting, fixed-arm and oval-based, the bugle itself beautifully modelled with a delicate mouthpiece and tassel both rather prone to break off. In about 1908 the figure was given a square base, but still without an embossed inscription underneath. After the First World War a new full-trousered, adult-height bugler was produced, with two alternate movable bugle arms, one at the carry and one to play. Set 30 usually included two of each.

The drummer boy was another short figure that matched the boy bugler. The first version of this figure pointed the toe of his right foot out sideways and so has become known as the pigeon-toed drummer boy. He was replaced c.1900 or a little before by an improved but undated version, which, again because of the position of

Another example of the Whisstock universal label illustrated on page 68, this time overprinted with the title for set 322. The labels for the larger boxes in the Britains' range tended to be much duller than the labels for the single-row boxes, although the contents, as in this instance, were much more exciting. Here, of course, the label is not nearly as big as the box, which contains three rows of troops, 25 figures.

the feet, is known as the heel-and-toe drummer boy. The heel-and-toe drummer was given a square base c.1908 and continued in use until 1934, when full-trouser figures of all these three models were introduced.

The buglers and drummers were used extensively to add some variety to infantry sets, and these musicians are described in context. They often appear with different facings or helmet colours from those used in sets 27 and 30, which indicates the sets to which they belong.

Set 37, The Band of the Coldstream Guards, drum major, three trombonists, three euphonium-players, one

Above: Massed bands of the Foot Guards and Infantry of the Line (see description on page 74).

Right: Close-up of the picture opposite showing the new thin side-drummer. He is called thin because of the shallow nature of his side-drum rather the thinness of the figure! It is interesting that, having made this excellent new drummer boy, Britains did not make any attempt to improve the ordinary fixed-arm drummer boy until 1955, when a new drummer boy with a plastic drum and a movable arm on the other shoulder appeared.

bombardon-player, four trumpeters, one cymbalist, one bass-drummer, one side-drummer, one bassoonist, four clarinetists and one fifer. The same bandsmen as in set 27 were used, but with Foot Guard heads. The paintwork was even more magnificent, and the price proportionately more expensive, since the 21 pieces cost four shillings. When the new 1.5.1911 bandsman was introduced, the bombardon was replaced by a bass horn.

Set 69, Pipers of the Scots Guards, seven pipers wearing glengarries. An improved figure dated 6.3.1912 was introduced, and just after our period a new model with a full-feather bonnet was made. Other than this figure, which was used for pipers in various Highland regiments, no attempt was made during our period to depict Highland bands. In box 130, the very big box of Scots Guards, there was a pipe, drum and bugle band which probably numbered 20 pieces: drum-major, 10 pipers, four side-drummers, bass-drummer and four buglers. It may well be that the contents of this box varied from time to time.

Box 73 contained a variation of set 27, the band of the line (illustrated on page 96). This contained 14 pieces. The second euphonium was replaced by a bombardon and

Drum and Fife Bands, described on page 74

Right: Boxes for set 30, *Drums and Bugles of the Line.* Top: *Early typographical box, **c.**1900.* Bottom: *Whisstock design for the set, one of his more elaborate efforts, with the set number and two illustrations incorporated. Since this set does not relate to a specific regiment, no regimental badge could be included. It is interesting that, although this set contained eight figures throughout our period, the box was always smaller than the normal eight-figure size. Was this because there were six boys in the set? When Britains brought out a set of Boy Scouts, number 161, that contained eight Scouts with a Scoutmaster, and was also in a smaller than normal box.*

the third trumpet was dropped, but a wind section of two clarinets and a bassoon was added.

Set 93, a large box containing Coldstream Guards and Horse Guards. This included a Band of the Coldstream Guards. This was a smaller group than in set 37, containing drum-major, trombone-player, euphonium-player, bass horn-player, two trumpeters, cymbalist, bass-drummer, side-drummer, fifer, two clarinet-players and a bassoon-player. Also in the set were two buglers.

Set 131 contained a Band of the Coldstream Guards, and this was larger than set 37, having an additional bombardon-player, fifer and bassoon-player, a total of 24 musicians.

Set 132, Band of the Line, included as part of this very large display set. I have never seen this and so have been unable to check which instrumentalists it contained.

In 1929 a new style of band was issued, a 17-piece Drum and Fife Band. Set 321 was the Band of the Line version, and set 322 was a Coldstream Guards version with eight additional Coldstream Guards at the slope included in the set. Each band contained eight new boy fifer figures, only 50mm tall, and also a new figure of a boy drummer, with one movable arm and a drum that looked half as

thick as the normal side drum. Hence this new figure is known as the thin side-drummer. The bands comprised drum-major, eight fifers, two thin side-drummers, five heel-and-toe side-drummers and a base-drummer. The new figures were in full-trousers, but the others retained their gaiters until 1934, when they too became full-trousered. All the bandsmen in these two sets had distinctive piping painted down each sleeve, so that the drum-major and drummers belonging to them can be quite easily distinguished.

There is something particularly enjoyable about a massed band display. Page 72 shows the Massed Bands of the Coldstream Guards and the Drums, Bugles and Bands of the Line, page 73 a display of four Drum and Fife Bands. On page 72, the Coldstream Guards bands are on the left, arranged as four bands of three files each. The earliest, *c.*1900, is on the left, the next dates from *c.*1909, and the third is a mixed band of gaitered and ungaitered figures dated 1.5.1911 without a drum-major. The last is the standard version from the 1920s.

On the right, the Infantry of the Line are more an assemblage of figures than actual distinguishable sets. The earlier figures are ranked on the left, with the drums and bugles in the front. All the types already mentioned in the text are included, except for those that fall outside our period.

On page 73, the four bands are laid out in square formation. Front left is the Drum and Fife Band of the Line, set 321, *c.*1930, showing the gaitered figures. Behind this is the Coldstream set 322, with the eight extra Coldstream Guards to the right. Note, however, that this is a full-trousered version and therefore dates from 1934 to 1941. The version with gaitered men was only in production for four years and is rarer than the later set.

On the right in front is a later version of set 321. This is an interesting variation, since the fifers are all the adult figure, as used previously with the ordinary bands. From time to time boy fifers from these sets can be found as the fifer in sets 27 and 37.

At the back is another Fife and Drum Band, made up almost exactly as sets 321 and 322, but with a bugler and a cymbalist instead of two of the side-drummers. This band has Fusilier heads fitted and has been specially painted up by Britains to represent the Welch Fusiliers. As these are my favourite regiment, my wife bought them for me as my engagement present. The band falls a few years past our period, but I thought it unfair to leave it out. The vast majority of items specially cast or painted by Britains to customers' special order were done between 1935 and 1940. On the back of the section dividers in the 1935 catalogue it states: 'Britains Limited are prepared to manufacture Special Lines to customers' own requirements provided the quantities are sufficient.'

Chapter 24
Scottish infantry

The four earliest sets of Highlanders that Britains produced all used the germanic plug-handed Highlander already described on page 39.

Set 11, The Black Watch, seven including the officer
Set 15, The Argyll and Sutherland Highlanders, seven including the officer
Set 77, The Gordon Highlanders, five including the officer, with two pipers
Set 88, The Seaforth Highlanders, twelve including the officer with two pipers, a double-row box.

In sets 11, 15 and 88 the plug-handed Highlander was replaced by the charging Highlander dated 17.12.1903, and the number of figures per row was increased from seven to eight. Set 77 changed to the marching box-pack Highlander figure dated 1.1.1901, also with eight pieces, still including two pipers, but without an officer. Later one piper was changed to a marching man.

Other sets of Highlanders are as follows:
Set 112, The Seaforth Highlanders, eight men marching at the slope. This was a new box using the box-pack Highlander.

Set 114, The Cameron Highlanders, eight men marching at the slope, a further set using the box-pack Highlander, but this time with a foreign-service order helmet. All the above marching Highlander sets were changed to a figure without a pack c.1913.

As part of its range of firing troops introduced in 1901, Britains eventually made four sets of Highlanders in foreign-service helmets:
Set 89, The Cameron Highlanders, a three-row box containing a standing and a kneeling officer with binoculars, two pipers and seven standing, nine kneeling and ten lying firing men. This was a similar set to set 90, the Coldstream Guards.

Set 118, The Gordon Highlanders, nine men lying firing with a kneeling officer with binoculars

Set 122, The Black Watch, nine men standing firing with a standing officer with binoculars

Set 157, The Gordon Highlanders, four standing and three each kneeling and lying firing

Set 212, The Royal Scots, eight men at the slope
Set 213, The Highland Light Infantry, eight men at the slope.
These sets were composed of two new figures at the

slope specially cast, one for each regiment, and are the only Lowland Scottish which appeared in Britains' catalogue during our period. Illustrations of these figures appear on page 37.

Set 437, Officers of the Gordon Highlanders, four on foot and one mounted. First made in 1933, this set was the first appearance of full-dress Highland officers. Britains probably also produced special-order lines of these figures in bulk for Scottish retailers, painted as various Highland regiments.

The Black Watch appeared at the slope in full dress in the Parade Series, set 449 (see page 188).

There were no Highlanders in the X series and only a single marching figure in the A series. Set 23b in the small size (also illustrated on page 116) purported to be the Camerons. In the early days the set was always painted as Black Watch in foreign-service order. In 1912, however, a new full-dress Highland marching figure appeared, dated 8.4.1912, painted as Cameron. This figure was also used by the Paris Office (see page 132) and in the W series in second-grade paint.

BOXES FOR SEAFORTH AND CAMERON HIGHLANDERS
Top to bottom: *1 and 2 Interesting variations in typographical box labels for set 112. Which might be earlier is difficult to say. They might both date from about 1905. 3 Whisstock design for set 112, with an illustration of an officer not included in the set. 4 Typographical label for smaller-size set 23B, c.1905. 5 Whisstock design for set 23B, showing a Highlander in foreign-service dress. As Whisstock started to do designs for Britains at about the same time as a new full-dress figure began to be used for this set, this illustration may be a good pointer to the exact starting-date of Whisstock's work, ie 1912.*

HIGHLAND SQUARE

Here is my version of this famous toy soldier formation, first popularized on the cover of the first edition of Len Richards' book **Old British Model Soldiers 1893 – 1918** (see Bibliography, page 6). In real life, square formations were used by the British Army during colonial campaigns as all-round defence against native warriors who did not possess sufficient long-range fire-power to pick off the closely packed British troops from a distance. The Zulu and Sudan campaigns are probably the best examples. In the illustration above are a number of Cameron Highlanders from several sets 89, showing differing variations and paint styles during our period. Set 89 was issued in 1901, and for a short period the officers were given heads with a smooth foreign-service helmet rather than one with a bump half-way down the helmet representing the pugaree.

These smooth-helmeted officers can be seen standing and kneeling in the front left corner of the square, and another view is provided in the close-up to the right. Starting from these officers, the figures are arranged clockwise in order of age of issue, the earliest versions first. The early-version figures are more intricately painted, with more stripes on the kilts. In fact one might almost make a correlation between the number of horizontal red stripes and the age of the figure. In the first version, *c.*1901, there are five or sometimes even six stripes. In the 1920s and 1930s there are three stripes. In the post-Second World War set 2025 containing the same figures (not shown here) the stripes are reduced to two. Note also the very light brown rifles on the front right of the square, characteristic painting of the late 1920s and early 1930s. The pipers in the centre of the square are arranged from left to right in order of age, the oval-based ones first. The close-up to the right gives a good view of the early 1930s style of figure in the foreground contrasted with the paint style of 30 years earlier behind them.

Examples of Highlanders, described on page 78

Box for set 88, a double row of the Seaforth Highlanders charging. The black label with gold printing on it is typical of many early Britains' labels for multi-row sets. Presumably they were intended to add a luxurious feel to the higher-price items, and in this they were following a tradition of gold on black labels started by the German manufacturers. Unfortunately the printing ink fades very easily, so it is difficult to find one of these labels in its original full glory. This particular label would be suitable for any larger box of British Army figures.

Highland figures: descriptions

Top row Figs 1–4 are Seaforth Highlanders, the two pipers being from set 88, *c*.1905 and *c*.1913. Fig 2, the new larger piper dated 6.3.1912, replaced the earlier oval-based piper on the left. The marching figures are from set 112, showing the box-pack Highlander *c*.1910 and the later standard version *c*.1925. Figs 5 and 6 are Black Watch, unusually in the marching position. Fig 5 comes from the Parade series set 449, *c*.1932, and fig 6 is a special painting *c*.1938. Note the extra detail round the coat on the special figure and the neater painting of the sporran. Figs 7 and 10 come from set 437, Officers of the Gordon Highlanders, *c*.1936. The greater care that needed to be taken with the painting of these figures meant that Britains could only afford to include four on foot and one mounted in a standard value box.

Figs 8, 9 and 11 came from set 77, in reverse order of age. Fig 11 is the box-pack type, of which a row can be seen in box 73, page 65. Fig 9 is the new type introduced *c*.1913, still in this year retaining the arm carrying the rifle with the loose sling. Fig 8 shows the same figure *c*.1930 with the later slope arm and tight rifle sling. The pipers to go with this set are shown immediately below in the 2nd row. Fig 14 is one of the early type, unusually with a square base, and fig 15 is a nicely painted example of the 6.3.1912 dated figure.

2nd row Fig 1–4 are various types of standing Black Watch officers with binoculars. Fig 1 is something of a mystery, since, instead of being painted in the standard black stripes on dark green, the kilt has light green stripes on dark blue. Since the collar is painted the correct blue facing colour for the Black Watch, I can only assume that the kilt is a mistake. Fig 2 shows a standard painting of the smooth-helmeted variation. Both must date close to 1901. Fig 3 shows an officer *c*.1910, still on a round base,

and fig 4 shows a square-based one *c*.1932. Note that the painting of the five tassels on the kilt has been simplified to two tails. All these figures came from set 122.

Fig 5 is a very odd small-size figure that I have been quite unable to identify. I have seen three or four examples, although only one of these was a private with rifle at the trail. They appear to be Black Watch in a spiked Infantry of the Line helmet, the one on view being an officer with gold facings. The nearest real-life uniform would have been a Canadian Black Watch. It may possibly be a very rare version of set 23b, the normal style of which is shown as fig 6. This set was titled Cameron Highlanders, but as can be seen the figure in the box was clearly a Black Watch. Interestingly, the engravings of set 23b used in Gamages' 1906 catalogue and in Britains' 1915 catalogue both show spiked helmets. Since Britains tended not to alter its engravings in line with the actual figures, it might well be that the figure in the white spiked helmet is the true first variation of set 23b. Since so few have survived, and since the set is known to have been in existence in 1902, the probability is that it was initially brought out immediately before the Boer War and was almost immediately switched into a Boer War uniform.

Fig 7 is a Gordon officer on a brown horse, which is unusual and may have appeared only in a large box, perhaps set 1350. The next figures, 8 and 9, show the second version of set 23b, a true Cameron Highlander at the slope, dated 8.4.1912, and the derived W series Highlander. Fig 10 is the normal A series Highlander, usually designated Black Watch, and fig 11 is the large-size Highlander 6h, although, since the gilt Highlander next to it (fig 12) is designated 1h, presumably these figures were first produced as a gilt line. Fig 13 is the gilt fixed-arm Highlander 2c. Figs 14 and 15 are the Gordon Highlander pipers, which have already been described with the others of the same set, in the top row.

3rd row Figs 1–5 are all Black Watch from set 122, showing various paint styles. Figs 1–4 all have an oval base and date from before *c*.1910. Note the different ways in which the tassels or tails are painted on the sporran. The easiest way of identifying a matching set of Highlanders is to check if the sporrans are all painted in the same style. Fig 5 is much later, *c*.1935. The extra flair of the kilt at the back shows it was made from a different mould. Figs 6–8, the lying firing Gordon Highlanders, could be from either set 118 or set 157. The first two show the earlier feet-together position, and fig 8 is the later feet-apart position introduced *c*.1934. The two kneeling Gordon officers are from set 122, the first being a smooth-helmeted variation. Fig 11 is the kneeling firing Gordon from set 157, *c*.1910, and fig 12 is the same figure *c*.1935. There seems to be no distinguishable difference between the two, except perhaps that the later figure's front foot is thinner. Fig 13 is the standing firing Gordon from set 157, with an oval base.

4th row This row is of the later charging Highlander types. (The earlier running plug-handed figures are shown on page 40.) Figs 1–3 are Argyll and Sutherlands from set 15. Notice that their sporrans, which all have yellow tops, are grey with either two long tails or six tassels. Fig 4 is a mounted officer of the Argylls, who does not appear in any catalogued set. Since he is not done up to a 'special' standard, it may well be that Britains produced Highland officers based on the castings for set 437 for all the Highland regiments to order, in standard paint. A similar mystery officer, this time of the Camerons on foot, is illustrated on page 37. Figs 5–8 are Black Watch from set 11. Fig 5 is the oval-based version, and fig 6 has gold collar and cuffs painted to represent an officer. Fig 8 is *c*.1925. Figs 9–11 show the Seaforth Highlanders from set 88. Fig 9 has an oval base, and fig 10 is a beautiful paint style from *c*.1912 on a square base. Fig 11 shows the paint style *c*.1930.

Chapter 25
Infantry of the Line

 As far as Britains' toy soldiers are concerned, Infantry of the Line (I of L) means infantry in red coats, blue trousers and a spiked helmet. All other uniforms worn by infantry in the British Army are discussed elsewhere. The first three I of L sets all consisted of on-guard fixed-arm figures.

Set 16, The East Kent Regiment, the Buffs, seven infantry standing on guard, marching officer, drummer and bugler, yellow facings and blue helmet. I have seen some kneeling on-guard figures with yellow facings. A possible explanation for these is that they appeared in set 132.

Set 17, The Somerset Light Infantry, contained four each of men standing and kneeling on guard, with marching officer and bugler, blue facings and green helmet.

Set 18, The Worcestershire Regiment, four each of men standing and kneeling on guard, with marching officer and drummer, white facings and white helmet.

A few of the very earliest sets may not have had a full complement of officer and musicians. The on-guard figures were improved in 1910.

Set 25, Soldiers to Shoot, four pieces. This is illustrated and described on page 65.

Display Set 29, included 15 figures of the Royal West Surrey Regiment unavailable elsewhere: viz, one officer, two drummers, two buglers, five standing men on guard and five marching at the slope. The marching-at-the-slope figure, which was a fixed-arm smallish type with the rifle on the right shoulder, was soon changed to the valise-pack movable-arm type and its successors.

Set 27, Brass Band of the Line, twelve pieces
Set 30, Drums and Bugles of the Line, eight pieces
Both sets are described on page 71.

Set 36, The Royal Sussex Regiment, was the earliest single set of marching figures, and at the start was reputed to contain nine marching men of the fixed-arm type, rifle on the right shoulder, with a bemedalled officer. A mounted officer on a head-down spindly horse was soon introduced, replacing two infantry, and the set may sometimes have contained both. The fixed-arm figure seems to have continued in this set until 1910, when it was replaced by the figure dated 24.2.1910. The early version of this set is illustrated on page 84.

Set 76, The Middlesex Regiment, seven men at the slope and an officer. In the very early days, this set was sometimes produced using the wasp-waisted officer figure given a trail arm instead of a sword arm. This set contained five men at the trail, two pioneers and an officer, all wasp-waisted. Normally, the set was based on the valise-pack marching figure, and most early sets included a pioneer as well as the officer. The figures in the earliest sets had white facings, but these were soon changed to yellow. Both this and the Royal Sussex were very popular sets.

Set 96, The York and Lancaster Regiment, seven men and an officer running at the trail. The first version of this set appeared in Soudan foreign-service dress (see page 117), but it was soon switched to full dress with white facings and a blue helmet.

Set 113, The East Yorkshire Regiment, eight men at attention. This was a companion set to 111, the Grenadier Guards.

Set 121, The Royal West Surrey Regiment, nine standing firing men and a standing officer with binoculars

Display Set 131, included 24 figures of the Worcestershire Regiment unavailable elsewhere: viz ten each marching and running with two officers and two further figures.

Set 156, The Royal Irish Regiment, four men standing and three each kneeling and lying firing, without an officer. This means that the only I of L kneeling officer with binoculars appeared outside our period in set 1908,

the Infantry Officers set made in 1940 only, thus being incredibly rare.

Set 206, The Warwickshire Regiment at the present, seven men and an officer. One figure had sword and scabbard arms to represent the officer. This was a companion to set 205, the Coldstream Guards.

Set 255, The Green Howards, officer, standard-bearer, drummer and six men marching at slope. This was one of the slightly larger sets brought out in the 1920s. The men wore blue helmets with green facings. A later version of this set is shown on page 84.

Set 321, Drum and Fife Band of the Line, seventeen musicians, described on page 74

Many I of L figures appeared in the X and A series. The first fixed-arm marching figure and first-version on-guard were in the X series, and the new on-guard and firing figures were in the A series, often with officers mounted on spindly horses. The firing figures in the A series are very rare today, presumably because the figures were not widely issued.

In the small size the I of L representative was the Manchester Regiment, set 20b. The first version of this was also used in the miniature encampment sets which appear in the 1915 catalogue. The second version with the square base was painted second grade in the W series.

Page 37 shows an enlarged example of each regiment made by Britains during our period. This makes a useful comparison of uniform details, such as facings and helmet colour, which are particularly confusing when considering Infantry of the Line.

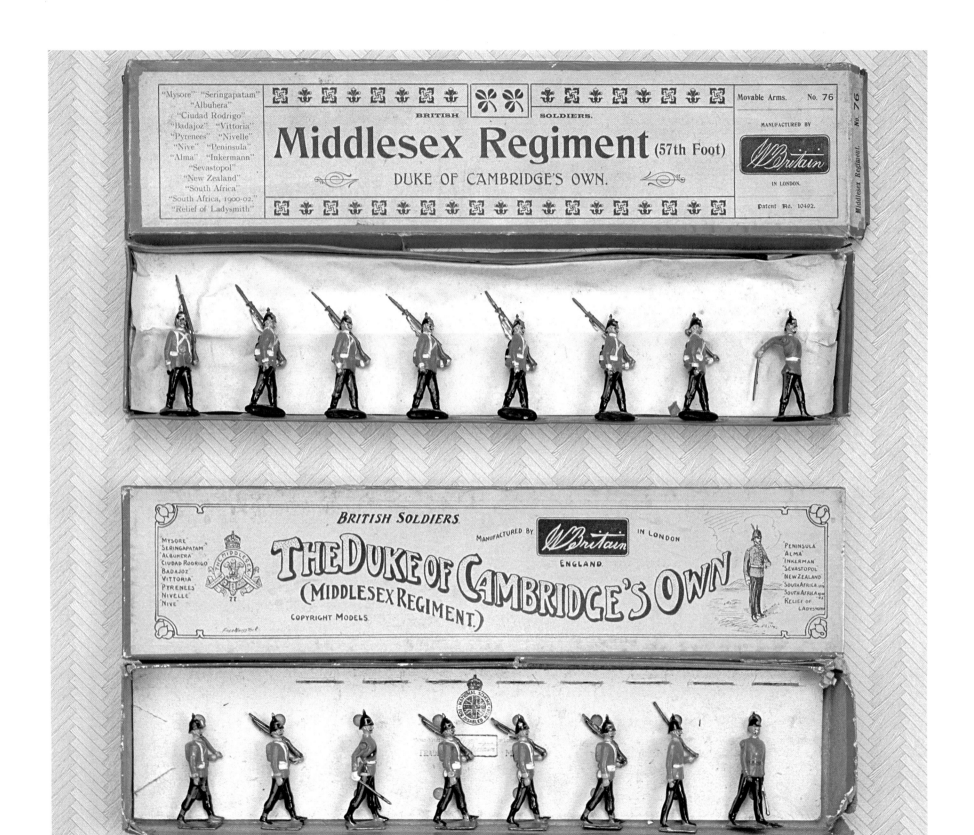

Top: Set 76 in original box, *c.1897.*   **Bottom:** Set 76 in original box, *c.1906. An officer and man from the version c.1911 are on the right.*

Examples of Infantry of the Line, described on pages 82-3.

Infantry of the Line: descriptions

Top row The figures in this row depict the four sets of Infantry of the Line on guard, numbers 16, 17, 18 and 29. (Early figures from set 16, 17 and 18 are shown on page 84.) Fig 1 is an officer of the Worcestershires with an oval base *c*.1906. Fig 2 is the later variation of the kneeling on-guard figure, without the little base protruding from the front foot. Fig 3 is a copy of the same figure, probably done by Hanks or Reka. Figs 4–7 show the later figures of the Worcestershires (set 18), *c*.1930. Figs 8–13 and 15 are types of the West Surrey Regiment from set 29. Fig 8 is the officer *c*.1922, fig 10 the matching on-guard figure. Fig 9 is the first version *c*.1905, in F paint condition. Figs 11 and 15 are full-trousered, *c*.1935, figs 12 and 13 are still gaitered, *c*.1914 and 1930, and also show slightly different head moulds, the brim of the helmet being wider in fig 13. Fig 14 is a second-grade Infantry of the Line on guard, *c*.1930.

2nd row Figs 1–3 show types of set 113, the East Yorks at attention. Fig 3 has the later arm with the rifle tucked into the side. Figs 4 and 5 show the round- and square-based officers for set 121, the Royal West Surreys firing, and figs 6–11 are firing men from this set in various painting styles. Fig 12 is the normal early lying firing Royal Irish Regiment from set 156, and fig 13 the rather unusual intermediate figure, *c*.1933. The legs were remodelled with the feet apart, but the boots still had gaiters rather than the legs having full trousers. Fig 14 shows the normal early kneeling firing figure for the same set.

3rd row Figs 1–6 show types of the Royal Sussex Regiment, set 36. Fig 1 is the early mounted officer *c*.1903, followed by the matching fixed-arm infantryman, eight of which made up the set. Fig 3 is a copy of the same figure, probably by Hanks. Fig 4 is the improved marching figure without the pack, dated 24.2.1912, and fig 5 is the normal figure for the 1920s and 1930s. Note that the arm has been changed. Fig 6 is the improved mounted officer for the set, which changed *c*.1912. This model has a blue helmet, which indicates that it belongs to the late 1930s when the helmet colour for the whole set was changed. Figs 7 and 9–11 show the marching figures from the Royal West Surreys in set 29. Fig 7 is the early bemedalled officer, fig 8 a Hanks copy of it. Fig 9 shows the fixed-arm man at the slope, the only time this figure appears in first-quality paint other than in set 36. The marching figures in set 29 followed the full sequence of marching types, from the first fixed-arm valise-pack type through to the 1910 figure without pack, shown on page 36. Figs 10 and 11 show the intermediate types. Fig 10 is the movable-arm valise-pack figure, which in this example has lost its bayonet, fig 11 the early oval-based box-pack figure dated 1.8.1905. Fig 12 is a later square-based box-pack figure with yellow facings denoting the Middlesex Regiment, *c*.1909.

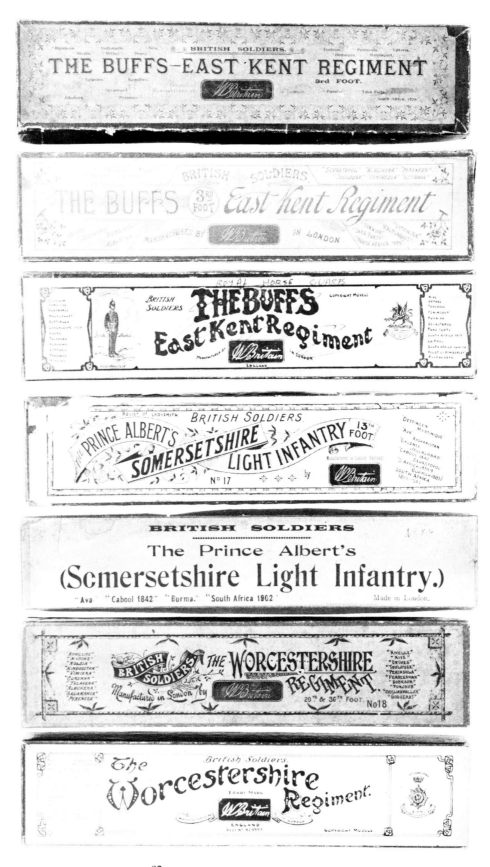

Left: **BOXES FOR INFANTRY OF THE LINE ON GUARD.**
*Top to bottom: 1 Highly decorative box from the early period before set numbering for set 16, **c.1895**. This was printed on a vivid pink, an unusual colour for a Britains' label. 2 Typographical box label for set 16, **c.1900**. 3 Whisstock pictorial design for set 16, showing a soldier at attention rather than on guard as they are in this set. 4 Typographical label for set 17, **c.1905**. Battle honours usually featured on Britains' boxes, but not often the entire roll. Sometimes they changed from label to label, not simply because extra ones had been awarded. 5 Second-grade box, **c.1910**. This box has no Britains' trademark, nor does it have an end label with an X series number as the similar cavalry boxes illustrated on pages 50 and 51. The figures inside, however, were Britains' Infantry of the Line on guard in second-grade paint, but with the green helmets that indicated that they were Somerset Light Infantry. 6 Typographical label for set 18, **c.1900**. 7 Whisstock design for set 18, complete with regimental badge.*

Opposite bottom: *Boxes for various regiments, all with labels designed by Whisstock. Top to bottom: 1 Set 113. 2 Set 156. 3 Set 206. In these three designs, Whisstock has included illustrations that capture quite faithfully the contents of the box, although there is no officer in set 113.*

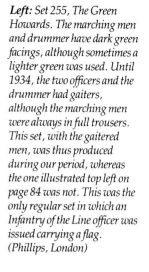

Left: *Set 255, The Green Howards. The marching men and drummer have dark green facings, although sometimes a lighter green was used. Until 1934, the two officers and the drummer had gaiters, although the marching men were always in full trousers. This set, with the gaitered men, was thus produced during our period, whereas the one illustrated top left on page 84 was not. This was the only regular set in which an Infantry of the Line officer was issued carrying a flag. (Phillips, London)*

4th row Figs 1–4 show types of the York and Lancaster Regiment. The first version of this set, which was always running at the trail, was in Soudan uniform and appears on page 118. Figs 1 and 2 show the same pigeon-chested figure with the rather later spiked helmet and square base, painted up in full dress with white facings, fig 1 being the officer and fig 2 the private, *c.*1912. Fig 3 is an odd figure, showing how 'wrong' differences stand out. Someone probably painted the white helmet at about the time the model was bought in 1909, and a short carbine arm has been substituted for the proper arm at the trail. The figure underwent further intensive active duty, during which the alterations took on the patina of authenticity. Fig 4 is a later version of the York and Lancaster, in the full-trousered closed-elbow version, *c.*1932. Fig 5 is a mounted officer for the W series set of Infantry of the Line, *c.*1930, based on the small-size first-version trotting horse.

Fig 6 is from a late second version of set 20b, the Manchester Regiment (the early version appears on page 37). It was only produced between 1912 and 1916, and after the First World War was reissued in second-grade paint as set 10w, an example of which is shown here as fig 7. Fig 8 is the standard A series second-grade Infantry of the Line figure. Fig 9 is a very interesting mounted Infantry of the Line officer on the head-down spindly horse, with the base moulded between the back pair of horse's hooves so that it can be inserted in a Parade Series slotted card insert. The figure appears to be a Royal Sussex Regiment officer. But so far as is known no set of these appeared in the Parade Series, and the blue helmet may have been overpainted white, so that the officer may therefore be from the Middlesex Regiment, set 481. Fig 10 is a second-grade painted Infantry of the Line mounted officer on a head-level spindly horse.

Below: A ROW OF INFANTRY

The long illustrations on the upper row are of an assembly of Infantry of the Line. They are arranged as a succession of sets, and are described, as usual, from left to right.

First is a late-version set 255, the Green Howards, with the distinctive standard-bearer that, so far as I know, was the only Infantry of the Line standard Britains produced. Since the officers have no gaiters, they must date from after 1934, when gaiters were abolished. A close-up is shown to the left.

Next is the mounted officer of the early version set 36, the Royal Sussex, who are marching forward to his right, with their rifles on the left shoulder. This is Britains' earliest infantry, with the exception of the plug-handed Fusilier (see page 38).

Next come a stalwart group of the early on-guard sets,

numbers 16, 18 and 17, the East Kent Regiment (Buffs), the Worcestershire Regiment, and examples of the Somerset Light Infantry. The Buffs are a very early set, without the drummer and bugler included later. The Worcestershires date from c.1898, having the early pigeon-toed drummer boy and the wasp-waisted officer. The little stands that the earlier kneeling on-guard figures possessed can also be seen clearly. In the back row of the group of F to P Somerset Light Infantry are a bemedalled and a wasp-waisted officer, with a standing on-guard infantryman and, in the front row, a boy bugler and three kneeling men on guard. These figures show the wide variety of greens in which the helmets in this set could be painted. Under normal circumstances, the lighter green signifies an earlier set.

Compare these figures with the six standing and six kneeling X series Somerset Light Infantry, using the same figures, pictured opposite on page 85. The impact of the second-grade paint is quite striking. To the right of the first six standing are examples of three other paint styles, the Worcesters, the Buffs and a gilt.

Next comes a group of the figures used before the First World War in the British Army Encampment sets illustrated on page 15 of the 1915 catalogue. These figures – cavalry, tree, gun and marching infantry – are as they appear in the set marked 06. The tent on the left is Britains' but the wrong shape. The tent on the right is the right shape, but not Britains'. So many manufacturers produced tents, which are in any case very fragile, that sorting out the survivors is difficult. Britains often

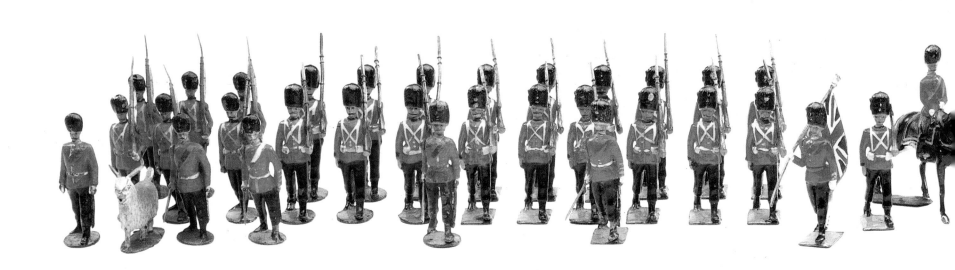

rubber-stamped the underside 'Seamless – Made in England Eng.Pat. No 9189', which of course dispels any doubt. The marching infantry are second-grade painted figures of the type used for set 20b, the Manchester Regiment (see page 37).

By contrast, the next figures are representative of the three larger scales of second-grade painted figures: X series West Surreys, Infantry of the Line number 4h, and Infantry of the Line number 1hh. The double h series men are 83mm scale, and were sold only during the late 1930s, outside our period. My one battered example is shown here to permit scale comparisons with the smaller figures.

A company of Fusiliers

The bottom picture on these pages is of types of the Fusiliers,

arranged stylistically into a company marching in line. There is normally no way of distinguishing an ordinary marching Royal from a Royal Welch simply by Britains' paint style. The figures on parade here show, from left to right, a complete range of paint styles from 1897 to 1966; on this occasion I have included the full spectrum of Britains' production to show the different finishes on figures produced during and after our period.

The appropriate officers appear in front of their contemporary men. On the extreme left is the fixed-arm bemedalled officer with the valise-pack men of 1897. With them are an early goat tinged with brown rather than the later cream or dead white, and to the right two wasp-waisted officers, one with the normal crimson sash, the other with a white sash. All these figures have the small early Fusilier head. Next come the

oval-base box-pack figures, rarer than the previous versions since they were only produced for about four years. Next to them are the square-base box-pack figures. Note that, although the first four files of box-pack figures have heads without a moulded plume, thereafter – perhaps from the end of the First World War – a plume is moulded into the right side of the cap. From 1905 on, the Fusilier figure retained the box pack until the end of production in 1966, the only marching British infantry figure to do this. All other production figures had changed to the 1910 model without the pack by 1938.

Near the middle of the company are a standard-bearer and pioneer from set 73 (for the earlier versions of these, see page 96). Then come two mounted officers. The first is a rare example of a mounted Fusilier officer to go with a Parade set, the base between the rear hooves of the horse allowing it to slot into the Parade baseboard. The second officer is a converted and repainted figure, the only other way of providing a company of Britains Fusiliers with a mounted officer.

With their officer, the first six men on the right-hand page represent the paint style c.1930. Until then Fusiliers all had gaiters, but from now on they have full trousers. The next six men and the officer show the paint style of the late 1930s, a pioneer once more being included. The moustache was done away with at this time, and the next group of six, from the 1940s, is clean-shaven. Finally, the group of six on the extreme right, with the officer and dead-white goat, were my first set of best-quality Britains, bought for me by my grandmother at Harrods in 1952. Notice the darker red of the coats and the rifles with the large protruding bayonet. The painted brass chin straps are not original but my own addition when young – an attempt to prevent caps being blown off! At that time I was convinced that these figures were Foot Guards.

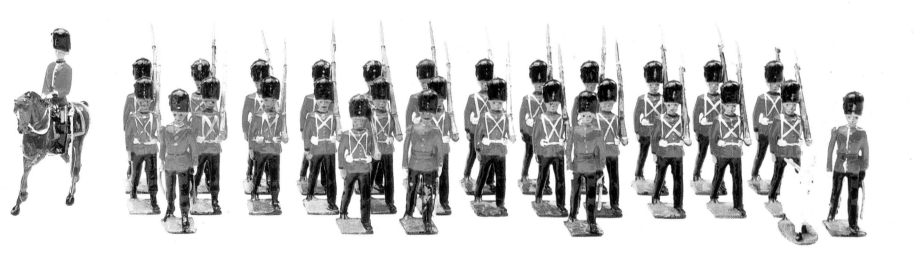

Chapter 26
Fusiliers and Rifles

The Fusiliers

The earliest Fusiliers made by Britains were the germanic types described on page 38. These were never given a set number. After that, only two sets were made during our period.

Set 7, The 7th Royal Fusiliers, seven men at the slope and an officer. Despite the low number of the set, which might indicate that it came out in 1893, the earliest version dates from 1897 and uses the valise-pack figures with the bemedalled officer.

Set 74, The Royal Welch Fusiliers, six men at the slope with an officer and a goat mascot. For a short time after the set was first issued in 1897, an extra man was included, so that in effect the goat was a free gift in addition to the normal value of eight soldiers for a shilling. The Royal Welch Fusiliers also appeared in set 73, which is illustrated on page 96.

The Rifle regiments

As with the Fusiliers, Britains only included two boxed sets of first-grade rifle regiments in its list during our period.

Set 9, The Rifle Brigade, seven men at the slope bayonets not fixed, with an officer. Like set 7, the Royal Fusiliers, set 9 was not brought out until 1897, using the valise-pack marching figure and the bemedalled officer. Recent research has vindicated Britains' original choice of the at-the-slope drill position (see page 11). The men and officers followed the usual sequence of types for marching figures, provided with rifle regiment heads wearing busbies. This set was not included in the catalogue after the First World War for very long.

Set 98, The King's Royal Rifle Corps, seven men running at the trail, officer running with sword. Very early sets wore a spiked helmet with their green uniform, but this soon changed to the rifle busby, and the figures were changed according to the usual sequence for running infantry.

In the A series there was a rifleman running, a rather tall fixed-arm figure in full trousers with the rifle carried level across the body. This was included in a number of A series sets, and was also available singly. There were no small-size models of Rifle regiments.

Types of the above sets are included in the illustration on page 88.

More Fusiliers were represented in the small size. Set 84 included a row of small 7th Royal Fusiliers, set 85 had a row of Northumberland Fusiliers, and set 86 was a double row of small Lancashire Fusiliers, 14 in all. Of the B series sets, 17b were Lancashire Fusiliers marching at the trail with white facings, 19b were Dublin Fusiliers running at the trail, and 21b were Northumberland Fusiliers in foreign-service helmets marching at the trail. An example of each of these three will be found on page 37, and some further examples are on page 65.

No Fusiliers appeared in the X, W or A ranges, and the only second-grade paint Fusilier was the large-size 5h figure (illustrated on page 65).

BOXES FOR FUSILIERS
Top to bottom: 1 Whisstock design for set 7. 2 Early pictorial design for set 74, without set number, c.1897, when they introduced these two sets. Britains evidently thought that it was worth making a special plate for the box label, as was later done for the Whisstock designs, rather than have the printer make them up. Other similar labels were made for early Lancer regiments and the West India Regiment, but this was not often done before Whisstock. 3 Even though set 74 already had a specially designed label, here is one put together by the printers, c.1905. Maybe the plate for the previous label had worn out or been lost. 4 Whisstock produced an excellent label design for the set, complete with an illustration of the mascot goat, and this was used from c.1913 until c.1952. 5 Early typographical label for smaller-size set 21B.

Chapter 27
The Royal Navy

Set 35, The Royal Marine Artillery (RMA), seven men marching at the slope with officer. The Royal Marines were the earliest numbered set of royal naval figures brought out by Britains. From its position in the list next to the Sussex Regiment one would expect the first version of this to be the fixed-arm marching figure. Len Richards showed one in his book, but it has since been discovered that this was an embellished second grade, and I have found no evidence for RMA figures earlier than the 1897 valise-pack figure, of which seven with the bemedalled officer made up a set. The officer followed the normal sequence of changes, but the RMA remained the box-pack type until about 1938, even producing a full-trouser version, following the Fusilier figure.

Set 97, The Royal Marine Light Infantry (RMLI), seven men running at the trail with officer. Early sets of the other branch of the Marines had a white helmet, although this was soon changed to blue, and only their blue facings distinguished them from the York and Lancaster Regiment. By 1934, the uniform had changed to blue, and the infantry helmet eventually gave way to a Marine tropical helmet c.1937.

The fixed-arm marching figure was painted in a blue uniform to represent an X series Royal Marine Artillery, and in the small size the similar infantry marching figure also appeared in blue in second-grade paint.

Set 78, Bluejackets of the Royal Navy, seven men and a petty officer.
Set 80, Whitejackets of the Royal Navy, seven men and a petty officer.
The Royal Navy's Bluejackets were first represented running at the trail. Set 80 contained the same figures painted as Whitejackets, although these were at the slope before the First World War, and usually the petty officer retained his blue uniform.

Set 79, Royal Naval Landing Party with gun. This set comprised eight sailors running with hands formed into loops to pull the ropes attached to the limber. In addition was a running petty officer and a mountain gun provided with a wire loop to fit over the limber's towing hook. This set is illustrated on page 108.

From c.1900 Britains made available the 4.7-inch Naval Gun which for 15 years was Britains' heaviest artillery piece (see page 145). It has no catalogue number during our period.

Set 151, The Royal Naval Volunteer Reserve (RNVR),

BOXES FOR THE ROYAL MARINES
*Top to bottom: 1 Early label for set 35, **c**.1900.*
2 Whisstock design for set 35.
*3 Early label for set 97, **c**.1900. 4 Whisstock pictorial design for set 97. Since it is relatively common, the early label for set 35 may have endured after the First World War. If Whisstock had done a label for the set before the two branches of the Royal Marines, the Artillery and the Light Infantry, merged, the title of the box would have been the Royal Marine Artillery.*

seven men and a petty officer. This set contained a new fixed-arm figure at the shoulder (dated 12.11.1907), although reminiscent of the Boer/US figure of 15.6.1906. A new petty officer was created to be in charge of these, and in very early versions of this set he had a movable arm. Soon afterwards, he was remodelled into a fixed-arm figure.

Set 207, Officers and Petty Officers of the Royal Navy. After the First World War, a set of naval officers was brought out containing two admirals and two midshipmen as well as four petty officers of the type in set 151.

Set 254, Bluejackets and Whitejackets of the Royal Navy with petty officer. In this set, the last introduced during

our period depicting the Royal Navy, four of the eight men of the shoulder-arms variety were painted as Whitejackets, and there was a petty officer in charge of the set of nine.

In the A series there was a very attractive fixed-arm sailor with a hat striding along swinging his arms, a figure later replaced by a rather smaller one with his arms at his side. The fixed-arm sailor at the shoulder arms from set 151 was also used with second-grade paint. Small-size sailors appeared in set 22b Bluejackets and set 24b Whitejackets. Each of these consisted of seven sailors marching at the slope, with a smaller oval-base and a larger square-base version of each. The larger versions went into the W series in second-grade paint as both Bluejacket and Whitejacket.

Examples of Riflemen, Marines and Sailors, described on page 90.

Top Left: *Set 316, Royal Horse Artillery at the halt. Although this set was current from 1929 to 1941, not many can have been sold, since it is extremely rare. So too are its equivalent sets for the RFA, set 317, and in service dress, set 318.*

Centre left: *Although at first glance this seems a normal Britains' Royal Horse Artillery gun team, in fact it is a copy by Renvoize. Based on the original Britains' gun team, it goes one better by providing the drivers with movable whip arms and improving the modelling of the gun. There are no bucket seats on the gun, but the limber takes two seated men. In all other respects the team is indistinguishable from Britains'.*

ROYAL FIELD ARTILLERY (RFA)

This illustration shows three gun teams of the RFA. On the left is the first version, introduced in 1906, from when until 1916 it had four men seated on the limber and gun. The gun was identical to the one used for the RHA. The distinctive uniform of the RFA is the red facings and the infantry-style helmet topped with a ball rather than a spike. This last item often gets broken off the model – hence the sometimes unfortunately worded description seen in auction catalogues: 'ball missing'. This has happened to several men in the photograph above. After the First World War, the bucket seats were removed from the gun, so that until 1924 the set was issued with two seated figures, as in the centre example above. From 1924, when the light-harness horse team was introduced, until the advent in 1932 of the new pattern limber, the RFA used the same plain-topped centre-pole limber that the RHA had been using since 1906, and there were no seated men at all. This version can be seen on the right above. All versions came with a mounted officer on the cantering horse originally dated 12.2.1903, and he carried a sword in an outstretched arm.

The Royal Navy: descriptions

Top row Fig 1 is the X series Royal Marine artilleryman once thought to be the first version of set 35. Figs 2–12 are all riflemen. Figs 2–4 are Rifle Brigade, set 9. Fig 2 is the first-version valise-pack marching figure, fig 3 the bemedalled officer to match, fig 4 the box-pack figure with an oval base. Fig 5 is a very unusual bugler boy who does not definitely fit specifically with set 9, but on the other hand is difficult to place elsewhere. Figs 5–12 are the King's Royal Rifle Corps, set 98. Fig 6 is the first-version pigeon-chested figure in the spiked infantry helmet and fig 7 the matching officer. Fig 8 shows the same figure now in a Rifles busby. Fig 9 is the full-trouser open-elbow figure, figs 10 and 11 being the matching officers, one without and one with the distinctive red Austrian knot painted on the cuff. Fig 12 is the late-pattern rifleman, the closed-elbow version of the running figure, in a later paint style, *c.*1949. Fig 13 is the A series rifleman running, a distinctly larger fixed-arm figure in about 56mm scale. Figs 14-16 are the later types of the Royal Marine Light Infantry and are dealt with in the description of the 2nd row.

2nd row Royal Marines: Figs 1–10 are types of the Royal Marine Artillery, set 35, starting with fig 1, the valise-pack private, and fig 2, the bemedalled officer, which together make up the first version. Figs 3 and 4 show the 1905 box-pack figures on oval bases. Fig 5 is a private *c.*1925, and figs 6 and 7 show the white infantry helmet style *c.*1930. Finally, on retitling as the Royal Marines, the distinctive Marine pith helmet appeared *c.*1932, fig 8, followed by fig 9, *c.*1937, without gaiters with a similar officer, fig 10. Figs 11–14 of this row and figs 14–16 of the top row show the sequence of set 97, the Royal Marine Light Infantry. Fig 11 is the early pigeon-chested figure, which has a small infantry helmet, painted white. Fig 12, the same figure *c.*1908, has a blue helmet, and is only distinguishable from the York and Lancaster Regiment (set 96) by its blue, rather than white, facings. Fig 13 is the matching officer. Fig 14 shows the first open-elbow full-trouser figure, and figs 14 and 15 of the top row show the change to the blue uniform. Sometimes these figures had an infantry helmet with a ball rather than a spike. Fig 15 of the top row shows the final form of this set *c.*1937.

3rd and 4th rows Types of the Royal Navy: on the 3rd row, figs 1–8 are small-size sailors. Figs 1–5 are Bluejackets, figs 1, 3 and 4 showing the first and second versions of set 22b. Fig 2 is a copy, probably by Reka. Fig 1, the earliest small sailor, has a rifle with fixed bayonet, a feature which appeared to be lost or was deliberately not moulded in later small-size figures at the slope, such as fig 3. Fig 4 is the later, larger sailor with a square base, and fig 5 shows the same in W series paint style. Figs 6 and 7 show the two versions of the Whitejackets set 24b, and fig 8 is the W series equivalent. Figs 9–11 show the two versions of Britains standard-size Bluejackets at the trail,

set 79, but fig 10 is a Renvoize copy with a distinctively different rifle. Figs 12–14 show types of the fixed-arm sailors used with the Naval Landing Party, set 80. The earliest figures of the ratings all had a comparatively small head. Figs 15 and 16 are petty officers of the type normally seen leading sets 79, 80 and 81.

4th row Fig 1 is the admiral and fig 2 is the midshipman from the set of naval officers, 207. Fig 3 is the A series sailor in straw hat. Figs 4–8 show Whitejackets from set 81, the early figures being at the slope. These were probably produced until the First World War. Figs 7 and 8 are *c.*1935, and the petty officer in white uniform is very unusual, since, although in this set they are leading Whitejackets, they were normally supplied in blue like fig 15 of the 3rd row. Fig 9 is the Royal Naval Volunteer Reserve figure dated 12.11.1907, and fig 10 is in the *c.*1930 style of paint with fig 11, a similar figure painted as a Whitejacket to make up set 254. The first petty officer made before the First World War had a movable arm, fig 12. But from then on they were fixed-arm, fig 13 1925 and fig 14 *c.*1937. Note that, *c.*1934, naval officers' brown gloves were replaced with white ones.

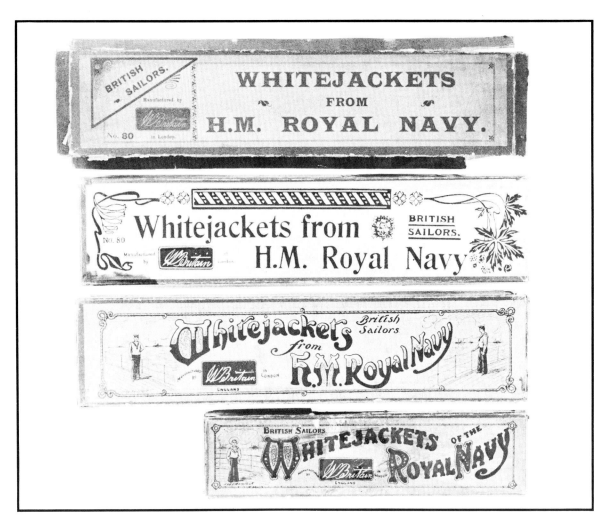

BOXES FOR ROYAL NAVY WHITEJACKETS

Top to bottom: 1 and 2 Early typographical labels for set 80. Both look as though the set number could have been added as an afterthought. These two box labels are another example of the diversity of labels produced by Britains before Whisstock took on the job of giving the whole range of single-row sets a consistent appearance. I find these very early boxes extremely attractive, although that may be in anticipation of what is to be found within when first recognizing the style of label on the box. 3 Whisstock label for set 80. This is a very attractive fully illustrated label surrounded by a rope motif. Whisstock often took a great deal of trouble with his borders, and incorporated items such as shamrocks for Irish regiments. 4 Whisstock design for set 24B. Although the design is similar to 3, even the illustration is a completely different one.

Chapter 28
The Royal Artillery

Britains' sets of the Royal Artillery are some of the most spectacular and sought-after items that they ever produced. In 1914, the Royal Artillery was organized in three branches, the Royal Horse Artillery (RHA), the Royal Field Artillery (RFA) and the Royal Garrison Artillery (RGA), which was in charge of the mountain batteries.

Set 28, Mountain Artillery, four mules, six men, mounted officer and gun. This was Britains' first artillery set, and probably resulted from the publicity accorded to the mountain gunners' sterling service on the north-west frontier of India since 1850 (see page 108).

Set 39, Royal Horse Artillery, six-horse team with limber, gun, mounted officer and four seated or mounted gunners, according to version. A complete battery of these guns is illustrated on pages 92 and 93, showing the various different versions.

Set 125, Royal Horse Artillery, small size, review order
Set 126, Royal Horse Artillery, small size, active-service order
These small-size sets had the same contents as set 39, with four mounted gunners. They are described and illustrated on page 116.

Set 144, Royal Field Artillery, six-horse team with limber, gun and mounted officer. This set, which was first produced in 1906, was at the walk, in contrast with the RHA teams, which were all at the gallop (illustrated on page 89).

Set 39a, Royal Horse Artillery, service dress
Set 144a, Royal Field Artillery, service dress
These sets were introduced in 1916 as part of Britains' representation of the khaki-clad British Army of the First World War. The contents of the sets were exactly the same as the full-dress sets 39 and 144, the men simply

having peaked caps and khaki uniforms. (See page 144.)

Set 211, Heavy Howitzer with Horse Team, ten-horse team, limber and gun. This set was produced in 1924, and is described on page 146.

Set 316, Royal Horse Artillery (see page 89)
Set 317, Royal Field Artillery
Set 318, Gun of the Royal Artillery with Limber and Horse Team, and standing and kneeling gunners (active-service order)
These three sets were all gun teams at the halt, and were first produced in 1929. They are extremely rare. Each set had a six-horse team, mounted officer, limber and gun, set 318 having in addition eight gunners on foot.

In addition to these sets, Britains sold their guns individually. During our period these had no catalogue numbers. They are discussed on page 143.

Set 39, the Royal Horse Artillery, second version with officer and mounted gunners, with original box, c.1908. (Sotheby's, Pulborough)

A battery of Royal Horse Artillery, described on page 94.

A battery of Royal Horse Artillery

Pages 92–3 show a battery of Royal Horse Artillery moving forward. Each gun team came complete with mounted officer and four gunners. In the early set 39, produced from 1895 to 1905, the gunners sat on the limber and gun, but in 1906 a new limber was introduced and the gunners were each given their own head-up trotting horse dated 12.12.1902 and equipped with a carbine.

The gun, representing the 12-pounder used during the Boer War, remained the same throughout our period, except for minor modifications when the holes for the bucket seats were omitted and later when an improved method of installing the spring was introduced. The bucket seats were mounted on thick wire pins pushed into holes at the top end of the trail of the gun. The seats were grooved, to take a flange cast on the bottom of the gunners, thus ensuring that the men did not fall out of their seats when moving at speed.

The early limber is known as the shafted limber as it has two shafts which take the unridden team horse nearest to the limber. By contrast, the 1906 limber is the centre-pole type, seen in the rear three teams in the picture. The pole goes forward between the rear pair of horses of the team. At first, before the First World War, limbers were painted grey, later and during the War they were khaki, and afterwards they were given a gun-metal finish, as shown in the near-most team.

Until c.1924 the team horses were all of the collar-harness type: the harness was attached to a large collar, against which the horses pulled with their shoulders. A further feature of the collar harness is the valise on the unridden horse. These details can be seen on all but the rear-most team at the back. This team has breast harness, often referred to as light harness; this was a much lighter harness that distributed the pull over the breast of the horse, making the load much easier to manage. This light-harness version was probably introduced as a result of the decision to make set 211 in 1924, as Britains tended to update previous sets on the same subject when doing the research for a new set (ICP). This also happened in 1906, when the Royal Field Artillery were introduced and set 39 was updated at the same time. All the RHA galloping gun-team drivers have fixed arms outstretched cracking their whips. On page 89 a Renvoize copy of a Britains' gun team is shown which reverses the usual state of affairs, for unlike the Britains original the copy has movable whip arms.

The RFA set 39 was sold at a premium price of six shillings, and to justify this the quality of the paintwork was better than Britains' usual standard. The frogging of the artillerymen was meticulously painted in, although as usual the rows of frogging decorating the chest were more ambitiously represented in early figures. Look at the seated gunners in the nearest gun team. The furthest gunner, which is earlier and original to this team, has at least four extra rows of yellow across his chest. The

piping down the seams of the shell jackets on the backs of these figures is also painted in, and the caplines are carefully painted round the busby. On the horses, the full details of the harness are painted, and their faces are shown with a pink nose, red mouth, eyes and eyebrows; the hooves are painted black. All this extra work made this set most attractive.

In looking at the gunners mounted on separate horses, note that the ones in the front row carry short carbines, whereas the ones at the rear carry long carbines. This tells us that short carbines were used for at least a few years after 1906.

BOXES FOR SMALL-SIZE ROYAL HORSE ARTILLERY GUN TEAMS
The labels for the standard-size artillery sets were uniformly dull (see page 91). In the small size, however, some most remarkable labels were produced for Britains' sets. Top to bottom: 1 Typographical label for set 125, printed in two colours, a very unusual occurrence. 2 Whisstock design for set 125. 3 Whisstock design for set 126. There is no doubt that these two labels were some of Whisstock's best work. 4 This box contained a Britains copy gun team, small-size, in foreign-service dress, probably by Reka. Examples of the contents of all these boxes are illustrated on page 116.

Chapter 29
Set 73

Having examined most of the British Army, we now come to what for me is one of the high spots of collecting. Set 73 was the first of the really large boxes of soldiers Britains produced, and it remained the most popular, enduring from 1897 until 1965, the penultimate year of lead soldier production, when I bought one of the last produced as my twenty-first birthday present to myself. I remember negotiating a reduction of twelve and sixpence as the lid was torn.

What a really large box meant as far as Britains was concerned was more than one layer. Apart from the mammoth sets 131 and 132, which because of their rarity are virtually unattainable, most of these sets had two layers and contained between 60 and 120 pieces. During much of our period by coincidence set 73 contained exactly 73 pieces, as follows:

14 Band of the Line	7 Royal Scots Greys
14 Royal Welch Fusiliers	7 17th Lancers
14 Gordon Highlanders	9 Royal Horse Artillery
7 2nd Life Guards	1 General Officer

Before 1906, and possibly for some years thereafter, the RHA was the version with seated gunners, which meant four more pieces, and at about the end of our period the RHA was changed to Royal Field Artillery.

In the first version of set 73, the 17th Lancers were in full dress on pony horses and the Gordons were the plug-handed figure running. By the time the set shown here was made, the foreign-service order Ulundi-style 17th Lancers from set 81 had been installed, and the new Gordon Highlander dated 20.1.1901 had arrived. There is no sign of the improved cavalry figures of 1902–3, however, so the date of the box seems to be 1901 or 1902. Some of the original contents of the box are missing, and in these cases a substitute has been included to simulate a full box. This will test readers' powers of observation, since it is such substitutions that collectors look for when determining a box's authenticity. Let us now, as an instructional exercise, undertake just such a rigorous examination of what is in front of us. What we are looking for is consistency row by row, as different paint styles may well be in the same large box, since the various regiments will have been painted separately by different people.

The box lid and the top lift-out tray are shown on the left-hand side. The tray has only three rows, as the RHA takes up the full depth of the box. The box is made of wood, and in this example the lid slides out from nicely constructed grooves in the top of the sides of the main box. Other examples from the 1900s I have seen have hinged wooden lids. Although the box continued to be made of wood after the First World War, the lid was converted to a cardboard lift-off style. All types were covered in the usual red paper. The carpentry on earlier boxes tended to be considerably better than on later ones. The infantry bases fit into slots in the cardboard packing, and the cavalry have individual card boxes nested with tissue paper.

The top row of the lift-out tray consists of the Band of the Line, composed of slotted-arm bandsmen, which have the early largish, somewhat squashed-looking face and so could well belong together in this set. The Band of the Line is rather different from the basic set 27, since one cornet and one euphonium have vanished and one bombardon and a wind section of two clarinets and a bassoon have been added. It is only in this set that these additional Line Infantry bandsmen are found. Unfortunately the top of the bassoon is missing (bandsman on the extreme left of the row). Note also the two men who have lost their helmet spikes.

The 2nd Life Guards are represented by the figure found in set 1, rather than, as one might expect, a row of figures from set 43. They seem perfectly authentic, however, and have been painted with the correct white sheepskins, thus providing another variation not available elsewhere. Later on in the career of set 73, the Life Guard at the gallop was used, but unusual variations of position or arm often did crop up in this row.

The Royal Welch Fusiliers formed the third row of the tray, and three figures not available elsewhere were included, two pioneers and a standard-bearer. Later, between the wars, the tendency was to equip this whole row with rifles without the bayonet fixed, thus creating another difference between this and set 74, the basic set of Welch Fusiliers. In the set on view, the two figures on the left do not match the rest of the Fusiliers, having brown-painted rather than metallic rifles, and white gloves rather than hands painted a flesh colour. The third figure from the left has lost his bayonet, but matches the remainder of the row.

On the lower layer, illustrated on page 97, the top row is of 17th Lancers in foreign-service order. These appear to be rather a mixed bunch. The officer and trumpeter have the same bright face paint as the Welch Fusiliers, unlike the three troopers on rocking horses, who have chin straps painted in gold, a trait from an earlier period. The two troopers on pony horses do not match each other or the others in the row. The one on the brown horse has a cross-grained arm-stud, whereas the one on the black has a centre-punched arm-stud. The brown horse is an early type without the ear pricked, and the lance pennon is a much darker red. Note also the following points: the yellow paint stripe down the trumpeter's leg is much brighter than on the other figures; there are only two centre-punched movable arm-studs in the row; and, unusually, there are more than two colours of horse among the troopers. Here there are, from the left, light brown, dark brown, light brown, black, dark brown. Conclusion: a mixed group, with no evidence that rocking and pony horses were ever included together in this way either in this set or in set 81.

The Gordon Highlanders in the second row are susceptible to the same sort of analysis. Although all bear paper labels dated Jan 20th 1901, figs 1–4, 6, 9 and 14 are in one paint style, with very pale faces matching the 2nd Life Guards in the top tray, while all the others except fig 11 are in the bright face-paint noted in the two right-hand 17th Lancers above. Fig 11, the dark green painted piper, is a total stranger. Note the different ways the tails on the sporran are painted; the tails on the first group extend further down than on the other. Cross straps and equipment are also painted far more neatly on the first group. As a matter of interest, note that the pipers are given fiery Scottish red hair, eyebrows and moustaches.

The Royal Scots Greys in the third row are a very motley group, ranging from F to P and with five tin swords, a leg, four ends of sword scabbard (hardly detectable in the photograph) and even a head missing. They are so different from the G to F condition of the rest of the box that they can be dismissed straight away as not matching the rest of the box, even if they are the correct type for the date. The face painting of the bucket-seat RHA team, on the other hand, matches that of the 'bright face group' seen in the top and second rows, and apart from one substitute gunner and a broken capline and a plume missing from the third driver's busby they are in good condition. The officer also matches the 'bright face group', and is nice, although his plume and front foreleg are bent. The substitute gunner is detectable because the frogging is more closely spaced across his chest, with far more lines than on his supposed comrades. The General Officer belongs to the 'pale face group' noted in the 2nd row.

The conclusion of this rather lengthy analysis is that this box contains figures from two different set 73s, one of the bright face group and one pale face. Looking back at the top tray, we find sadly that the face-paint of the Infantry of the Line Band and the Fusiliers belong to neither of these groups. This is not conclusive evidence that these two rows are not original.

For me, even a non-matching box such as this still looks really attractive, and can be treasured until – if ever – something better turns up.

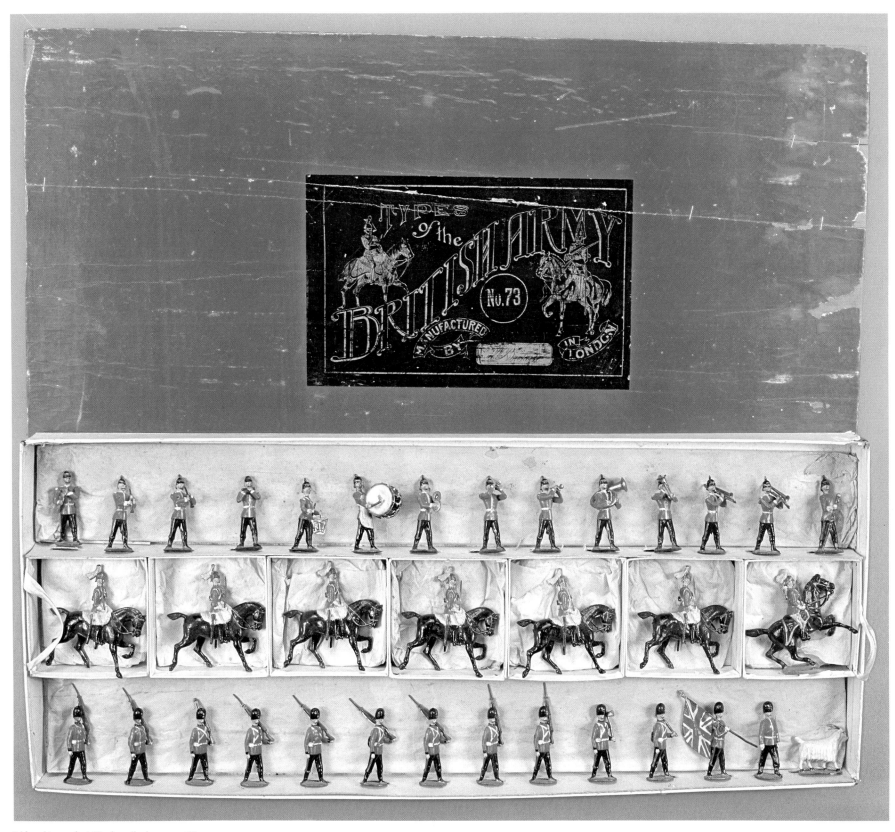

Lid and tray of set 73, described on page 95.

Lower tray of set 73, described on page 95.

PART FOUR
THE BRITISH EMPIRE

Britains was much influenced by contemporary events, and often produced toys that mirrored these events for their young clientele. In 1893, the British Empire was at its height. Over the next 20 years, sets of toy soldiers were produced showing troops from the West Indies, Egypt, the Soudan, India and Australia, as well as British soldiers engaged in conflicts throughout the far-flung imperial territories and the enemies they had to face. Chapter 30 gives details of the colonial troops, Chapter 31 shows how the British went to war in the Empire, and Chapter 32 describes the toys produced as a result of the Boer War.

*Below: **BOXES FOR INDIAN EMPIRE CAVALRY***
*Top to bottom: 1 Early un-numbered pictorial label for set 66, **c.**1896. 2 Most attractive pictorial label for set 45, **c.**1900. It is interesting to sort out the many early labels into stylistic groups, eg those including reversed-out lettering in black scrolls as seen here. 3 Later label for set 45, when the title had changed, **c.**1935.*

Chapter 30
Colonial troops

Britains depicted various troops of the British Empire as the occasion arose.

Set 19, The West India Regiment, eight men and a mounted officer. This regiment became topical when the Victoria Cross was awarded to a sergeant after the third Ashanti War of 1893–4. For a time it included a bemedalled officer on foot, possibly on occasion as well as the mounted officer, rather than instead of him. The mounted officer was the same figure as the Mountain Artillery officer, starting on the head-down spindly horse and changing c.1920 to a sturdier fixed-arm figure on the former X series head-up spindly horse. The foot figure was fixed-arm carrying the rifle at the shoulder, and remained the same throughout production except that it changed from an oval to a square base c.1920. Later, the set became just eight foot figures, without any officer. The box label designed for this set in 1894 when it entered production was considered so good that it was not changed throughout the life of the set.

Set 38, The South African Mounted Infantry. For details of this set, see page 115.

Set 48, Egyptian Camel Corps (see page 107)

Set 49, The South Australian Lancers, four troopers and an officer. For a discussion of the origins of the South Australian Lancers, see page 11.

Set 115, Egyptian Cavalry
Set 116, Soudanese Infantry
Set 117, Egyptian Infantry
These three sets are fully described on page 107.

After the First World War, three more interesting sets were added to the list of imperial troops.
Set 202, Togoland Warriors, eight pieces, illustrated on page 136
Set 214, The Royal Canadian Mounted Police, in winter dress at the slope, eight pieces
Set 225, The King's African Rifles, eight pieces
None of these sets had an officer, and all three were newly-made castings for their set. The reason why these sets were introduced is no longer known to us.

The part of the Empire that excited most interest were the vast Indian territories, where an almost independent military tradition had grown up. Britains produced ten regiments from the Indian Army during our period. The names of Indian regiments are rather confusing, since

BOXES FOR COLONIAL TROOPS
Top to bottom: 1 – 3 Boxes for set 19. Note that in 2 the set number has been added top right. This shows that the top box is pre-1898, when set numbers were not shown on boxes. The original pictorial label for this set, 1, was so well designed that Britains retained it throughout our period, with the addition of the set number, 2, and the enlargement of the elements of the design to cover the whole box, 3. The set was originally produced to commemorate the Ashanti Wars, and the Britain family commissioned some really good pictures to mark the occasion on this label. 4 – 6 typographical labels for set 49. At first glance, 4 and 5 seem identical, but the lettering for 'Movable Arms' has been changed. 4 and 5 are c.1897. 6, c.1901, has a little sticker added, proclaiming copyright models. 7 Whisstock design for set 214.

many were reorganized, and so both the original and the revised titles are listed below. Cavalry regiments were represented by five cavalrymen including a trumpeter, and infantry regiments by seven men and an officer at the trail until c.1921, then by eight men at the slope using a different figure.
Set 45, 3rd Madras Cavalry, 28th Light Cavalry, **7th Light Cavalry**
Set 46, 10th Bengal Lancers, Hodson's Horse
Set 47, 1st Bengal Cavalry, Skinner's Horse
Set 64, two-row set with 2nd Madras Lancers, 16th Light Cavalry, and **7th Bengal Infantry**, 3rd battalion, 7th Rajput Regiment

Set 66, 1st Bombay Lancers, 13th Duke of Connaught's Own Lancers
Set 67, 1st Madras Native Infantry, Corps of Madras Pioneers
Set 68, 2nd Bombay Native Infantry, 4th Bombay Grenadiers
Set 123, the Bikanir Camel Corps, three men on camels
Set 197, Gurkha Rifles, 1st King George's Own, the Malaun Regiment. These were eight to a set of a figure specially produced as a Gurkha.
Set 271, 1st Duke of York's Own Lancers, Skinner's Horse. This was really the same regiment as set 47, but for a time Britains did not realize it (see page 11).

BOXED SETS OF THE INDIAN EMPIRE

Top left: *Set 67. In the box is a set, c.1912, with no pioneer, followed to the right by a sepoy showing an earlier paint style, a pioneer and a copy, most apparent from the different rifle.*

Top right: *Set 68. The figures in this box do not match. The differing colours of the straps and pouches show this.*

Bottom: *Set 123. Most of the lettering on the two box lids shown is exactly the same, but the lower one does not show the set number, and has 'England' added beneath the trade mark. The camel shown on the left is the first version with wire tail and*

detachable rider, c.1910. The two on the right, which match the box interior, are the second version, c.1926, with the riders soldered on and the tails of the camels moulded into the body.

Centre right: *Set 47, c.1906. Until c.1935 the troopers carried swords, and the jackets were a warm ochre colour. The troopers in this set have the arm with the early thick sword; the swords became much thinner, c.1924. Until 1935, Britains did not realize that 1st Bengal Cavalry are also Skinners Horse, and so produced set 271 (**bottom right**). This confusion may have been caused by incorrect source material (see page 11). Britains must*

have realized the mistake in about 1935. Set 271 was dropped from the range (thus becoming rather rare) and the yellow-coated Lancers were given a new home in set 47, substituting for the ochre-jacketed men with swords. Set 47 then remained popular until the end of production in 1966. Even though this top is spoilt by the addition of sticky brown paper, it is worth collecting. The six box labels show the range of colours on to which the label designs were printed.

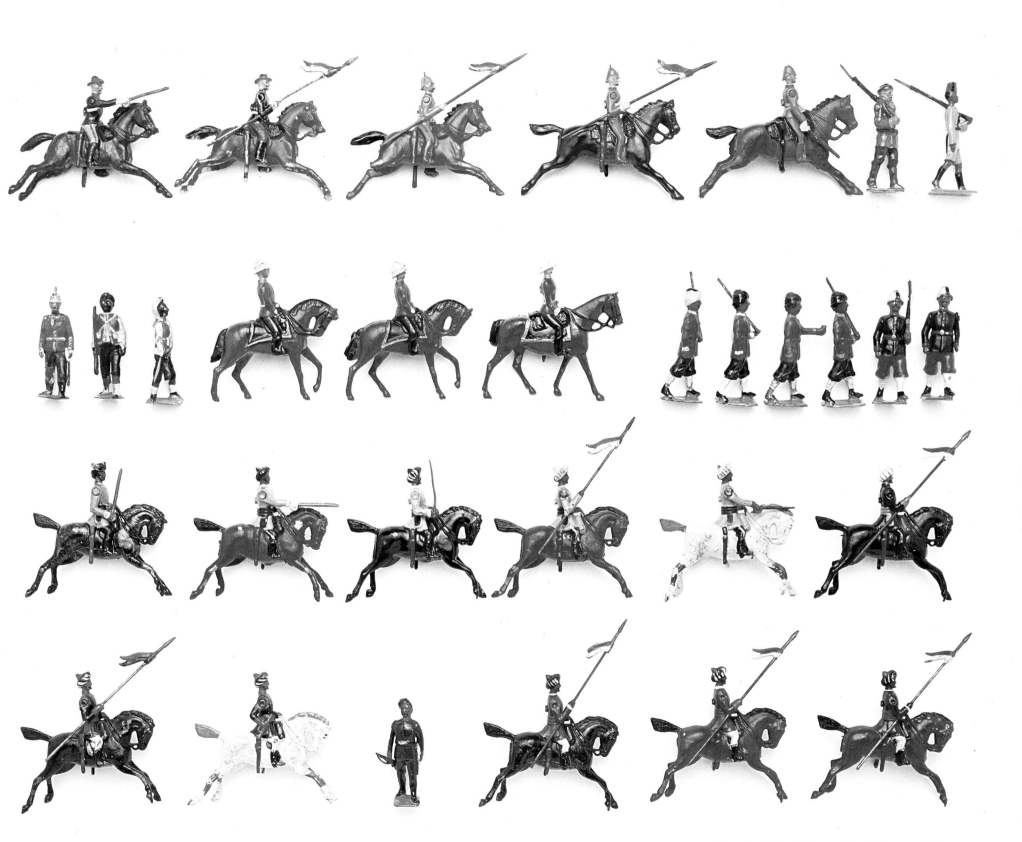

Examples of Colonial Troops, described on page 102.

Colonial troops: descriptions

Top row Figs 1–5 show types of the South Australian Lancers. Fig 1 is the officer for the first version, and fig 2 a trooper from the same version. Note the considerable colour difference in the breeches, which indicates that they are not from the same set. Fig 3, which has one leg missing from the horse, shows another rocking-horse mounted trooper, this one, c.1900, in the uniform of the Adelaide Lancers. (See page 11 for a discussion of this set's uniform.) Fig 4 is a trooper c.1905 on the improved one-eared horse dated 1.1.1903, and fig 5 is the matching officer. Fig 6 is the Royal Canadian Mounted Policeman in winter dress from set 214, and fig 7 the King's African Rifles figure. Neither set had officers, and although colours vary somewhat no major changes of paint style were made during the production of either set, making it very difficult to tell, in the case of the King's African Rifles, whether a figure is pre- or post-Second World War.

2nd row Figs 1–6 show types of set 19, the West India Regiment. Fig 1 is the early officer on foot, indistinguishable from a bemedalled officer of the Worcestershire Regiment. Fig 2 shows the oval-based private, which remained on an oval base at least until the First World War, and probably for several years afterwards. Fig 3 is the square-base type, turned to show the profile of the figure, which remained the same as the earlier one. Figs 4–6 are the mounted officers, c.1897, c.1905 and c.1930. They follow the same sequence as the Mountain Artillery officer and the officer of the Sussex Regiment. Compare the early beehive hat on fig 4 with the more correctly shaped fig 5.

Figs 7–12 show types of the second-version Indian Infantry introduced c.1920. Fig 7 is an unusual paint variation of set 67 with a white turban, fig 8 being the more usual figure. Fig 9 appears to be an officer for the set, equipped with a sword arm with the sword broken off. Sets of Indian Army Infantry using this version figure usually do not have an officer at all. Fig 10 is a man from the 7th Rajput row of set 64, c.1935. The distinguishing mark of the 7th Rajput is the yellow facings, as opposed to the similar set 67, which has white facings. Fig 11 is a man from set 68, c.1935, at this date called the 4th Bombay Grenadiers.

3rd row Figs 1–3 show types of the 3rd Madras Cavalry, set 45. Fig 1 is c.1900. Note how thick the sword is compared with one carried by fig 3, c.1937. On fig 1 too the black paint of the horse is very thin, giving a sort of metallic shine to the finish where the bare metal shows through. This often happens with Britains' black and blue paints, especially in the early years. Fig 2 is the officer for the set with his outstretched sword arm. Fig 4 is an early 2nd Madras Lancer from set 64. Note the shape of the early lance-head and pennon of this figure as opposed to fig 6. The change took place c.1908. Fig 5 is the only officer for set 64, c.1902, and fig 6 shows the much

darker painting of the set, retitled 16th Light Cavalry, that was standard c.1938.

4th row Figs 1 and 2 show the early trooper and trumpeter of set 46, 10th Bengal Lancers, later Hodson's Horse, c.1900. Fig 3 is a Gurkha at the trail from set 197. The paint style in this set hardly varied, except that after the Second World War the face was more mud-coloured

and less rich chocolate, as shown here, c.1935. Figs 4–6 show styles of paint for troopers from set 66, the 1st Bombay Lancers, later Duke of Connaught's, c.1904, c.1930 and c.1938 respectively. Note that fig 5 has no cuff facings painted. In all Indian Cavalry regiments, brown and black troopers' horses alternated in each row of five. If there was a trumpeter, he was on a grey horse, if an officer he was on a black or a brown horse.

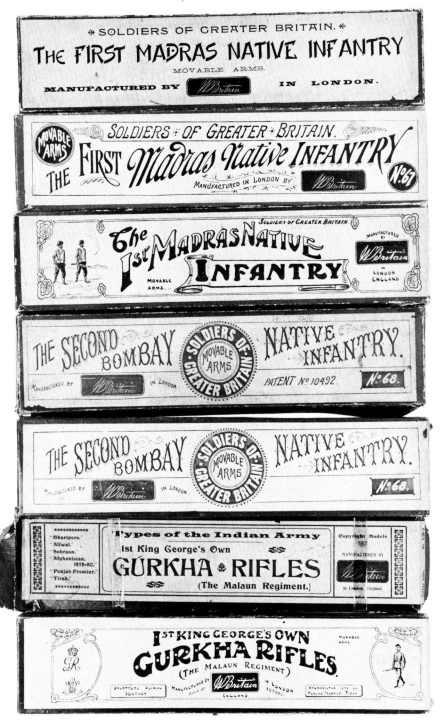

BOXES FOR INDIAN EMPIRE INFANTRY
*Top to bottom: 1 Early unnumbered typographical label for set 67, **c.**1896. In the early years, Britains liked to call the Indian troops 'Soldiers of Greater Britain'. 2 Ornate typographical box label for set 67, **c.**1900. 3 Whisstock design for set 67. 4 and 5 Early typographical labels for set 68, **c.**1898. 4 is identical to 5 apart from the addition of the patent number. The Indian sepoy figure was the earliest infantry figure with the movable arm.*
6 Typographic label for set 197. Since this set was only issued in 1916, it is a little surprising to find a typographic label for it at all. One might have expected the box to start with a Whisstock-designed label. This set was probably issued while he was enlisted, and his design for the set had to wait until after the First World War. 7 The Whisstock design for set 197.

Chapter 31
On campaign

In modern warfare, parade-ground drill is far removed from the manoeuvres of the actual battlefield, but this has not always been so. In the Crimean War (1853–6), the British Foot Guards advanced into battle in their bearskin caps, and the 93rd Highlanders met the charge of the Russian cavalry at Balaklava arrayed in the 'thin red line'. Field manoeuvres at home in Britain tended to reflect this custom until after the Boer War at the end of the century, and Britains' sets of infantry firing, running and on guard would have found their real-life counterparts in the same full dress while practising.

Abroad, however, it was a different story, especially in tropical climes. After the Indian Mutiny (1857) British troops in India increasingly took to using white uniforms stained to khaki, a word derived from the Persian word for dust. The last campaign in which British troops abroad appeared in red coats was in the Sudan in 1885. While parade-ground drill was still applicable to some extent in dealing with native tribesmen, against the Boers it turned out to be worse than useless, and the British Army divorced parade-ground and battlefield completely.

This divorce was mirrored in Britains' toy soldiers when the first set in khaki was produced, set 94, the 21st Lancers in the foreign-service order of 1898, as at the battle of Omdurman. This was followed by further sets during the course of the Boer War and later.

At about the same time, small groups of adults were beginning to take toy soldiers more seriously in Britain. This was in part a result of interest in the *Kriegsspiel* (war games) developed by the German General Staff to help instruction in tactics. Another factor was the Boy Scout Movement, which began with quite warlike aims, including war-gaming. The availability of Britains' toy soldiers encouraged these interests, and Britains itself produced a war-gaming booklet even before H.G.Wells wrote *Little Wars*, published in 1913, in which Britains' troops were used throughout.

Recently, the popularity of war-gaming has grown again, although figures smaller than 54mm scale are normally used. However, collectors of Britains' toy soldiers have found it interesting to use parts of their armies specifically to show the toy soldier on campaign, thus following one of the toys' original uses and utilizing a good theme for a dramatic presentation. In the following pages we show three such scenes, in chronological order of the actual event: the Zulu War; the Sudan campaign of 1898; and finally the campaign in China against the Boxers to relieve the Peking Legations in 1900. Britains did not make any sets specifically depicting this last campaign, and it provides a good

example of what can be done with a mixture of contemporary units and some more modern items. Since it provides the best opportunity to develop the largest campaign collection, with a considerable number of models available, the Boer War is discussed in a separate chapter.

We start, however with the Zulu War, which gives us a very good excuse to introduce to the story of Britains the American Inventor Charles William Beiser.

BOXES FOR ZULUS
*Top to bottom: 1 Early typographical box for set 147, **c.**1906. 2 Later box for set 147. The elements have been changed somewhat, but the main lettering remains the same. Whisstock never designed a label for this set. 3 On the other hand, set 188 produced one of Whisstock's most ambitious pictorial designs, also probably one of the first he ever produced for Britains.*

Zulu campaign, described on page 106.

Zululand

THE BEISER SETS

In 1907, Britains produced two sets of soldiers with a baseboard and clip system patented by an American, Charles William Beiser. The soldiers could be knocked over with toy gunfire, but, because the base of the figure was secured in hinged tin clips, when they fell down they remained attached to the baseboard and could be stood up again instantly by turning the baseboard through one revolution. For a collector, this goes against the grain, and in any case if a figure is loose in its clip it can drop out. But the idea does work. Britains must have been very impressed, and the device probably appealed to their traditional bent for mechanical toys. They came to an agreement with Beiser to market his invention in Great Britain and supply him with toys to fill his sets in the USA. I suspect that the at the ready and marching at the shoulder figures dated 15.6.1906 were created specially.

The snag was that the youth of England did not want eleven soldiers, a mounted officer and a small cannon for two shillings and sixpence when they could buy sixteen or twenty infantry for two shillings. Nor, I suspect, did they really enjoy the rather static target practice involved. It was far more fun to have the soldiers loose and then fire at them. The whole idea was too clever by half, and received the commercial thumbs down, which is why so few sets remain today. Britains quite often dabbled in special packings and mechanical parades, for instance the Parade series (see pages 188–9); outside our period, set 1396 was a Marching Board of Grenadier Guards. However, try as they might, they could never sell any of them successfully.

Britains may have had grand ideas of fitting many of their sets into Beiser clips – which meant that the bases of all their figures would have had to fit the clips. Set 147, the Zulus, is the last with oval bases, and the next two numbers are the Beiser sets, so this makes sense from the number sequence. Britains probably thought that square or rectangular bases were an improvement in any case, since oval bases were abandoned on all but a very few infantry figures in a relatively short time, and all newly produced figures had square bases.

The Beiser sets were 148, the Royal Lancaster Regiment, shown on its baseboard to the left of the preceding pages, and 149, American Soldiers (see page 152).

Set 148, The Royal Lancaster Regiment, nine pigeon-chested figures, of which three were at the slope, three at the trail, officer, standard-bearer and bugler, two gunners at attention, mounted officer and gun. That the Royal Lancaster Regiment in foreign-service dress follows the Zulus can hardly be a coincidence, especially since the second battalion took part in the Zulu Wars, although they were not present at the battle of Ulundi, 1879. In the absence of the proper bugle-arm fitted to the later adult bugler figure, the bugler was equipped with a

NEW MILITARY DISPLAY AND GAME

ENGLISH SOLDIERS

(Royal Lancaster Regiment)

Directions :

"BRITAIN'S 4.7 NAVAL GUN"

MANUFACTURED BY   Britain   IN LONDON.

No. 148.

Patented in England, United States, and Germany.

Lid of the box for set 148. The label included instructions for playing the game.

cavalry trumpet. The standard-bearer featured a furled flag, later reintroduced for the Scots Guards colours and others to replace the previous flat flag. The two gunners were based on the at-attention figure dated 20.1.1901, with a new ramrod arm. The small gun was the same as that used for the small-size gun teams, but without the hole bored to take the towing hook. The mounted officer was based on the original officer on the prancing horse, but given a movable arm and a rectangular base to fit the clip. Once this new officer had been created especially for this set, other sets with an officer of this type changed to include the new figure. Note that one man is shown knocked over.

The lying firing figure in the foreground is a mystery. It was inside a toy Edwardian wooden fort which I purchased at auction, but does not fit into any Britains' set I know. In style it matches the Royal Lancasters, but I have never seen any other Line Infantry with red coats wearing the foreign-service helmet with pugaree. It may have been a 'counter line' (see page 63) – it is certainly genuinely original.

Set 81, 17th Lancers in foreign-service dress, four troopers and a trumpeter; sometimes an officer in full-dress uniform on a horse at the halt was included instead of the trumpeter or the fourth trooper. These figures supporting the Royal Lancasters in their charge towards the Zulus are as they would have appeared at Ulundi. There is no obvious reason why this set came out in 1897. The earliest figures are on the right at the back, on the rocking horse. The trumpeter and troopers changed to the pony horse before the set finally changed to the head-up trotting horse dated 12.12.1902, the trumpeter also being on the same horse. On the right of the picture are three troopers with carbines instead of the usual lances, and behind them are a trumpeter and officer on the cantering horse, who may well be Britains

specials from 1932. The 17th in foreign-service order also appear as a row of seven in set 73 (see page 97). Sometimes the composition of that set was changed for variety, which may explain why unusual 17th Lancers turn up from time to time.

Set 147, Zulus, eight charging figures with movable arms, four with knobkerries, two holding spears over-arm and two under-arm. At first these had oval bases dated 23.5.1906. The loincloths were painted in three different colour schemes, as Britains always did for native troops or irregulars who might not be expected to wear uniforms.

Set 188, Zulu Kraal, six Zulus, two huts, two date palms and a coconut palm. This was an attractive additional set of Zulus which came in the scenic box shown on the right. The huts, made of papier-mache, and the palms appeared for the first time in this set.

On the extreme right is one of the later cast metal huts which may have been introduced after 1932. Originally the Zulus seem to have been equipped with Beiser clips, although the 1915 catalogue description specifies 'securely wired', so my set may have been the victim of experimental conversion into a 'knock-down' set. The figures are certainly not spaced correctly to be tipped over. The Zulus by this time had rectangular bases, and there was a little nick in each side of the base, so that they could be 'securely wired' to the box. Between the two world wars some of the Zulus seem to have been painted with brown bases rather than green. Finally, just in front of the metal hut, is a second-grade Zulu, a fixed-arm figure waving an ugly-looking spiked knobkerry, variously catalogued as 4R or 28C, or, with inferior third-grade paint, as 21P, when sold singly between the wars.

The Sudan campaign

The British Empire was heavily involved in Egypt, the staging post to India, and undertook two expeditions up the Nile, the Gordon relief expedition in 1885 and the reconquest of the Sudan from the Dervishes by Kitchener. The later expedition was famous for the battle of Omdurman in 1898, at which occurred the heroic charge of the 21st Lancers. This was commemorated late in the same year by Britains in set 94, the 21st Lancers 'Heroes of Omdurman', in khaki uniform with foreign-service helmets. Set 96, the York and Lancaster Regiment, should be included here, but has generally been included in the Boer War (see page 117).

Other troops suitable to serve in a Sudan campaign were sets 115, Egyptian Cavalry, 116, Soudanese Infantry, and 117, Egyptian Infantry, all produced in 1901. The Egyptian Camel Corps had already been issued as set 48 in 1896. All these, together with the Mountain Gun and Naval Landing Party Gun, are shown in the campaign picture on the preceeding pages. Britains never produced any Dervishes; perhaps the closest they came was with their Abyssinian Tribesmen, produced in 1936. The Dervish forces, therefore, have to be represented by Arabs, set 164 on horseback, set 187 on foot and set 193 on camels. The box label for 193 was marked Types of the Enemy. Completing the picture are two British Camel Corps figures from the enormous display set 131, which included nine in its total of 275 pieces.

In the illustration, the Egyptian Infantry lined up on the extreme left are the first version with round bases, and have paper labels with the 20.1.1901 date of the basic attention figure. These figures are painted a much darker colour than the later ones which can be seen to their right. Passing by the gunners and naval figures described on page 110, the Soudanese Infantry are marching forward in the foreground. These are based on the Slade Wallace equipment marching figure also dated 20.1.1901, and, again, the earliest figures on the left at the back of the column have oval bases and paper labels. Unlike all the other sets based on this figure, this mould was used for the Soudanese until the Second World War

Behind the Soudanese are two sets of Egyptian Camel Corps. The earlier, on the left, has the distinctive wire tail of the first-version camel. The row in front shows the moulded tail of the more modern camel. During the 1920s and 1930s the rider was soldered on to the camel, but before and after those dates he was separate and could be taken off.

The Egyptian Cavalry are shown as three sets. For a short time they used the pony-horse figure, at the rear on the left, before changing to the cantering horse dated 12.2.1903. The front rank is composed of a 1930s set. Note that the paint becomes more glossy on later sets. In front of these are the two British Camel Corps figures, which unfortunately have lost their rifles. These figures are extremely rare, which makes one wonder how many of the gigantic set 131 were ever sold. The similar figure in

Top: **BOXES FOR EGYPTIAN AND SUDANESE TROOPS**

Top to bottom: 1 Whisstock pictorial design for set 115. This label remained in use well into the 1950s. 2 Early typographical design for set 115, c.1905. 3 Whisstock design for set 117. 4 Typographical label for set 116. Whisstock did not produce a design for this set.

Left: **BOXES FOR LANCERS IN FOREIGN-SERVICE DRESS**

Top to bottom: 1 Early box for set 81. 2 Whisstock box for set 81. 3 and 4. Boxes for set 94, for which Whisstock never did a design. The label at the bottom is more elaborate than the one above, and the title 'Empress of India' has been added. Only the 17th and 21st Lancers, among all the British cavalry regiments, were offered the honour of a standard-size set in foreign-service order.

The Soudan campaign, described on pages 107 and 110.

Len Richards' collection had a red collar and cuffs, but these two have been left plain khaki.

Behind the Egyptian Cavalry, leading the charge, are some examples of the 21st Lancers in foreign-service order, set 94. Left to right are two troopers and a trumpeter on the first rocking-horse version, then a trooper and trumpeter on the one-eared horse dated 1.1.1901. At the start of the First World War, this set was given steel helmets. Foreign-service helmets were usually painted white, although the trooper on the extreme left has an original khaki helmet, and sets sometimes turn up with this variation. The lance is shown without a pennon, which was simply clipped off. This was the only set to be depicted with furled lance pennons.

Set 164, Arabs on horses, two with jezails, three with scimitars
Set 187, Arabs on foot, eight marching at the slope with jezails
Set 193, Arabs on Camels, six, holding jezails
The Arab figures were never changed, and the only dated figure was the horseman, 17.7.1911. Their colours are of interest: in the box of five horsemen were one with a blue and two with a red bernouse, all three with scimitars; the other two were in green and carried jezails. In the box of eight men on foot there were normally three red, three blue and two yellow. The box of six camels contained two each in red, green and blue. Even though the riders could not be demounted it is surely a strong contender for the title of Britains' most magnificent figure. All the infantry and camel-riders were armed solely with jezails.

The date and coconut palms in the background come originally from the Zulu Kraal set, but were included in an assorted Arab Display set 224.

Right: **BOXES FOR MOUNTAIN AND NAVAL ARTILLERY**
Top to bottom: 1 Splendid label designed by Whisstock for set 28. 2 Early typographical box for set 79, c.1899. The set number looks as though it was added later. 3 Later typographical box for set 79, c.1905. The set number is on the label stuck to the end of the lid. 4 Whisstock design for set 79. Notice once more the rope motif with which Whisstock bordered his boxes for the Royal Navy.
Far right bottom: *This example of the British Camel Corps figure is one of the most famous figures in the collector's ken. This one was sold in the Richards collection and at the time made a world-record price for a single figure. It has red collar and cuffs, although others, including those illustrated on the previous page, have no facings at all. The most frequently observed uniform details for this figure include white crossbelt, brown puttees and black boots. Set 131, the giant 275-piece box from which these figures come, contained nine of them, nested in a specially sized set of compartments. The figure was not included in any other set.*

Top: *Three examples of horsedrawn vehicles, **c.**1921, in excellent condition. The saddles and harness are in bright orange and all have the collar harness and valises of the first version. The Pontoon Wagon is one of the first made, for this set was only issued in 1920, and since the team changed to the second-version light-harness horses **c.**1924 the collar-harness team Pontoon Wagon is comparatively scarce. It is a little surprising to find bucket seats and four seated men on the Royal Field Artillery team at this date. The change to two seated figures only and none on the gun version must have come quite quickly, as there was*

*another change to a light-harness team without any seated men **c.**1924, and yet I have seen a number of the teams with collar harness and only two seated men. Of course the difference between a gun with or without bucket seats could simply be the result of substitution, and it would be wrong to assume that this second version of the set actually exists. As no catalogues specifically relating to this period exist, it is a difficult matter to verify. (See page 89 for a picture of the supposed three versions.) The khaki Ambulance Wagon 146a presents no problems, since this was introduced in 1916. Had no Pontoon Section been*

present, the temptation would be to ascribe these vehicles to 1916. This picture teaches us to be aware of how known timings can help us to discover when version changes took place. (Phillips, London)

Bottom: *Limber and gun from the Royal Naval Landing Party, set 79. The gun has a towing hook, while the otherwise identical one for the Mountain Artillery does not. During our period the gun wheels have eight spokes, while later models had twelve.*

The China campaign, described on page 114.

Special Services of the British Army

ROYAL ARMY MEDICAL CORPS

DOCTORS & NURSES

MANUFACTURED IN *Britains* IN LONDON ENGLAND

TRADE MARK   COPYRIGHT MODELS

BOXES FOR THE MEDICAL CORPS

Top: Label for set 320. This set contained two doctors and six nurses in their long dresses. The doctors were the same as those in set 137. The label is made up using a wood-cut block of medical staff which also frequently appeared in Britains' catalogues. The set first appeared in 1929.

Bottom: The standard gold-on-black printed label for the Army Medical Service, set 137. I have not seen any other label for this set, which lasted from 1905 until 1941, although occasionally the label is found printed on red rather than on black.

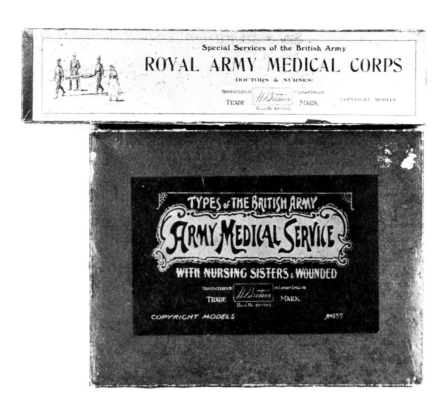

The China campaign

The Boxer Rebellion and the siege of the Peking Legations in 1900 were the occasion of a great deal of military activity in northern China. Here, if one is not too fussy about the uniforms, is a good excuse to parade together nearly all the European troops made by Britains, since the relief column was a joint effort almost without parallel in the history of warfare. In fact, almost anything can fit into this expedition, so I have taken the opportunity to include in the illustration a number of items not previously considered. Those in full dress are strictly out of context, but one of the good things about campaigning with toy soldiers is that accuracy down to the last detail is not necessary.

Set 137, The Army Medical Service, four nurses, three stretcher-parties of two men and a stretcher, one senior medical officer, two doctors and eight wounded assorted over three types – head wound, leg wound and arm wound. On the left foreground of the illustration is a field dressing-station manned by figures from this set. Examples of each figure are shown here, although the oval bases of the stretcher-party hurrying towards the station are obscured; they had paper labels or were dated 20.3.1905. The standing medical officers retained their round base throughout the production of this popular set. The later style of nurse, introduced *c.*1935, is shown by way of comparison to the right of the tent, which is not by Britains.

Set 145, Royal Army Medical Corps (with ambulance

waggon). Four-horse team wagon with canvas tilt, and two seated drivers. The four-horse ambulance that goes with set 137 was produced in the next year, 1906, and two examples of the collar-harness version are shown. Note that the men seated on the wagon in the foreground have Red Cross armbands, the only paint detail that distinguishes them from seated field artillery gunners. Seated Army Supply Corps figures have a white stripe down the trouser rather than a red one. To the right of the ambulance in the middle of the illustration, some of the men who sit on the ambulance are taking a rest on a Britains' log. Of the two facing the camera, the man on the right is the early figure with the crossbelt over his left shoulder and his feet together. The later figure on the left has no crossbelt and his feet are rather further apart. The two figures seated to the left with their backs turned are a rear view of these same two figures.

Set 146, The Army Service Corps (with wagon), two-horse team, wagon and two seated drivers. At the back left of the illustration are shown two of this set, which Britains never supplied with four horses. The wagon on the left is the early collar-harness version, the right-hand one a light-harness version, introduced *c.*1924. The heavy collar has gone and the wagon is pulled from the horse's breast rather than from its neck and shoulders. The valise on the riderless horse was removed at the same time.

The finish on the wagons gives another clue to their date. Early wagons were finished in light grey paint. Before and during the First World War, they appeared in khaki paint. After the war, Britains started to produce a gun-metal finish for wagons and artillery by 'smoking'

the castings in the greenhouse at Lambton Road and hanging them up in wire baskets with pots of spirits of salts mixed with zinc. These fumed copiously and sealed the surface of the metal, which was then finished off with 'Nugget' boot polish. Apparently the neighbourhood was unbearable after a fumigating session, as Bill Seago, in charge of metal production in the 1950s, remembers from his younger days. From about 1933 the guns and wagons were again painted in a variety of khakis and dark greens: perhaps the neighbours complained.

On the right of the illustration are pontoon wagons with their teams of four horses and Royal Engineer drivers. The full set included a wooden boat and two sections of roadway. The roadway was made of a single piece of wood, split into several planks down the length of the grain, and backed with glued cheesecloth, with two small wooden strips glued on the upper surface as edging. This rolled up for transport on the wagon. At each end of the roadway section small holes were drilled that fit over the spikes protruding from the centre section of the boat. This can be seen in the span going over the 'river'. In fact the 'mint' colour of the plank roadway is more the colour of the piece on the left of the bridge that has come unglued from its backing. The central section has become very dirty. The boat to the right of the river is a reproduction, the genuine original being to the left.

Set 203, Pontoon Section, with pontoon and two roadway sections, four-horse team and wagon. This set probably appeared in 1922, when the collar-harness team horses were still in use. The change to light harness took place two years later, and collar-harness Royal Engineer teams are relatively rare. Behind the light-harness version, note for comparison the service-dress set, although this is numbered 1254 and did not come out until 1933.

Britains' Chinese (see page 124) are rather disappointing for China Campaign displays, so I commissioned Jan Scroby, the eminent military sculptress, to model some contemporary Chinese troops to my specifications. Some of these are shown on the extreme right, surprising the Empire forces in the act of securing the pontoons at their moorings. A great deal of extra fun can come from collecting Britains if one enhances the originals with the excellent compatible models currently being produced for this very purpose. The Pontoons cry out to be handled by the party of Indian Sappers shown in the picture, produced by Albion, and the reinforcements of Royal Welch Fusiliers and Sikhs marching up the 'road' are by Bastion. Another alternative is to convert original Britains figures to a new purpose, which is what has happened with the Royal Artillery in the central foreground. These are simply the later steel-helmeted Britains' gunners issued with recast foreign-service helmets and a recast Renvoize gun

All this produces a much more enjoyable pseudo-Victorian war-gaming scene than if one were limited solely to original Britains figures.

Chapter 32
The Boer War

The Boer War (1899–1902) was the biggest military event involving the British Army in the first twenty years of Britains' production. Naturally, Britains made sets of the troops involved. Foreshadowing the war, at the end of 1895, there took place the Jameson Raid, in which Dr Jameson attempted a *coup d'état* in the Transvaal which would have replaced the Boer government with one headed by British nationals.

Set 38, Dr Jameson and the African Mounted Infantry, four mounted fixed-arm figures with rifles, and one the same but with a pistol representing Dr Jameson. Although Dr Jameson is now best known for his raid, he had taken part in the Matabele Wars of 1893, so it is quite possible that Britains had already produced this set coincidentally a few months before the raid itself. The set with this label is extremely rare, sales having perhaps taken a nosedive on the news of Jameson's surrender to the Boers. Set 38 was always titled the South African Mounted Infantry thereafter, although exactly the same contents were included. A second version of the set used the figure first made for set 276, US Cavalry in action (see page 153). Since this second version only existed from 1928 to 1940, this would account for the the second version with movable arm and no officer being rarer than the first version.

Set 6, Boer Cavalry, four with rifles, one with pistol. These were the same figures used for set 38, and it is not known exactly when they were first produced. They could have been made in 1896 to go with set 38, or they might have joined the list on the outbreak of the Boer War in 1899.

Set 26, Boer Infantry, eight men, or variations as given below. The first version was the 1897 valise-pack marching figure with the same head used for the US Infantry in set 91, which came out in 1898. This would suggest that the Boer Infantry set was first produced in 1899. The Boer Infantry at first used the ordinary movable arm with rifle at the slope and bayonet fixed. Occasionally Britains seem to have clipped the bayonets off the rifles, as it was quite well known that the Boers did not use bayonets. Sometimes the trail arm was used, and sometimes the arm at the slope without bayonet fixed. Occasionally, the set included a figure with a sword arm to represent an officer. Boers both mounted and on foot were painted light khaki with black hats. Occasionally the valise-pack marching Boer is found fitted with a slouch hat head rather than the US Infantry head.

When new US Infantry figures on guard and at shoulder arms were made dated 15.6.1906, both types were used as Boer Infantry, though not mixed within sets. When the set used the on-guard figure, an officer based on the figure with sword and pistol from set 104, the CIVs, was included. Both these versions are very rare, and were probably only in production for two years, since the Britains' list attributed to 1909 no longer mentions Boer Infantry or Cavalry. All the other sets produced for the Boer War are of the British Army.

Set 96, The York and Lancaster Regiment, seven men and an officer running. For a short time, this was produced in foreign-service dress, using the pigeon-chested figure with a foreign-service helmet, the uniform being light khaki. Although this set is generally accepted as a Boer War set, its numerical position in the list would suggest that it appeared earlier, possibly as a companion set for the 21st Lancers in the Sudan. Shortly after the Boer War this set was changed to full dress (see page 81).

Set 104, The City Imperial Volunteers, nine fixed-arm men on guard and an officer with pointed pistol and a movable sword arm. The CIVs were the first of the sets produced specifically for the Boer War, and also the first figures to be dated, having paper labels with 1 Jun 1900 on them. They wore slouch hats, puttees and bandoliers.

Set 105, The Imperial Yeomanry, five fixed-arm cavalrymen. This was the cavalry counterpart of set 104,

Left: Set 38 with box, c.1920. When this set ceased to be titled Dr Jameson and the African Mounted Infantry, a rather plain label was made up for it out of type. Whisstock never designed a label for the set. Compare this set with the earlier Dr Jameson set illustrated on page 119 and note that the two are to all intents and purposes identical apart from the labels on the boxes. (Phillips, London)

Britains' set 26 with a splendid early typographical label. The box for this set is especially rare. This is the first version, c.1900, at the slope with fixed bayonets and 'Montana' hats. One man is missing from this set. (Phillips, London)

SMALL-SIZE ARTILLERY

Sets 125 and 126, Royal Horse Artillery Teams in full and service dress. The latter is one of the nicest sets associated with the Boer War. The service dress is the style that units serving in South Africa wore, where they won great public acclaim for bravery under adverse conditions in engagements such as the battle of Colenso, December 1899. The team horses of both sets are dated 1.11.1901. Britains never made a standard-size gun team in Boer War service dress, something that many collectors have regretted.

In the picture above, a half battery of each type is shown, service dress on the left, full dress on the right. At the rear left the other small-size items in khaki service dress are shown. At the back are two sets 23b, the so-called Cameron Highlanders which were painted as if they were Black Watch (see also page 77). These are at the trail, and one figure has its rifle clipped off to represent the officer. Interestingly, each of the two sets has one white cross strap painted across the opposite shoulder from the other.

In front of the 'Camerons' is an assortment of figures from the small-size display set 85, which contained a row of 5th

Dragoon Guards in service dress. All these are on first-version horses. In front of these again is a second-version set 12b, 16th Lancers in Service Dress, a set of four including a trumpeter and mounted on the walking horse dated 11.8.1904. All the troopers in these two groups carry lances.

Of the three gun-teams in foreign-service order, the one furthest to the left, with only two team horses, is a copy, probably by Reka, as are its attendant gunners and officer. Nearer to the centre of the picture are the two genuine Britains' teams, followed by the two versions of mounted gunners. In the first version, the gunners ride the first-version head-down small-size cantering horse, while the officers are on the first-version walking horse. In the second version, officers and men were all on the full-stretch galloping horse dated 9.5.1904. The first version escort thus only had a production life of just over two years.

The full-dress teams that appear to the right of the picture also went through the same two versions, and both sets were the only survivors of the first-grade small-size figures after the First World War, remaining in the company's catalogue until 1939.

Examples from the Boer War, described on page 119.

117

and the men were also wearing slouch hats. The figure was dated 1.6.1900, and was one of the few fixed-arm cavalrymen to be produced right through till 1941. The dating was not shown after *c.*1920. The set included two men on brown horses, two on black and one on a grey, and some of the horses often had socks or points painted in.

Set 108, The 6th Dragoons, five identical fixed-arm cavalrymen, three on brown and two on black horses. This was simply the Imperial Yeomanry figure with a normal smooth foreign-service helmet instead of the slouch hat. The paint style was exactly the same except that the grey horse was changed to a brown one and the set also lasted until 1941. These were the only Britains models of the 6th Dragoons.

Set 109, The Dublin Fusiliers
Set 110, The Devonshire Regiment
Each set contained eight men without an officer. Both sets were based on a new figure marching in Slade Wallace equipment dated 20.1.1901. The movable arm was on the right shoulder, presumably normally intended to take an arm at the trail. Both regiments started out with smooth foreign-service helmets but very quickly changed to the type with the pugaree wound round it, like the Highlander firing. The Dublins were at the trail, while the Devons were at the slope, and the jacket and trousers of the Dublins were always painted in different colours, while those of the Devons matched each other. This distinction continued right through the careers of these sets, although after the First World War both sets switched to the figure with the webbing equipment, retaining the helmet with pugaree, and both sets carried their rifles at the trail. After our period, the two sets adopted the Wolseley pattern wide-brimmed helmet for a time, until production ended in 1941.

Set 114, The Cameron Highlanders, marching in foreign-service dress, eight men without an officer. This set was based on the new marching Highland figure, also dated 20.1.1901, in kilt and also with Slade Wallace equipment, though with a more marked box pack. The earliest of these figures were also equipped with smooth foreign-service helmets, but these are very rare indeed, and most appear with the pugaree. After the First World War a new figure was adopted for this set corresponding with the new Highlander marching in full dress.

Set 119, The Gloucestershire Regiment, standing firing, ten men without an officer. This set used the figure dated 1.7.1901 adapted to the Boer War campaign with puttees and the foreign-service helmet with pugaree. By the time this set was issued, the smooth foreign-service helmet was no longer being used, so it probably only had a life of some six months.

Since all these sets were painted in khaki, it is worth mentioning that Britains never hit upon a standard khaki

Above: Army Service Supply Column wagon with the canvas cover removed, showing two of the six cardboard supply boxes that came with each wagon. Note the early oval-based infantry of the escort. The officer appears to have had his arm replaced, since the sword is suspiciously thin for the age of the set, and the position of the arm should be outstretched rather than bent at the elbow. (Phillips, London)

Above: Top: CFE Army Service Supply Column wagon, with mounted officer and four infantry with oval bases, and Britains' set 145, Medical Ambulance Wagon. As so often happens, the mounted drivers of the ambulance have lost the balls from their helmets. The Britains' origin of the wagon on the left is immediately apparent. Bottom: Set 105 Imperial Yeomanry, *c.*1912. There was nearly always one figure on a grey horse, probably intended to be an officer. (Sotheby's, London)

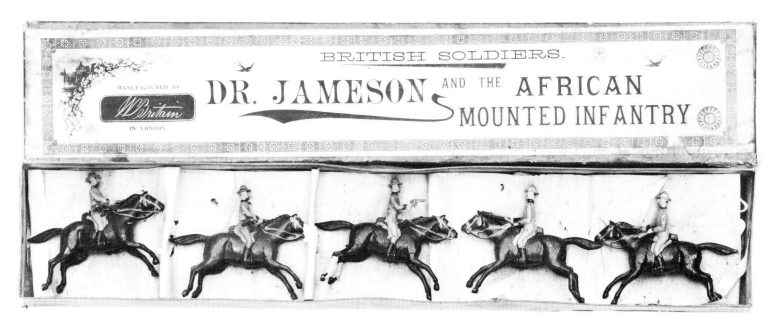

Set 38, Dr Jameson and the African Mounted Infantry. Even though the set, under this title, was so short-lived, Britains managed to design a variety of labels. Compare this label with the one illustrated on page 121. The set shown here is the better set, since all the figures match each other in paint style. Indeed, it is difficult to justify calling five figures in a box a set unless the paint style does match perfectly, since, if differences are detected, they suggest that the figures and box did not leave the Britains' factory in company. (Phillips, London)

colour. A large variety of shades was used, as the illustrations show, a practice in which Britains followed the British Army. Even the helmets varied from white to quite a dark brown. At least this makes it easy to determine whether a group of figures is a matching set.

The rarest and most famous Boer War item is strictly not Britains at all, although it was manufactured by them. This is the 'Army Service Supply Column', marketed by a company with the initials C.F.E., about which nothing else is known. The set comprised a mounted officer on a Scots Grey horse, with an outstretched sword arm, ten infantry at the trail, and two four-horse wagons with seated men, each containing six ammunition boxes made of card marked ASC (Army Supply Corps). All the men had slouch hats like the CIV figures. The men on foot sometimes appear with oval bases, so the set cannot have been produced any later than about 1908. It also appears in the 1913 Gamages' catalogue, and so seems to have lasted for at least five years. There have been rumours of an ambulance matching the supply column, but I suspect that this was simply a very easy conversion, done by transferring the ambulance tilt from a regular Britains ambulance. This would leave the original ambulance looking like a four-horse supply wagon, although Britains only produced these with two horses (see page 114). C.F.E. appeared to make quite a profit on its set. The cost of two RAMC wagons was two shillings and fourpence halfpenny each, and ten infantry and a mounted officer cost one shilling and threepence. The ASC set retailed for eight shillings and ninepence, however, a 45 per cent mark-up for a fancy box.

The Boer War: descriptions

Top row Figs 1–7 are Britains' Boers, of which there were many different versions and variations. Fig 1 is the original type, based on the valise-pack figure with rifle at the slope and fixed bayonet. It is the same casting as the US Infantry figure in Montana hat, made for set 91. On page 65 are pictures of a Boer officer and man with a different head with a slouch hat, these figures not being available when this photograph was taken. Fig 2 is the same as fig 1 but fitted with a rifle without bayonet. Fig 3 has a rifle that once had a bayonet that is now clipped off. Whether Britains did this to a number of sets, having been told that Boers did not use bayonets, or whether it was accuracy-seeking purchasers it is hard to tell, but I have seen a number of different sets so clipped. Fig 4 is a Boer with an arm carrying his rifle at the trail. Later Boer figures are based on the US types dated 15.6.1906, and these figures have the slouch hat sometimes used on the valise-pack first version. No matter which hat it carried, it was always painted black. The officer for the on-guard later version (early sets only rarely included an officer) was taken from the officer figure made originally for the City Imperial Volunteers. An example is fig 5. Fig 6 is the on-guard Boer figure, and fig 7 the shoulder-arms type, otherwise only used in American Soldier Company sets (see page 151). Figs 8–10 are types of the first-version set 96, the York and Lancaster Regiment, fig 8 being the officer.

2nd Row Figs 1–7 show varieties of the Devonshire Regiment, with two stragglers, fig 13 of this row, and fig 7 of the 3rd row. Note the smooth helmets of figs 1 and 2. On fig 1 the helmet is painted to match the uniform, while on fig 2 it matches the equipment. Fig 13 also has a smooth helmet, though fitted with a trail arm, while fig 3 has a helmet with pugaree but an arm at the slope. Various examples show that no strict time sequence governs the appearance of these variations or even the incidence of paper labels or engraved bases. Fig 4 shows

the ordinary Devon of the 1920s, the figure having changed to the First World War webbing-equipment figure marching at the trail but still with the foreign-service helmet with pugaree. Fig 5 is an unusual officer for the set (which normally did not have an officer) based on the 1920s officer for set 160 with a change of head. Fig 6 is the later figure with the Wolseley helmet, *c*.1937. Fig 7 is a colour variation from the 1920s, the arm being missing.

Figs 8–12 show a similar sequence of figures for set 109, the Dublin Fusiliers, a regiment which was always shown marching at the trail, and whose jackets and trousers were always painted different colours.

3rd row Figs 1–6 show the sequence for set 114, the Cameron Highlanders. The smooth-helmet type on the left is extremely rare, since this set, although using the same date as sets 109 and 110 for its kilted marching figure, was probably issued a little later. Figs 2 and 3 with the helmet with the pugaree are normal for the years 1902 to 1912. Note the decreasing number of horizontal stripes on the kilt as the later models economize. Figs 4–6 are based on the standard Highland marching figure introduced in 1913 or a little later. Towards the 1930s the khaki became much darker, and fig 6 shows the Wolseley pattern helmet, *c*.1937. Fig 7 is an errant Devon (see above).

Figs 8–12 show the sequence of set 119, the Gloucestershire Regiment Firing. Fig 8 is the early oval-based type. Once the figure had been converted to a square base, it remained the same until production stopped in 1941. Later sets tended to have matching jacket and trousers, as seen in figs 10–12.

4th row This shows types of set 108, the 6th Dragoons. The figure was not changed throughout its production life, 1900 to 1941, but, as can be seen, the painting style varied considerably.

Top: Britains' British troops during the Boer War, in slouch hats. In the mind of the Britains' collector, the slouch hat has always been associated with three most popular sets: the Imperial Yeomanry, the City Imperial Volunteers and the Army Service Supply Column. The first two mentioned, sets 104 and 105 in the Britains' list, were not only the first sets to be produced specifically in response to the Boer War, but also the only Britains' sets to depict British troops wearing slouch hats. The picture shows a column of troops in slouch hats escorting a wagon. In front are examples of the City Imperial Volunteers (CIVs), which were always on oval bases. Early sets, however, have the officer (to the left) also on an oval base, whereas from *c.*1908 he was on a square base as shown here. Behind the CIVs are samples of South African Mounted Infantry, who also wear slouch hats. The two on the right are the second version with movable arms, based on the US Cavalry in-action figure introduced in 1928. The example to the left is fixed-arm and has an orange hat band, which is unusual. Next to the left are four Imperial Yeomanry. The one on the grey horse is a late painting, *c.*1940, and it is interesting to note that the khaki used on these troops matches the changes of khaki that Britains used for First and Second World War troops right down to 1941. Next comes the Army Service Supply Column wagon, one of two in the set which was packed and sold by the mysterious company CFE. These initials are taken from the box label, and I may even be mistaken in thinking that they refer to the firm undertaking the sale of the set! The infantry escort is of men with Slade Wallace equipment marching at the trail and, of course, wearing slouch hats, like the officer mounted on Scots Grey horse and the two seated drivers. On the ground near the rear wagon wheel is one of the six cardboard supply boxes which formed the load for each wagon. They are painted grey with the initials A.S.C. on each. At the rear are more slouch-hatted troops converted from Mountain Artillerymen.

Opposite top: *Set 105, Imperial Yeomanry, in original box. Although there is no difference in the casting and no rank insignia, Britains only included one man on a grey horse, and he may well be meant to be the officer. In the actual Boer War, officers soon learned not to ride grey horses since they made far too good a target. This early painting was beautiful, c.1903, with an orange and white hat badge and white gaiter buttons.*

Opposite bottom: *Set 6, Boer Cavalry in original box. Nothing much like these regular uniformed black-hatted Cavalry existed in real life. The facings are orange, and the horses are all coloured differently, one of the black ones usually having white fetlocks. In common with the Boer Infantry, the set was discontinued at an early date, probably in about 1910.*

Above: *Set 38, Dr Jameson and the African Mounted Infantry. Even in the short period (1895-6?) during which this set was issued with this title, Britains managed to have more than one different label printed. Compare the one above with that shown on page 119. This is not actually a matched set. For instance the colour of the trousers is markedly different in the second and last men from the left. All these men have the normal blue hat band, although an orange band (see top of page), or no band at all, does occur from time to time. The title 'African Mounted Infantry' might, I suppose, stem from the time when Rhodes had visions of a British takeover of all Africa, as distinct from the later, less ambitious, 'South African Mounted Infantry'.*

Above: *Close-up of the Army Service Supply Column wagon and infantry escort, showing the strikingly orange boots of this period of paintwork. The twisted wire traces of the wagon and the magnificent moustaches of the men can be seen clearly. It is possible to date the first appearance of this 'non-Britains' set quite closely, since the escort was first produced with oval bases, which are probably not after 1907, and the wagon was first made by Britains in 1906. The oval-based figures, which are considerably rarer, are seen to the left. Note that they are carrying rifles with magazines, while the square-based figures to the right are carrying rifles without magazines. The extremely light colour of the hat on the leftmost man is probably the result of bleaching by sunlight.*

PART FIVE
ARMIES OF THE WORLD

Britains' 1933 catalogue was the first to contain a section entitled 'Armies of the World'. But thereafter the heading always appeared in catalogues until the end of production in 1966. Before 1933, Britains featured foreign armies strongly – hence the inclusion of Armies of the World in this book. Figures were made to record the Spanish-American War in 1898, the Russo-Japanese War in 1904–5, the Turkish-Italian War in 1911 and the more general Balkan conflict in 1912. Britains' Paris Office provided a 'French Connection' from 1905 to 1923, there was an 'American Connection' via Charles Beiser from 1906 (see pages 150–1) and major export initiatives were launched to Argentina in 1925 and the USA in 1927. Britains also produced models of Prussian troops from 1908 onwards.

Part Five deals with all foreign armies except those of the Americas, which are discussed in Part Seven.

Chapter 33
Russia and the Far East

One of the most striking examples of Britains' response to a contemporary war is the range of models produced in 1904 to illustrate the Russo-Japanese War of 1904-5. A comprehensive collection of cavalry and infantry from each side was soon on offer in both standard and small size, a total of eight different models.

Sets were as follows:
Set 20, display set including all four standard-size sets
Set 65, display set, Russian Infantry and Cavalry

Set 95, display set, Japanese Infantry and Cavalry
Set 133, Russian Infantry at the trail with officer, eight figures
Set 134, Japanese Infantry charging, eight figures
Set 135, Japanese Cavalry with officer, five figures
Set 136, Russian Cossacks with officer, five figures

SMALL-SIZE SETS
Set 11b, Japanese Cavalry with officer, four figures
Set 14b, Russian Cossacks with trumpeter, four figures

Set 25b, Japanese Infantry, seven figures
Set 26b, Russian Infantry, seven figures

Russia and the Far East: descriptions

Top row This consists of the small-size figures. Figs 1 and 2 are the trumpeter and trooper of the Cossacks, figs 3 and 4 the early and c.1912 versions of the Japanese

Far Left: SMALL-SIZE JAPANESE AND RUSSIAN BOXES.
1 Typographical box label for set 11b. 2 Ornate design for set 14B. 3 and 4 Two slightly different typographical labels for set 25b. 5 Typographical label for set 26b.

LEFT: BOXES FOR JAPANESE AND CHINESE TROOPS
1 Typographical label for set 134. 2 Typographical label for set 135. 3–5 Three different typographical labels for set 241, all after 1927 when this set was first issued. Whisstock appears not to have designed a label for this box.

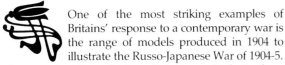

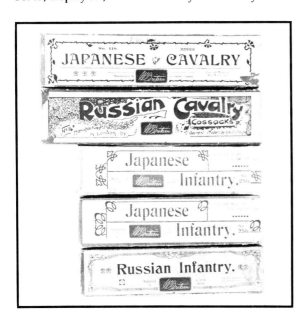

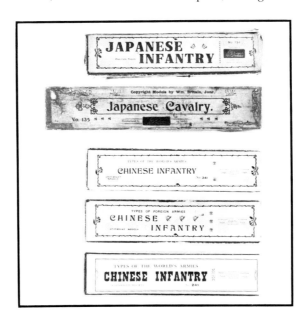

infantry at the trail, the latter extremely rare. Figs 5 and 6 show the officer and trooper of the Japanese cavalry. There were no first-version Russian or Japanese cavalry, as the sets were introduced after the improved small-size horses were in production. The Russian infantry in smaller size are shown as figs 1 and 2 of the 3rd row. The marching-at-the-trail figure is rare, and the running-at-the-slope man is the usual one in the box.

2nd row Russian infantry in standard size. Before the First World War, the set included some figures at the slope and some at the trail with the officer. Between the wars, the arms were all at the trail, but some sets appeared with red hat bands rather than the normal blue. It is interesting, too, that Britains switched the title of the box labels to 'United States of Soviet Russia', an unusual mistake on its part. Maybe at the time the now familiar term 'Union of Soviet Socialist Republics' was not so well known. Fig 1, c.1904, is painted the early light green colour, swiftly changed to the more correct dark green. Fig 2, c.1907, is an officer with the end of his sword broken off. Figs 3 and 4 show officer and man c.1910, still with oval bases but with heartier complexions. Fig 5 is c.1930 and shows an example of the red hat band.

To the right of the Russian infantry are shown figures from set 241, Chinese Infantry, a set that one might have expected to be issued at the time of the Boxer uprising in 1900; why it came out in 1927 is not readily apparent. As usual with irregulars, they were offered in three different colours in the same set, red, green and blue, with the additional variation of yellow or dark green caps. I have also seen a rare small-size Chinese at the slope, which appeared perfectly genuine, being the early marching Bluejacket painted up in a lively Chinese fashion.

3rd row Figs 1 and 2 are smaller-size Russian infantry (see above). Then come examples of standard-size Russian Cossacks, this time in green rather than red. This is one of Britains' most popular sets. The early figures, 3 and 4, did not differ much from the later ones, 5 and 6, except that they were dated 7.9.1904 and the officer's horse was painted in an ochre colour typical of this early period. The early figures are c.1908, the later ones c.1930.

4th row Figs 1 and 2 are Japanese infantry, which always had oval bases. Fig 1 shows the distinctively different small early kepi, contrasted with the normal one on fig 2, c.1930. Both the small and larger kepi figures can be found with paper labels. The cavalry figures to the right are the standard-size Japanese cavalry. Fig 3 is the officer, followed by two troopers on varying shades of brown horse with short carbines. Fig 6 shows the not very different paint style c.1930, with the long carbine on a black horse. The set was made up of two troopers on brown horses and two on black as well as the officer. The much-sought Japanese types in dark blue coats were not produced in our period, belonging to the years c.1935–41 and to the period just after the Second World War.

BOXES FOR RUSSIAN TROOPS

1 and 2 Spot the difference between these two early typographical boxes for set 133, c.1905. Clue: examine the border. There are other differences as well, although the arrow shape in the top design has been inked in by the purchaser. Differences between labels such as these show that a batch of labels must have been made by sending a previous label to the printer, who then used the blocks he had used previously, such as the block on the right of the label, together with other bits and pieces, such as the underline for the headline, which he happened to have in his type case. 3 and 4 Whisstock labels for set 133. 3 is

the original Whisstock design, but during the 1930s Britains felt that the new Soviet state deserved some recognition, so the lettering on the box has been changed, although the contents were not. The initials USSR have not been given their usual meaning. 5 Early typographical box for set 136, c.1905. Notice the same typeface for the headline as 1 and 2, and that an incorrect S has been used for the second S in 'Russian' for 2 and the first S in 'Russian' in 5. 6 and 7 Whisstock labels for set 136. The same change has taken place as with the labels for set 133, 3 and 4 above.

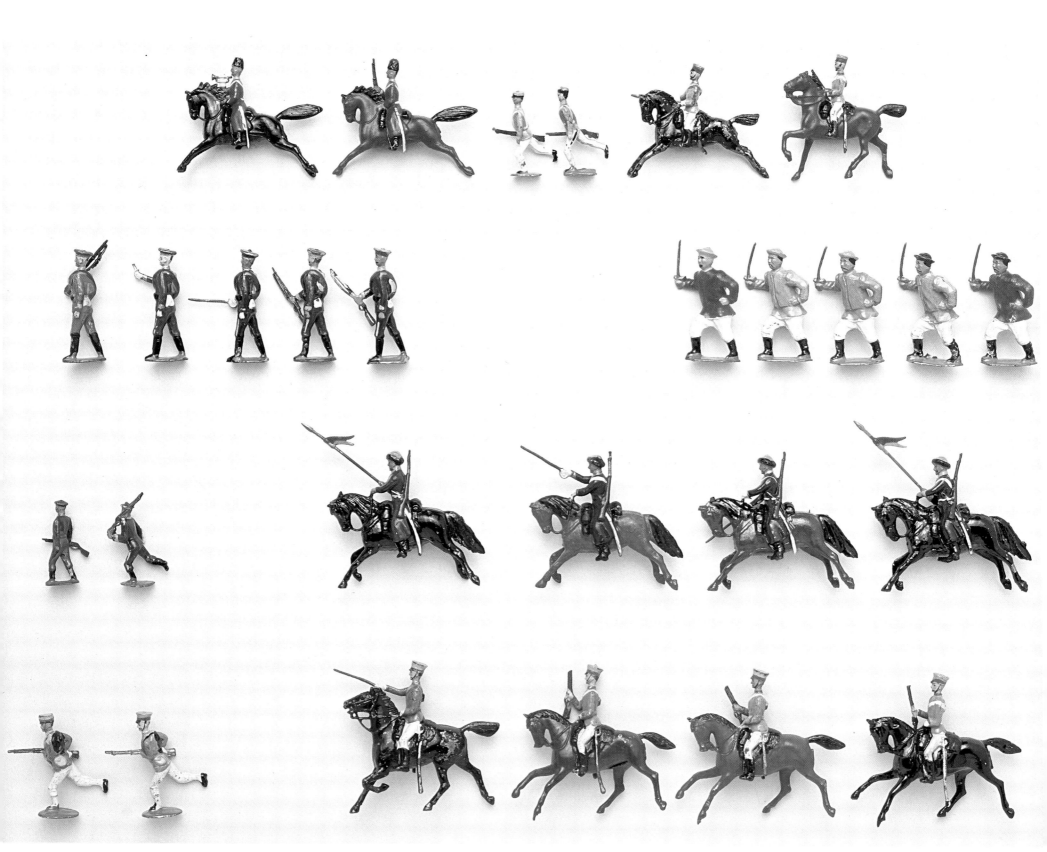

Examples of Russia and the Far East, described on pages 122 and 123.

Opposite: *Examples of European nations, described on page 126.*

Chapter 34
Austria, Turkey and the minor European nations

At the end of the nineteenth century, politicians and soldiers were still very much aware of the presence, however weakened, of the Turkish Empire in Europe. The emerging Balkan nations, variously helped or hindered by Russia, Austria and Italy, regularly tried to alter the balance of power in the north-eastern Mediterranean at Turkey's expense. It is the long-standing British interest in Egypt, however, that probably accounts for the early arrival of Turkish cavalry on Britains' list as set 71. The other sets represented in the illustration on the previous page are as follows:

Set 92, Spanish Infantry with officer until 1924, no officer thereafter
Set 167, Turkish Infantry with officer to 1916, no officer thereafter
Set 170, Greek Cavalry with officer
Set 171, Greek Infantry with officer
Set 172, Bulgarian Infantry with officer
Set 173, Serbian Infantry
Set 174, Montenegrin Infantry with officer
Set 175, Austro-Hungarian Lancers with trumpeter and officer
Set 176, Austro-Hungarian Dragoons with trumpeter and officer
Set 177, Austro-Hungarian Infantry of the Line with officer
Set 178, Austro-Hungarian Foot Guards with officer
Set 189, Belgian Infantry, review order
Set 190, Belgian Cavalry with officer
Set 196, Evzones
Set 218, Spanish Cavalry with officer
Each of these sets comprised eight infantry or five cavalry.

Austria, Turkey and the minor European nations: descriptions

Top row Figs 1–3 are Bulgarians from set 172. They are modelled on the Russian infantry figure but have a new head. Fig 1 is a private c.1930, and fig 2 an officer of similar date. Note that someone has given the sword a coat of silver paint – not Britains, since it never did this, although sword scabbards were painted, as these were covered in other colours during the painting process. Fig 3 is an officer c.1939. Note the much lighter face colour compared with the deep tan on figs 1 and 2. Face paint for Balkan nationals was normally darker than on western Europeans, but it seems that in the late 1930s Britains stopped making this distinction.

Fig 4 is a Greek Evzone from set 196. During our period they appeared in red coats. Figs 5–7 illustrate the Greek Infantry, set 171, which were based on the British infantry figure running at the trail with a new head. Figs 5 and 6, officer and man, are pigeon-chested, and fig 7 is a closed-elbow full-trousered figure c.1932. Figs 8–10 show types of the Greek cavalry, which are one of the rarest European regiments. I have never seen this set equipped with short carbines, so these had probably been discontinued by the time this set was put on the list. Figs 8 and 9 are troopers on a black horse and a tail-less brown horse, and fig 10 is the officer, all c.1930.

2nd row Fig 1 is the Serbian infantry figure, of which there was only one version. Figs 2 and 3 show Montenegrins in their grey uniform with shallow red fez. They are based on the Russian figure, and like the Bulgarians it is quite natural to find them at the slope, or

as mixed slope and trail during the early years of production. The rest of this row shows Turkish troops, figs 4–6 being the cavalry from set 71, troopers on a brown horse and a black horse and the officer on a grey horse. These are the Indian cavalry figure with a new head. The early style of the lance arms suggests that these date c.1902. Figs 7–9 show the infantry from set 167, the officer dated 18.3.1909 appearing only in sets before the First World War. The early infantry on-guard represented by fig 8 is based on the British on-guard figure dated 17.1.1910, and fig 9 shows the paint style c.1930.

3rd row This row shows types of the Austro-Hungarian Army. Fig 1 represents the first version of the infantry, which is the Prussian officer figure dated 16.2.1908 with a new head. The officer for this set was the same figure equipped with a sword arm. The Foot Guards, which wore the uniform of fig 2, also had a first version using the model of fig 1, and both sets then converted to the 1910 marching type from the British Army. As a result they look very similar to the Italian infantry (see page 133), except that the Austrian regiments had fixed bayonets. The officers in the second version were also based on the 1910 figure with a sword in the left hand. Figs 3 and 4 show a trooper and trumpeter, of the Lancers, figs 5–7 show trooper, trumpeter and officer of the Dragoons. The sets have English-style horse furniture and are based on the Scots Grey horse, short-rein variation, and the head-up trotting horse

*Examples of Austrian Cavalry and Infantry. **Top row:** Lancer officer, set 175; Dragoon officer and trumpeter, set 176; Lancer trumpeter, set 175. **2nd row:** Austrian Infantry of the Line, set 177; second-version man, first-version man, second-version officer, first-version officer, set 178; Austrian Foot Guards, first-version officer, second-version officer, first-version man, second-version man. Although there were very distinct first and second versions of the infantry, the cavalry were always just the one type, though after about 1928 the swords were markedly thinner. (Phillips, London)*

respectively. Both sets included three troopers with swords, a trumpeter and an officer. The examples shown here are c.1930.

4th row Figs 1–4 show the types of the Belgian Army. Fig 1, the Belgian trooper, is at the halt carrying a carbine, but as in the French cavalry the officer is on a grey horse at the canter. The infantry were never given an officer and used a new great-coated figure on guard, fixed-arm, for all eight pieces. In the early paint style, the kepi had a wide black band round the base, but later as in fig 4 more red showed. Fig 5 is a duplicate trumpeter of the Austro-Hungarian Dragoons. Comparing it with fig 6 in the 3rd row, one can only marvel at the constant excellence of the paintwork in set after set. Fig 6 is the second version of the Spanish Infantry brought out c.1925 to replace the first version, which is illustrated on page 153. Fig 7 shows the Spanish Cavalry, set 218, an attractive restyling of the Scots Grey figure.

Chapter 35
France

Production of models of the French armed forces started with a batch of six sets in 1905. This probably resulted from the conclusion of an agreement with a sales agent in France. Certainly the opening of the Paris factories did not take place until 1912. The first five sets of French figures are all dated 9.5.1905, and were presumably ready for the Christmas market of that year. The sixth set, the Matelots, at first bore a paper label dated Mar 20th 1905, the same date as the RAMC set 137. The cavalry all bore two dates, the date of origin of the figure on which they were based, and the 9.5.1905 date of their conversion to a French figure with continental horse furniture.

Set 138, the Cuirassiers, four men and an officer. This was the famous French heavy cavalry, the equivalent of the British Household Cavalry. The troopers were based on the Scots Grey horse of 1.11.1902 with the long rein, and the officer was on the cantering horse dated 12.2.1903, as indeed were all the French cavalry officers. In early sets the peak of the helmet includes a small extra crest.

Set 139, Chasseurs à Cheval, four men and an officer, based on the head-up trotting horse dated 12.12.1902. These carried short carbines to start with, followed at the appropriate time by a change to the long-carbine arm.

Set 140 was perhaps the most attractive set of the three cavalry boxes, being the 'Dragons' (Dragoons in English), four men and an officer. These had helmets similar to the Cuirassiers', but no breast- and back-plates, and they were at the halt, based on the horse dated 18.8.1903. Before the First World War, a long carbine, cast separately, was plugged into a hole in the back of the figure and passed under the flowing plume across the back. This feature is known as the 'plugged carbine'.

Coming to the infantry, the first box, **set 141**, eight men, was the ordinary **French Infantérie de Ligne**, the French equivalent of the British Army figure in spiked helmet. Two versions of this were issued, both dated 9.5.1909, one of which had full trousers and an oval base, the other gaiters and a rather squarer base. After the First World War, the full-trousered version was discontinued. Both versions appear to have been issued in a dark blue coat as well as the usual horizon blue, although the reasons for this are not known. Occasionally a set is found which was issued with an officer, as shown in the 1915 catalogue, but normally the set comprised just the eight men at the slope.

Set 142, the Zouaves, seven men and an officer. This was a new fixed-arm, charging figure of the famous French regiment. In deference to their Algerian origin, Britains often painted the figures of this set darker than normal. The set was issued with a walking officer, a fact that occasioned some comment since at that pace he could hardly be leading from the front. This state of affairs was only corrected by the removal of the officer after the First World War, although he continued to appear on the Whisstock label design, and the Zouaves had to wait until c.1952 to gain a mounted officer capable of keeping up with the troops.

BOXES FOR FRENCH ARMY CAVALRY
Note that all the titles for French sets are in French, eg Dragons rather than Dragoons. Top to bottom: 1 Early typographical label for set 138, c.1905. 2 and 3 Later typographical labels for set 138 in the 1920s. The border in 3 was used for a number of sets, simply by replacing the titling within, a step towards the universal type of label issued after the 1920s. 4 Early typographical label for set 139, c.1905. 5 Whisstock design for set 139. This was the only set of French cavalry for which Whisstock designed a label.

French Infantry of the Line in full dress, described on page 130.

French Dragoons, described on page 130.

French Infantry of the First World War, described on page 130.

Paris Office Spanish Dragoons, described on page 130.

Set 143, the Matelots, the French sailors, eight men, just as ready to form a landing-party as their British counterparts. The early set of eight was running with the long French rifle at the slope. Although derived from the British naval figure, as already mentioned, early sets have a Mar 20th 1905 paper label, signifying the reworking of the mould, but in fact the same date as that of set 137, the RAMC. The significance of this is not apparent. Later, the Matelots were given a British rifle at the trail, which made them resemble the Royal Navy much more closely, except for their red and white striped jersey and red pompom.

Two sets were added to the list of French troops available in England in 1916, among the last to be added to the range before production ceased for two years.

Set 191, Turcos, eight men

Set 192, French Infantérie in steel helmets, eight men Both sets were in horizon blue, although the paint for the Turcos settled down at a lighter shade than for the infantry. The Turcos were exactly the same basic figure as the Zouaves, painted in a different uniform. The Infantérie were as the full-dress types in gaiters, but given a head with a French-style crested steel helmet and painted horizon blue with brown equipment.

Set 225, French Infantry in Action, 14 men. Finally in our period, the last set of French troops produced was a set of French Infantérie in steel helmets firing. The set comprised four each of standing, kneeling and lying firing troops, with two French Hotchkiss machine gunners. All were in horizon blue matching the marching troops of set 192. It seems most likely that these had already been produced by Britains' Paris Office and were thought suitable to offer to the British market as well. At this time there were no equivalent First World War figures of British infantry available, and in 1924, when the set was introduced, Britains was probably concentrating on producing moulds for the Home Farm, and thought that this was a good way of introducing a new set without much effort.

French Troops: descriptions

FRENCH INFANTÉRIE, FULL DRESS

The top picture on page 128 is organized in six rows of four infantry marching left to right and slightly towards the camera. The two last rows on the left are eight 'Infantérie à grande tenue', or full dress, which were produced by the Paris Office. They are a different model altogether from the normal Infantérie and have a short coat and epaulettes. They are in fact repainted, but so expertly as to be almost indistinguishable from the originals. The officer which best seems to match them is at the front left. This is a Britains' revival of a Paris Office mould for their picture-pack Foreign Legion foot marching officer 1367B in 1954. He is still dated 9.5.1905, even though the necessity for dating had long since passed, and was himself a Paris remodelling of the officer to his right, which is the original fixed-arm French foot

British officers of the First World War period produced in the Paris Office. The walking one was derived from the Chauffeur dated 19.8.1908, the standing one from the medical officer. (Phillips, London)

officer issued by Britains in 1905 with the Zouaves, and sometimes with the Infantérie. This officer matches the full-trouser Infantérie which form the second two rows of four behind him, the leftward row showing the more usual horizon blue coats.

The front two rows of four are of the most usual Infantérie figure, the standard horizon blue style once more being behind the unusual dark blue. It seems probable that the dark blue style was not done after the First World War, although many sets of horizon blue coated troops were certainly produced before the First World War. At the front of the column is the later French Infantry Officer with movable arm and blanket roll, dated 18.3.1909. In the same row as this officer are two Infantérie in a smart dark blue uniform with blue kepi and trousers trimmed in yellow, one of the smarter uniforms issued by the Paris Office. A matching mounted officer on a 'Scots Grey' horse converted to continental horse furniture is directly behind them. The mounted officer to the right on the horse at the halt is the figure usually associated with the later French Foreign Legion, set 1711, but the paint style suggests that this is a Paris Office issue c.1922.

FRENCH DRAGONS

Below on page 128 is a row of three sets of French Dragoons, number 140. I feel this is one of Britains' most pleasing figures. The set on the left is made up of early Dragoons with the plugged carbine clearly seen over the left shoulder. This set is well matched, considering that it is not really a set at all but put together one by one over the years. The second set with the lances held up dates c.1930, and the glossier set on the right, with the lances lowered, is c.1936.

FRENCH INFANTÉRIE, ACTIVE SERVICE

At the top of page 129 is a group of French Infantérie which, in contrast with those opposite on page 128, are closed up and going to war. On the extreme left is a rank of Infantérie in kepis with full trousers, painted by the Paris Office in horizon blue all over. With them is an officer in a matching tunic, though not the officer meant to go with them, I suggest. The next rank shows the usual figure from set 192, the Infantérie at the slope in steel helmets, c.1930. Note that the rifles for these figures only have a bayonet guard projecting on one side, whereas the rifles for the Infantérie in full dress have projections on both sides. The next rank to the right is the same figure, but with a very strange rifle-arm put on them, c.1920. In front of these again is a pair of steel-helmeted troops with rifles at the trail, a variation in khaki produced by the Paris Office. To their right are two Infantérie without arms, but showing the early slightly lighter horizon blue and same smaller head with marked helmet strap as the Paris Office figures beside them. To the right again is a complete set 225 of 14 figures, c.1930. Charging on the extreme right are three Turcos from set 191 and a Paris Office Infantérie in steel helmet. This was later revived by Britains as a Foreign Legion figure in set 2095 after the Second World War.

PARIS OFFICE, SPANISH DRAGOONS

Below on page 129 I show again the superb Paris Office figures of Spanish Dragoons, a highlight of Len Richards' collection. These figures are probably examples of the Paris Office's policy of offering the troops of neighbouring countries (see page 162). Obviously there was once a wagon to which the team horses and the seated men belong. The two troopers and the trumpeter are a straight repaint of the 1837 Life Guard from set 72, but why the troopers are carrying a British infantry rifle at the trail is a bit of a puzzle. The infantrymen are based on the attention figure dated 20.1.1901. The officer is the most beautiful and unusual piece. He is based on the cantering horse dated 12.2.1903, but the Paris Office went to the trouble of adding a throat plume to the mould, the only time that a throat plume appeared, so far as I know, on any figure other than the officer on prancing horse.

Opposite: **BOXES FOR FRENCH INFANTRY ON ACTIVE SERVICE.**

Top to bottom: 1 Typographical box for set 192, c.1916, one of the few box labels to include a date in the set title. 2 Whisstock label for set 192. This is one of the boxes signed L/C (Lance Corporal) Fred Whisstock, implying that he himself was on active service when this label was produced. 3 and 4 Typographical labels for set 215, c.1924. 4 has the words TRADEMARK REGD No. 459993 added. Possibly they were left out of 3 by mistake, or perhaps the trademark was first registered in about 1924. If the latter were true, it would give a valuable dating clue for label design.

their type, all these figure must have been made after 1912, and most likely they were issued in France during the early part of the First World War. One might have expected these figures to have been manufactured in France, but figs 3 and 9 are both dated 1.7.1912 and state underneath 'Made in Great Britain'. This establishes that French figures continued to be supplied from London and suggests a later date for the French factories. Figs 10–13 show types of a set of French small-size cavalry in khaki, presumably of about the same period. Figs 10 and 11 use the figure already met in Britains' portrayal of Edward VII and the Life Guards, *c*.1902 (see page 64).

2nd row Fig 1 is rather a mystery, being a cavalryman on a horse at the halt with British horse furniture, a Belgian-style kepi and red trousers. The paint is in such bad condition that it is difficult to decipher, but it could well be a Paris Office figure. Much the same applies to fig 2, based on the Prussian Officer figure. Fig 3 shows an Infantérie de Ligne figure from set 141. Figs 4–6 are Matelots from set 143, fig 4 being the early at the slope version which sometimes had a paper label dated 20.3.1905. Fig 5 shows an unusual early variation at the trail with the rifle with magazine, and fig 6 is the standard between the wars style, *c*.1928. Figs 7 and 8 show the Zouaves from set 142, fig 7 being the oval based version *c*.1908 and fig 8 the style of *c*.1928. Figs 9–11 are Paris Office productions, probably during the First World War. Fig 9 is a lying, firing British infantryman of 1914, in the feet-together position, but in full trousers as opposed to the normal gaiters. Fig 10 shows a similar Frenchman, not in the normal long coat. Fig 11 shows the kneeling officer in binoculars that probably went with a set of fig 10. Fig 11 was revived in Foreign Legion uniform to go in set 209 after the Second World War.

3rd row Fig 1 is a most interesting figure, being a French Cuirassier, continental horse furniture and all, equipped with a short carbine and painted by the Paris Office as a British Royal Horse Guard. The only explanation I can think of for this is that it was produced in 1917 or 1918 when no products from London were available and the Household Cavalry moulds were not available in Paris. Figs 2 and 3 and 5 and 6 show types of the French Cuirassiers. Figs 2 and 3 have the small early crest to the front of the plume. For some reason, fig 2 has a much darker face than normal, with a beard painted in which *looks* original. Fig 4 purports to be a French Dragoon with a trumpet arm, but examination of the face reveals that it was originally a gilt figure (q.v.). Figs 5 and 6 show the officer and trooper of the Cuirassiers *c*.1930.

4th row These are all French Chasseurs à Cheval from set 139. Fig 1 is gilt. Figs 2–4 show two troopers on different coloured horses with the officer in the middle. The troopers have short carbines, so this style should date *c*.1908. Figs 5 and 6 show the trooper and officer, *c*.1935. Notice the completely different style of paint in the grey of the officer's horse. All the officers for the three French cavalry sets were on the same type of grey horse.

French Armed Forces: descriptions

Top row Figs 1–9 show examples of French small-size figures, none of which appeared in the UK catalogue. Fig 1 is the full-dress Highland figure used for late versions of set 23b, but in this instance painted khaki. Fig 2 is an Infantry of the Line set from set 20b, also painted khaki. Fig 3 shows a later Infantry of the Line painted field grey, presumably to represent a German. Figs 4–6 show French Infantry at the slope, fig 4 being in a steel helmet. Fig 7 is the Northumberland Fusilier in foreign-service order at the trail, second version, painted to look like a French Marine. Figs 8 and 9 show types of French Infantérie in full dress at the slope and the trail. From

Examples of French troops, described on page 131.

Chapter 36
Germany and Italy

The Prussian and German armies

Two sets of Prussian troops were made in 1908:
Set 153, the Hussars, four troopers and an officer
Set 154, the Infantry, seven infantry and an officer
They were probably made more with an eye to exports to Germany than as a result of any specific event.

The figures of Hussars were extremely colourful and one of Britains' favourite figures among collectors. They are shown on the left of the picture. They were based on the cantering horse of 12.2.1903, and were double-dated, the other date being 16.2.1908. They normally carried lances, the officer was on a brown horse, and the troopers alternated between brown and black. The officer carried a sword and had a tall plume to his busby, as can be seen on the second mounted figure from the front. Figs 3 and 4 of the Hussars are unusual in being equipped with swords, the only examples I have seen that do not carry lances. Fig 5 is their matching officer, which, although in poor condition, does not appear to have any non-standard features.

The infantry, a normal box of eight, were based on two completely new figures for the officer and men, dated 16.2.1908. These appear in the left-hand file of infantry with the officer in the lead. The bases were markedly rectangular, unlike the normal Britains' figure, and the men were stepping forward with their right feet, another abnormality. In the early days, a special rifle arm was used, but later the normal British rifle arm without bayonet sufficed. The officer had a drawn sword in his right hand, and sported a weighty scabbard at his left side. This figure was used shortly afterwards for both Austro-Hungarian Infantry sets, but the Prussian private was never used for any other set. Sometimes the set was issued without an officer. (See also page 65.)

The other file of the Prussian Infantry shows an alternative figure based on the marching figure with box pack, dated 1.8.1905. For no known reason sets of these were issued from time to time, but I cannot isolate any particular period during which all production was based on this model. The set in the illustration appears to be *c*.1920.

Set 432, seven men and an officer. Finally, in 1931, Britains brought out a set of First World War **German Infantry in steel helmets**, which appear on the right of the illustration. Why they were so long delayed after the war is a mystery, unless there was an antipathy to bringing out troops of the erstwhile enemy. The officer figure was similar to the men, except that the movable arm was on the opposite shoulder; note that the sword has been broken off and lost in this example. After our period, this German infantry figure with its breeches was used as the basis for many other sets.

The Italian army

Britains' three sets of Italian troops made during our period were brought out in 1911.

Set 165, Italian Cavalry, four men and an officer
Set 166, Italian Infantry, seven men and an officer
Set 169, the Bersaglieri, eight men
Doubtless production was provoked by the conflict between Italy and Turkey, Italy declaring war on 29 September 1911.

Types of the Italian cavalry are shown at each end of the lower picture on the previous page. They were at the halt, based on the horse at the halt dated 18.8.1903, and come with a number of variations. Most of those on the left have retained the English horse furniture of the original horse at the halt, whereas the continental horse furniture first seen in the French Dragoons, which is more usual for this set, is shown on the right. The normal correct head-gear for this set is a square kepi with a small round pompom at the front, but sometimes a Belgian chasseur-style kepi with a bent plume was used instead. The cavalryman on the extreme left, with continental horse furniture, is an example of this; he has the type of lance arm normally associated with a moving horse. The officer was the same figure with a sword instead of a lance.

The infantry was based on the marching figure dated 24.2.1910, and is one of the few figures I have seen issued with this date shown. The early pre-First World War painting shown on the left of the picture is delightful. An oval-based officer shown on the extreme left front of the infantry based on the French officer dated 9.5.1905 shows that the transition to square bases was by no means complete by 1911. The officer three files in at the front is also based on the French officer, but has a square base. Note that both the officers have epaulettes, whereas the original French figure in set 142 does not. In the centre are the Bersaglieri, *c*.1925. In the centre of the front rank is a puzzling painting that could well be a Paris Office style, maybe of a French or Swiss Alpine regiment.

To the right are the Italian infantry of the 1930s. The officers were by then based on the ordinary British officer originally dated 16.11.1905.

*Below: **BOXES FOR ITALIAN TROOPS***
Top to bottom: 1 Whisstock label for set 165, printed on dark purple and torn in the top right corner. 2 Early typographical label for set 166. The set number appears on a separate label on the end of the box. 3 Whisstock pictorial label for set 166.

PART SIX
THE FIRST WORLD WAR

As for the rest of the country, the First World War was a traumatic time for Britains. Shortages of raw material, young workers joining up, rampant inflation and the eventual change to munitions manufacturing all rudely interrupted the steady growth of the business. In addition, there was the psychological shock as the horrors of the war brought the whole morality of manufacturing toy soldiers into question, a dilemma typified by the story of the exploding trench (page 142).

In this part, chapter 37 on the Charterhouse Series introduces the war toys made at this time, while chapter 38 gives examples of various Britains troops in khaki before, during and after the war. Chapter 39 deals with equipment, and chapter 40 concludes by telling the story of the aftermath of the war and reaction that led Britains to develop the Home Farm series.

Chapter 37
The Charterhouse Series

C.E.T. and Co. (what the initials stood for is not known) was a company that specialized in assembling and marketing under its own label interesting sets and displays of various models chosen from the items produced by a number of toy manufacturers. The resulting sets were generally much more ambitious (and expensive) than the regular lines produced by the original makers. On page 29 a whole page of a catalogue showing items sold by C.E.T. and Co is reproduced. A listing of the known sets is as follows:

St John's Ambulance Set (one size)
Charterhouse Sandbag Fort (two sizes)
Charterhouse Tank Warfare (two sizes)
Charterhouse Trench Warfare (three sizes)
Charterhouse Battlefield (one size)
National Guard
Milk Float

Undoubtedly there would have been other sets, as C.E.T. and Co was a type of distributor well known in the toy trade. The company thought up good ideas for marketing toys, arranged with other toy manufacturers for the supply and packaging, and then sold the finished items into the retail trade. The National Guard set contained Wellington Toy Company figures, and was presumably for sale in the United States. The Milk Float appeared to date from the 1930s. It is interesting to speculate whether C.E.T. and Co has any connection with the mysterious CFE, who offered the Army Service Supply Column under what must have been a similar arrangement with Britains.

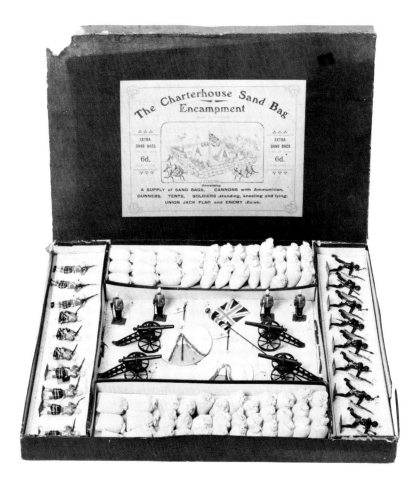

THE CHARTERHOUSE SANDBAG FORT
This set is quoted as being available in two sizes, and assuming (ICP) that the same label was used for both this should be the larger size. One would expect the label to be made the correct size to cover the smaller box and then to be centred on the larger box lid, as shown here. It is not conclusive that the set shown here is the largest set, since the picture on the label might suggest otherwise. There are 17 Zulus and 25 Highlanders visible. This may be artist's licence, or it may be indicative of a larger set containing, for instance, two Britains' equivalent sets of each type of figure. It may just have been to encourage youngsters to fill the sandbag fort by buying more soldiers. The illustration shows a fort made of about 200 sandbags, all this being before the days of the Trade Descriptions Act. (Phillips, London)

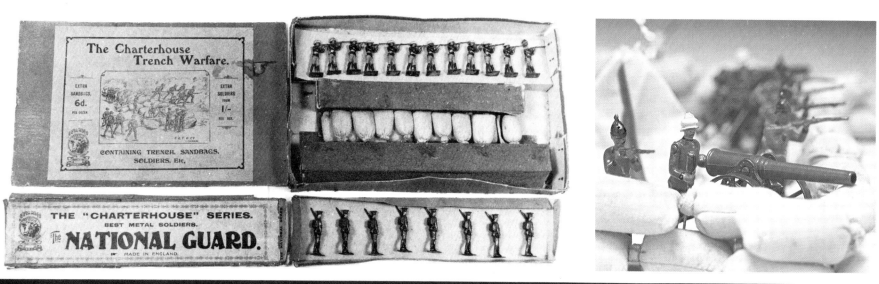

The Charterhouse Sandbag Encampment. See captions on pages 135 and 137.

Opposite top right: *Detail from the Sandbag Fort layout below.*

Opposite bottom: *The Charterhouse Sandbag Encampment set out ready to be played with. In this set the contents are completely different from those shown on the label, Britains sets 121, Royal West Surrey Regiment firing, and 142, French Zouaves. The label states that the set contains SOLDIERS (standing, kneeling and lying) and ENEMY (Zulus), so clearly the sets substituted here are an emergency measure because supplies ran short. Another set I have seen purports to have a complement of firing Foot Guards. The rest of the set comprised 72 sandbags (spare ones were available at six pence for a dozen), four gunners of the Lancaster Regiment originally used in Britains set 148, two small fabric tents, four brown Rivolet cannon imported from France and a large fabric Union Jack on a hatpin. Also shown in this picture, although not part of the set, are Britains Togoland Warriors, set 202. This set was added to the list shortly after the First World War, during which the warriors had gained notoriety as British allies during the campaign in German East Africa.*

Left: *Here we see the Trench Warfare set put out for use. The Gloucestershire Regiment seem a little inappropriate, but again (ICP) it was probably a question of what was available on the day. The titling for these gift sets does not commit the distributor to any particular content, other than in the Sandbag Fort, where it seems to have been ignored anyway. The German troops surrendering were not part of the set.*

Opposite top left: *The black and white photograph shows at the top the Charterhouse Trench Warfare Set as packed in its original box. This is the same set illustrated in colour on this page. Presumably a much larger range of figures was included in the larger sizes of box. Below the Charterhouse Trench Warfare Set is shown the single-row box entitled 'National Guard', which would seem to refer to the US military organization that is the equivalent of the British Territorial Army. The figures that came with this box are by yet another manufacturer, the Wellington Toy Company, and are khaki-clad with peak caps, marching at the slope. (Shire Publications)*

Chapter 38
Troops in khaki

Apart from troops produced for specific campaigns (eg the Soudan and Boer Wars), Britains' first troops in khaki were sets 159 and 160, respectively the Territorial Yeomanry Cavalry and the Territorial Infantry.

Set 159, Territorial Yeomanry cavalry, four men and an officer

Set 160, Territorial Infantry, six men and mounted officer.

Both these sets were in peak caps. The cavalry carried swords on the head-up trotting horse dated 12.12.1902, with an officer on a grey horse, and the infantry were based on the Slade Wallace equipment marching figure at the trail. Early versions still had the oval base, and the officer was the same as the cavalry, but on a brown horse. In 1914, this box was renamed British Expeditionary Force.

Set 195, British Infantry in shrapnel-proof helmet, seven men and an officer. When this set came out in 1916, with a new figure with webbing equipment, set 160 was changed to match, although it retained the peak cap. The men and the officer, whose arm had a baton, were the same figure. Set 160 was give a new fixed-arm officer on foot in peak cap and riding breeches.

Set 194, Machine Gun Section, lying with guns, six pieces. This was the first set of machine gunners, also introduced in 1916. At about this time the version of set 94, 21st Lancers in active-service order with steel helmets, and service-dress versions of sets 39, 144, 145 and 146 were introduced, each with the 'a' suffix to designate the khaki version.

Immediately after the war, Britains had much to do to restock all their outlets and develop the Home Farm series, and so new military sets were introduced slowly. Franco-British Entente displays, Motor Homes, Royal Flying Corps and British Army Encampments with Sandbags had been grandiosely promised in 1916, but they never materialized, and it took until 1927 to produce the RAF and until 1934 to produce the motor lorries. Only six more first-grade sets in khaki were introduced between the end of the war and 1932. These were:

Set 198, Machine Gun Section sitting, a nice set of four separate machine-guns, each with a peak capped gunner to sit behind it

Set 433, Royal Air Force Monoplane in original box. As originally packed, the monoplane was held in place with wads of tightly folded tissue paper. (Phillips, London)

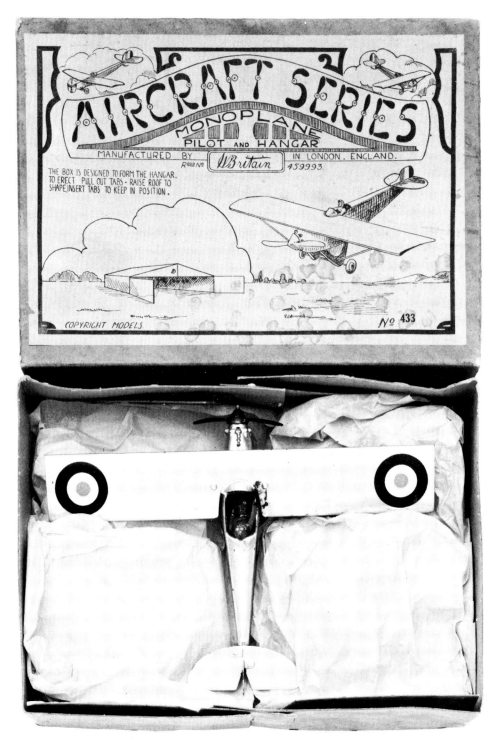

FIRST WORLD WAR TROOPS IN PEAK CAPS WITH THEIR BOXES
Top to bottom:
1 Typographical box for set 194. 2 Typographical box for set 160, c.1916. 3 Modified Whisstock design for set 200. 4 (to the left) Whisstock design for set 199. 5 (centre) Typographical box for set 159, c.1916. 6 (to the right) Whisstock design for the box to take four seated machine gunners, set 198. Of the figures that belong in these boxes, shown in the foreground, the mounted officer on the brown horse is for set 160 and the one on the grey horse for set 159. There are two extra men present for set 160. (Phillips, London)

Set 199, Motor Cycle Machine Gun Corps, described on page 142

Set 200, Motor Cycle Dispatch Riders

Set 203a, Royal Engineers Pontoon Section in service dress

Set 258, Infantry in Shrapnel-Proof Helmets and Gas Masks, eight marching without an officer

Set 313, Team of Royal Artillery Gunners in service dress, four standing and four kneeling with empty hands.

Set 318 RA Gun Team at the halt in service dress with teams of gunners.

Some interesting figures came out as second-grade lines, as the examples overleaf show. But the steel-helmeted infantry familiar in the First World War were not issued in any quantity until quite near the Second World War.

Troops in khaki: descriptions

Top row Figs 1–6 are all second-grade paint. Figs 1–4 are of First World War Highlanders, and it seems that Britains called figs 1 and 2 'running' and figs 3 and 4 'charging'. They are rather bulky figures and look a little larger than standard size. It is a strong possibility that the types in glengarry were made first, and that the ones in steel helmets only appeared during the 1930s. Fig 3 is in the earlier paint style and is designated 20c in the 1931 catalogue, where it is illustrated. This second-grade paint included brown belt and black boots with a green base. Fig 2 shows the minimum paint acceptable for the P series, with only three colours on the figure. These

figures also appeared in A series sets. Fig 5 is a similarly styled running figure in a peaked cap. The other in this style is the rifleman (see page 88, top row, fig 13). Fig 6 is the kneeling firing second-grade peak cap figure with gaiters, part of the group of firing figures in the row below. Fig 6 shows the early version of the peak cap seated machine gunner from set 198, with his maxim gun. The gun is clearly completely different from the later gun shown with fig 8 in the 2nd row, which is a Vickers.

2nd row Fig 1 is a second-grade British cavalry in khaki figure on a head-up spindly horse, c.1930. Fig 2 is the second-grade boy drummer that appeared in larger sets with the firing figures. Fig 3 is the East Kent Regiment on Guard, service dress, from set 326a. Figs 4–6 show the standing and lying peak cap firing figures to go with the kneeling figure in the top row. Note the two different foot positions of figs 5 and 6. Fig 7 is a lying machine gunner from set 194. Figs 8 and 9 show the second-grade machine gunners. Machine gunners always cost more than the ordinary single figures, but their fire power was such that I expect most boys did not mind.

3rd row Figs 1 and 2 show types of set 159, the Territorial Yeomanry, the officer dated c.1912, always being on a grey horse. The trooper is in the very yellow khaki, c.1925; note the completely different shape of the head. Fig 3 is not an original Britains painting, but very neatly repainted, as set 159 was never issued with lances, and the paint style is c.1938. Fig 4 shows the early mounted officer for set 160, the Territorial Infantry. He is exactly the same as fig 1 but on a brown horse. Figs 5–8 show the

infantry and foot officers of the Territorial Infantry, fig 5 being the Slade Wallace equipped figure c.1912, and fig 6 the webbing equipped figure c.1930. Fig 7 shows a normal officer for set 160, although there appears to have been some embellishment on the lapels and hat band, and fig 8 is a second-grade painted casting used in large A series boxes.

4th row Fig 1 is rather a peculiar figure which looks like a cross between a 21st Lancer and a South Australian Lancer. More I cannot say, since it is carrying a carbine, which belongs to neither: every now and then one comes across these interesting mysteries. The figures in this row are cavalry from set 94 in its later version and infantry from sets 195 and 258, all in steel helmets. They show a representative selection of the amazing variety of khakis in which Britains painted their khaki sets, paralleled by the inconstancy of the average Quartermaster's Stores. Figs 2 and 3 show the nice pale-sand coloured helmet with dark khaki and brown equipment. Fig 4 is a great contrast, with very yellowish khaki and dark green equipment. Grey is the most common colour for steel helmets in this period; it was changed to a khaki to match the tunic c.1938. Figs 3 and 10 show the trooper and trumpeter of the steel-helmeted set 94, the 21st Lancers. For the time being, c.1920, this set was still on the one-eared galloping horse, standardized to the two-eared version c.1925. The trooper retains the lance with furled pennant that has always been a feature of this set. Figs 4 and 5 show different-coloured infantry in steel helmets, set 195. Figs 6 and 7 are types of set 258, the infantry in gas masks. Figs 8 and 9 are officers for set 195, set 258 being without officer.

Examples of troops in khaki, described on page 139.

Chapter 39
Trenches, vehicles, aircraft and guns

Of all the images popularly associated with the First World War, perhaps the most common is of the first major deployment of machine guns, tanks and aircraft.

Tanks

Britains waited until 1932 before producing a tank, and even then it was only a very small one, the Carden Loyd. Only in 1957 was a large tank, the Centurion, brought on to the market, although this superb model did justify the wait.

Aircraft

Britains promised to produce aircraft in its 1919 catalogue but as with the tanks they were a long time coming.

Aircraft were issued in 1931, both in RAF and United States markings, and the picture above shows one of these in Royal Air Force colours, with its box, set 431. The aeroplane is described simply as a monoplane, and, although it is obviously a somewhat more advanced type than those used in the First World War, the difference in appearance is not all that great. The pilot

could be removed from the cockpit, and the propeller could be swung. This version of the monoplane is known as the 'square-wing' version, from the square cut tips to the wings, unlike the later version outside our period, which had rounded wings. The box for the aeroplane was rather special, in that the tray unfolded to form a hangar for the aircraft, as shown.

With the aeroplane are two men and an officer from set 240, the Royal Air Force, which contained two officers and six men. The officer is a completely different casting from the men, with a moulded open jacket showing a shirt and tie.

DIRECTIONS.

WORKING THE GUN.

To elevate or depress the muzzle rotate the Hand Wheel either to the left or to the right.

To LOAD THE GUN.—Raise the Breech to a horizontal position by pulling the Loading Lever on the right hand side of the carriage over from the position shown in Fig. 1 until it is in the position shown in Fig. 2.

Fig. 1.   Fig. 2.

Then open the Breech by pulling the Locking Lever to the left, until the Breech-Block swings clear, insert the shell and case in the breech so that the stud of the case enters the slot on the left hand side of the breech, close the Breech-Block and replace the Locking Lever.

Return the Loading Lever to its original position as in Fig. 1, and the gun will be restored to the elevation at which it was previously set, and it is ready for firing.

To fire simply pull the Firing Lever sharply over to the right.

Care should be taken to see that the cross wire in the base of the shell case is in an horizontal position, otherwise damage may be done to the breech block whilst trying to close it.

RE-CHARGING SHELLS WITH LOADER.

Hold the loader by the base in the left hand with the opening in the raised part upwards. Place the shell case in it so that the cross wire in its base lies in the groove of the loader, and the stud on the case points to the letter A. Now take the shell in the right hand, place the open end over the spring, and press down until it enters the shell case, so that the arrow on the shell case and the arrow on the shell are exactly opposite one another, maintain the pressure, and at the same time turn the shell and case in the holder until the stud on the case points to the letter B, when the shell can be removed and is ready for use.

To obtain a rotary twist on the shell, similar to that given by the rifling in a gun follow directions as already given, but when the arrows are in line, take one half turn with the shell towards you, so that the **second** arrow on the shell is in line with the one on the shell case and continue as above.

PATENT Nos. 114326 AND 105728.

TRADE  MARK.

Regd. No. 459993.

Machine guns and vehicles

Apart from the sitting and lying machine gunners shown on page 140, Britains brought out set 199, the Motor Cycle Machine Gun Corps. This was a box of three combinations like the example shown to the left of the RAF. The motorcycle is the same as the one used for set 200, the Dispatch Riders, and the side car and third-wheel castings are attached to it by two pieces of wire. The gunner is removable, and often gets lost.

On the extreme left of the picture is a First World War Supply Wagon, which first appeared in the catalogue in 1916 as number 146a. This is simply set 146 with the personnel given peak caps and painted khaki. Collar-harness versions of this set, as shown here, are rather rare, as they were only made in 1916 and between 1919 and 1923.

The Exploding Trench

This is a most interesting item that Britains produced in about 1915 or 1916; it appears never to have had a catalogue number. The only existing boxed example known to collectors is the property of G. M. Haley, and I am indebted to him and to the *Old Toy Soldier Newsletter* for permission to reproduce the pictures and information that first appeared in that publication. The model measures 13 inches long by 4 inches wide by 2½ inches tall (33 x 10.2 x 6.4 cm), and is made from textured green card nailed to a heavy wood frame. The frame encloses a platform pivoted on two nails at each end of the trench. A spring is attached to one of these nails, held in place by a swinging brass trigger, which in turn is attached to a tall flagpost with a red flag. The instructions read as follows: 'The flag should be fired at by one of Britains 4.7" Naval guns, when, on securing a hit, the trench will immediately explode with a loud report.' The result of hitting the flag is to release the trigger. This causes the trench platform, propelled by the spring, to swing sharply backwards and so throw out any occupant. At the same time it releases a hammer attached to the trigger, which strikes an amorce cap, thus producing a satisfactory explosion.

The toy was patented in 1915 – not a good time to try to market it, when many of the nation's men were undergoing just this sort of experience in real life. Judging by its extreme rarity, it can hardly have been sold at all. Doubtless Britains learned the lesson in bad taste, which led directly to the later development of the Home Farm, and a playing down of the military side of the business for some years.

Guns

At the onset of the First World War, the calibre of Britains' toy artillery was increased. The illustration overleaf shows all the standard-scale artillery pieces made by

Britains during our period. They are:

The Royal Artillery Gun, sold separately at one shilling. The guns are in the right foreground, with the grey early finish on the left. A variety of label colours is shown and a different painting on the extreme left. The gun metal RA gun has a different casting for the trail, the spring being clipped in with a pin. The RA gun is also shown on pages 92, 93 and 97, behind RHA and RFA teams, and there the versions in khaki finish and with bucket seats can be examined. The RA gun is probably modelled on the RA 12-pounder breach-loader.

The Mountain Artillery Gun, shown in the central foreground, is probably modelled on the 2.5-inch jointed RML gun, better known as the 'Screw Gun'. It takes to pieces in three sections, the barrel, wheels and trail, for loading onto mules. It is shown disassembled on page 108. Fitted with a towing loop, it also appeared in set 80, the Naval Landing Party, where it was pulled by eight sailors with a limber. This gun was not available separately.

Top left: The Gloucestershire Regiment defending a Britains' Exploding Trench (see text on page 142).
Centre left: The box lid for the Exploding Trench, complete with instructions for use. One can imagine the reaction of parents invited to buy this toy for boys whose elder brothers were currently being blown to bits in an exactly similar situation in real life. Recently toy manufacturing history repeated itself when a games' maker produced a bomb-defusing game at a time when British Bomb Squad members were being killed by the IRA in Northern Ireland.
Above: A view of the trench-exploding mechanism. (These pictures courtesy of Ged Haley and the **Old Toy Soldier Newsletter**.)
Bottom left: Top: Early label for Garrison mounted Heavy Howitzer, at four shillings an expensive item for those days. At first there was no number at all for the gun, **c.**1916. Below: Later label for the same gun, using a reduction of the same illustration, and now showing the numbering Gun no. 1.

Top: Britains set 39a, Royal Horse Artillery in service dress.
Bottom: Britains set 144a, Royal Field Artillery in service dress.
Opposite: Guns etc, described on pages 143 and 146.

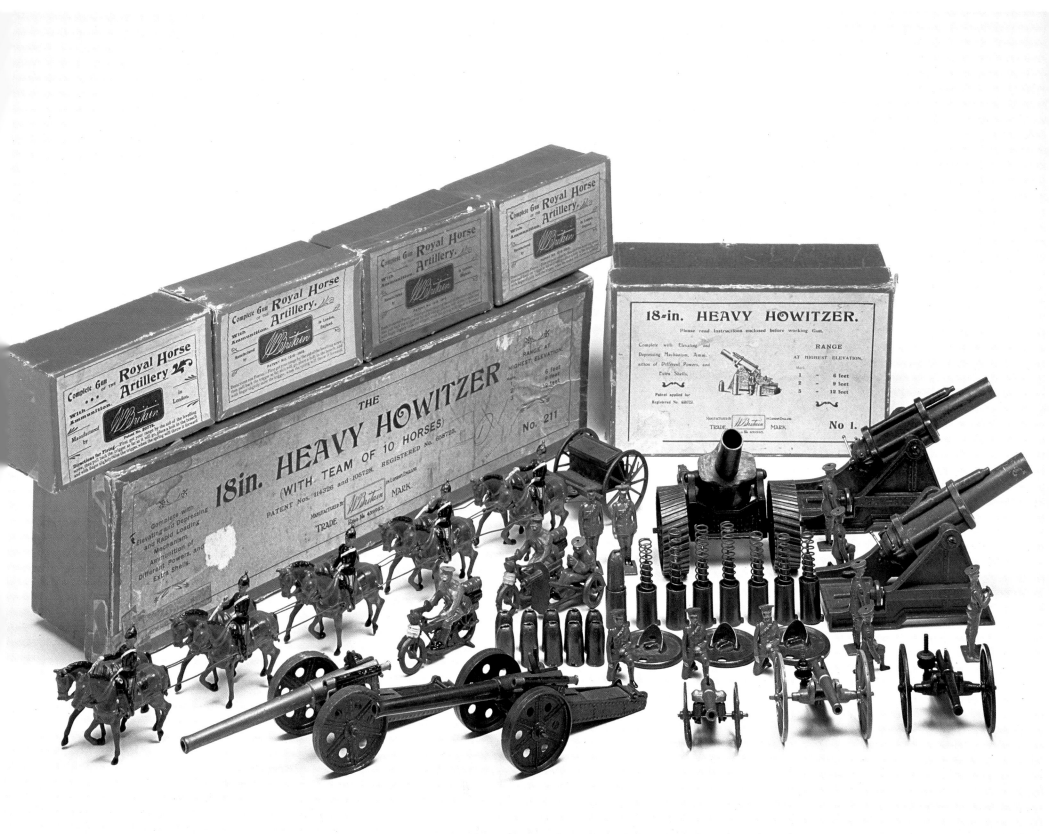

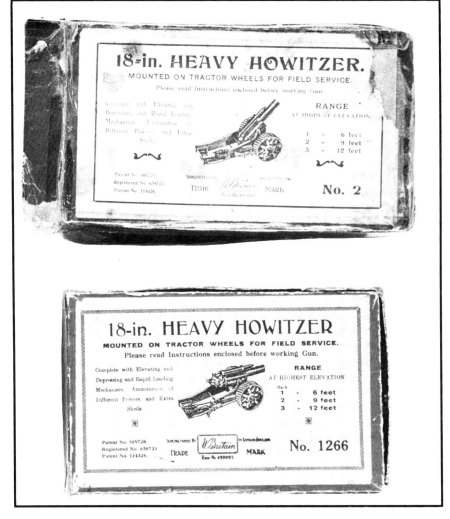

Above: A fairly early set 144a, Royal Field Artillery in Service Dress. As it has collar harness, it was made before 1924, but the earliest sets, before and immediately after the First World War, retained bucket seats and two extra seated gunners on the gun, as illustrated on page 144. It is noticeable that the galloping gun team in service dress, 39a (see page 144, top), is much rarer than set 144a, especially in the collar harness version. (Sotheby's, London)

Right: Top: Label for the tractor-wheeled version of the Heavy Howitzer, termed Gun no. 2 by Britains. At seven shillings and sixpence, this was a very expensive toy. But it was popular, and so as a collector's item today it is much less expensive to acquire than many shilling sets of soldiers. Below: A later label for the same gun, c.1933, when a main series number, 1266, was allocated. The illustrations of the gun in each label are both used in the instructions enclosed in the box, which are reproduced on page 142.

To the left are two of the impressive 4.7-inch **Naval Guns**, normally purchased separately for two shillings. This gun – H. G. Wells' favourite artillery piece – was based on the guns that did sterling service in the Boer War, and was certainly available from 1902 onwards. The grey gun and gun-metal models shown here are both 'open-spring' versions with the spring secured with a pin and open through the top of the trail. The earlier version, not shown, was the 'closed-spring' version, in which the spring is soldered in and totally enclosed by the top of the trail, presenting a flat covered surface.

Britains' most ambitious gun yet, patented in 1916, was the '18-inch Howitzer'. To the left is the first, No. 1 gun, which was mounted on a garrison mounting. The gun in front is a later khaki finish, as both models started life in gun-metal finish. The instructions reproduced opposite give a good idea of the work that went into the gun and its ingenious firing mechanism: hence its cost, four shillings. The box for the gun is shown behind it. In the centre is shown the No. 2 gun with tractor wheels and a mobile mounting, which was teamed up with a 10-horse team in set 211. The team and box are shown at the back to the left. The limber used was given an extra long hook to accommodate the gigantic trail. The ammunition for the giant guns is set out in front of them, with figures from set 313, Royal Artillery Gunners in peak caps, which contained four each standing and kneeling. The officer with binoculars comes from a later set, 1289.

Protecting the gun team are a dispatch rider from set 200, which contained four, and a motor cycle machine gun combination from set 199, which contained three combinations. I do not know why the 10-horse team itself is not in khaki, except that it was produced a few years after the war. The team was not available in a collar-harness version, and indeed may have been the occasion for the introduction of the light-harness horse.

Chapter 40
After the war: civilians

For most of 1919 one can imagine Britains busily resuming toy production after two years manufacturing ammunition. Re-filling all the shops with stock must have consumed most of their time, let alone estimating the effects of lost employees and returned servicemen. Prices, too, were running at well over 100 per cent above the 1914 level.

A profound feeling of relief at the end of the war gripped the country, and after this 'war to end all wars' the toy market was not in the mood to sell too many toy soldiers. Britains' thoughts, along with those of their contemporaries, turned thankfully towards peaceful pursuits. Before 1914, Britains had already brought out footballers, railway figures and Boy Scouts. In 1923, after a great deal of hard work on numerous completely new moulds, Britains unveiled its Home Farm.

It is not within the scope of this book to delve into the minutiae of Britains' civilian figures, but it is useful to realize that the main thrust of the company's expansion was in this field, if only to explain why the years 1919 to 1926 offered so few new military items. The proportion of military to civilian models in Britains' production has tended to decrease ever since (except for a slight upward surge during rearmament in the late 1930s), and today (1985) about 90 per cent of the factory's output is agricultural and other peaceful items, typified by the superb new hospital sets.

Overleaf, I show in the lower illustration a selection of farm and civilian items, including: farm wagon; huntsmen with hounds; lady railway passenger in red; various farm figures, including a village idiot in a light blue smock; boy on pony; cricketer, made by Britains for a cricket game manufactured by someone else, since he does not appear on the Britains list; timber wagon; mounted gentleman farmer; various animals; churns; male railway passenger in a Scout-type hat; and the railway driver and fireman with shovel. In the background are fences, signposts, scarecrow and Britains' set of four trees, number 204, fir, cedar, oak and elm.

Paramilitary organizations

Although these bodies do not belong to the army, they derive their organization from the military. Britains produced various sets of the Salvation Army, Scouts, Guides and Police during our period which are shown in the top illustration overleaf. The Police are on the left. One policeman was included in the set of civilians,

number 168, before the First World War. After the war, policemen featured individually in the Home Farm series, and set 319 provided an assorted box of mounted, foot and traffic police. Those on foot wore tall helmets, and, as far as I know, the policeman directing traffic in a peaked cap (fig 5) only appeared in set 428, which was a box of USA Police, all in peaked caps.

Boy Scouts were contained in sets 161, Boy Scouts with Scoutmaster, 162, Boy Scout Encampment, 163, Boy Scout Signallers, 180 and 181, Boy Scout Displays. These figures are shown in the middle section of the picture. The trek cart breaks down into a camp table and a ladder, which is assembled by hooking the sides of the cart together. The tree behind the cart was part of the Boy Scout display set, useful for climbing up, as can be seen, and for propping up the ladder. It says a lot for the

popularity of the Scout movement that Britains was prepared to devote so much energy in 1909 and 1910 to creating all the new models necessary for these sets. Even the slightly larger fixed-arm Boy Scout carrying his stave horizontally was created before the First World War, being dated 23.3.1911.

Britains' enthusiasm for the Salvation Army, on the other hand, appears to have been somewhat misplaced, since by 1910 Alfred Britain was complaining that it had not 'taken on'. The figures of men (set 10) and women (set 14) were created in 1906, dated 3.5.1906, and appear in the 1906 Gamages catalogue. These figures are shown on the right of the lower illustration. Britains made new figures of the Salvationists in about 1934, but these appeared after our period. The Salvation Army sets do not appear in the 1909 or 1915 Britains' listings.

Not many of these magnificent Whisstock labels for Britains' Home Farm sets are to be found, as they were replaced early in the 1930s with new designs. The smithy, well, barrow and haystack in the foreground are not Britains' products. (Sotheby's, London)

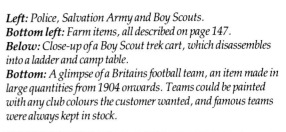

Left: Police, Salvation Army and Boy Scouts.
Bottom left: Farm items, all described on page 147.
Below: Close-up of a Boy Scout trek cart, which disassembles into a ladder and camp table.
Bottom: A glimpse of a Britains football team, an item made in large quantities from 1904 onwards. Teams could be painted with any club colours the customer wanted, and famous teams were always kept in stock.

149

PART SEVEN
THE AMERICAS

 Britains' production of troops from the Americas, and its sales of toy soldiers in the continent, have been somewhat spasmodic. In about 1906, Britains became involved with Charles William Beiser (see page 106), and I surmise that an agreement with this gentleman kept them out of the

United States market until 1927. A few sets depicting US Infantry, Cowboys, Indians and Mexicans were made and distributed in Great Britain before the First World War. In 1925, an opportunity arose to do business with Argentina, and from then on there were quite a number of South American sets in the Britains range. From 1927 onwards, Britains made and exported to the United

States a large range of American troops, although models of the American Civil War had to wait until 1951. Export to America received much more attention at times such as 1939–41 and immediately after the Second World War, when it was official British policy to encourage exports. Canada, of course, was treated as part of the Empire (see page 98).

Chapter 41
The United States

Britains' first models of US soldiers were made in 1898, depicting soldiers taking part in the Spanish-American war in Cuba.

Set 91, US Infantry at the slope, seven men with officer, 'Montana' hats. A very early version of this set has been found with full-dress white infantry helmets. In c.1907 this set was changed to contain seven men on guard with campaign hats, and an officer with sword and pistol. For the companion Spanish Infantry set 92, see page 153.

The next US set was inspired by the Beiser connection, and was a display tray and game.

Set 149, American Soldiers. The contents were exactly the same as set 148, the Royal Lancaster Regiment (see page 104), but the troops were US Infantry in dark blue 'bell-crown' caps rather than British infantry in foreign-service helmets (see below).

Expansion in the USA
Charles William Beiser and the
American Soldier Company

We have already met Mr Beiser on page 106 in considering the 'knockdown' sets that Britains issued to the British market in about 1907. The second of these, the American Infantry, set 149, is illustrated on page 153. Beiser's agreement with Britains appears to have been an

interesting commercial arrangement, and in effect Beiser virtually opened a New York office for Britains, who had itself just opened its Paris Office. The transatlantic arrangement, however, was of necessity more at arms length. Britains were to supply Beiser and his sole agent A.S. Ferguson and Company of 381 Broadway, New York, with toy soldiers, and in return obtained the rights to use Beiser's patent hinge mechanism in the United Kingdom. I would suppose (ICP) that the arrangement precluded Britains from selling at all in the USA, except at second hand via Beiser's American Soldier Company, an idea that is supported by the absence of most of Britains' regular pre-First World War lines in the USA. It may be coincidental that Britains started to make and ship a new series of sets of US figures to the USA in 1927, but it could be (ICP) that the original agreement was for 20 years, the American Soldier Company appearing to have been dissolved shortly after 1927.

The course of the relationship was probably subject to some stresses, and the contents of the boxes put out by the American Soldier Company were by no means exclusively Britains models. One explanation for this could be supply problems in 1917, when Britains went over to war production while the American Soldier Company went on supplying its customers normally. New local sources of supply brought in then would have tended to continue after the war.

Britains' figures used by the American Soldier Company started with the two new figures dated 15.6.1906, one marching at shoulder arms and one on guard. Both of these wore a slouch hat, and were never,

so far as I can trace, issued with any other headgear, either for the USA or in sets 26 or 91. To go with these, the prancing-horse officer was restyled to include a movable arm and rectangular base suitable for insertion into a Beiser hinged clip. This would not have been dated, since it was merely an alteration to an existing figure pre-dating 1900. From already existing figures, Britains supplied variations of pigeon-chested running soldiers and at-attention figures in bell-crown caps similar to those included in set 149, but with a different colour scheme, together with standing firing Infantry of the Line style figures and a marching officer to match. A prancing-horse officer with this helmet was also produced. Extra figures with slouch hats included a variation of the drummer boy and an at-attention figure with a furled standard of the type carried by a running figure in set 149.

These may well not be the only figures produced by Britains for this series, and many may yet be awaiting discovery. The American Soldier Company was in business for some 24 years, and a set number 107 has been found, suggesting at least that number of sets. Many of these could have been supplemented by US-produced figures such as the officer, standard-bearers and drummer included in the large set illustrated.

It has sometimes been suggested that these extra figures were made by Johillco, but I know of no evidence for this. ICP suggests that it would have been easier to enlist the aid of local competitors to enhance the American Soldier Company's sets than to search out a new British source of supply. It could be that the development of the US toy soldier producers McLoughlin Ideal and Barclay owes something to this connection. (See page 60, 4th row, fig 2 for an early Barclay prancing-horse figure.)

Virtually all the sets so far discovered by collectors fall into three colour variations. The first represents regular US Army units and comprises a brown slouch hat, blue 'bell crown' cap or black pickelhaube spiked helmet, with a dark blue coat and light blue trousers. The second shows either 'the enemy' or the 'Red Regular Army', though whose army is not specified. This colour scheme is like the first, but with a red coat rather than a blue. The third is a plain khaki, without as much detail as is normally added to Britains' regular khaki figures.

Beiser obviously had further schemes for 'knockdown' soldiers, since he patented an idea for another clip in which the soldier itself would have two hinge pivots moulded into the base, thus making the tin clip to enclose the base redundant. As far as I know, none of these were ever made.

In preparing the above information about Beiser, I have relied heavily upon the articles published by Will Beierwaltes, Joe Wallis and Scott Morlan in the *Old Toy Soldier Newsletter*. The large set is illustrated now in the collection of Ed Ruby. See also page 159 for Cowboys and Indians.

In 1927, Britains decided to enter the US market itself properly for the first time, using a distributor, George Bougfeldt and Company. Since the Second World War, the distributorship has changed to Reeves International, who still handle Britain's products in the USA at the time of writing.

This decision resulted in the creation of a number of basic sets of types of the United States Army as follows:

Set 226, West Point Cadets in Winter Dress at the slope, eight men

Set 227, US Infantry in service dress at the slope, seven with officer. These were in campaign hats and are known as the 'Doughboy' figure. The officer was fixed-arm in a peaked cap.

Set 228, US Marines at the slope in Blue Uniform, eight men, one of whom had a sergeant's chevrons painted on the movable arm.

Set 229, US Cavalry in Service Dress. These were based on the 'Scots Grey' horse, had peaked caps, and the set of five included no officer figure.

Set 230, US Sailors, Bluejackets at the slope. These had no officer.

This was the first group of US sets, and they proved extremely popular – so popular, in fact, that more than 44 sets of first-grade US mixed display sets were created between 1927 and the end of our period. These were followed by many more both before and after the Second World War, creating in the USA a market for Britains' soldiers second only to that in Great Britain itself and an equivalent interest in collecting the models after

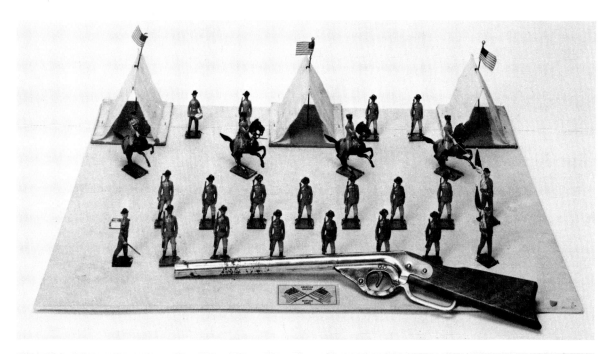

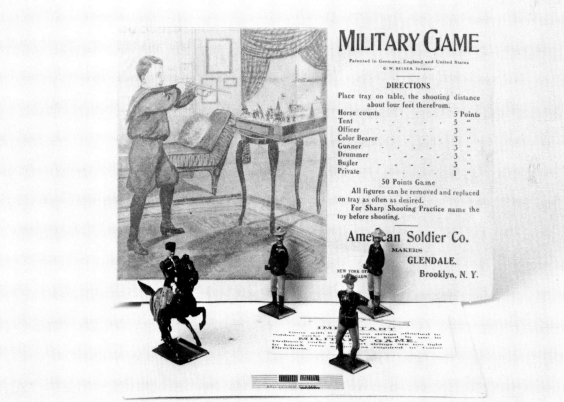

Top: American Soldier Company Beiser patent clipboard with military game, tents and pop-gun. The pop-gun was provided in many of the sets issued by this company, and replaced Britains' advice to use a 4.7-inch Naval Gun when playing with sets 148 and 149. The tents, officer, drummer and standard-bearer in the set illustrated were not Britains, nor indeed was the pop-gun.

Above: American Soldier Company instructions for a military game set, with Britains figures that were also used by Britains itself in sets 149 and 91. (Christie's, New York)

production finished – an interest that is still increasing at the time of writing.

In addition to the first group of basic sets, the following sets introduced further US types to the growing collection:

Set 276, US Cavalry in action, five men. This was a figure in a campaign hat mounted on a new galloping horse, which was also used for the second version of the South African Mounted Infantry and later for the Royal Canadian Mounted Police. Once more there was no officer figure.

Set 299, West Point Cadets in Summer Uniform at the slope, eight men. This was simply a new painting of the figure from set 226.

Set 323, a massive 73-piece diaplay set that included 'U.S. Artillery, Dispatch Rider and Officers'. These were presumably British figures, which may or may not have been painted differently for the US set. From my own observations, the only figures that were differently painted were the US Machine Gunners that appeared in sets 324, 359 and 475.

Set 324, another major display set of 81 pieces, containing Machine Gunners, Infantry in Gas Masks and officers.

Set 330, USA Aviation officers in short coats, eight officers. This set was the first of a number of sets of USA Aviation, all of which were new figures, mostly eight of each to a box.

Set 331, USA Aviation, officers in overcoats, eight officers

Set 332, USA Aviation, aviators in flying kit, short coats, eight aviators

Set 333, USA Aviation, aviators in sidcot suits, eight aviators

Set 334, USA Aviation, privates in peaked caps, eight privates

Set 335, USA Aviation, review order at the slope, 16 privates. For some reason this was a two-row set.

Set 359, USA Machine Gun Section. This was a basic set of six of the machine gunners lying, which I assume first appeared in set 323.

Set 399, USA Marines, active-service order, eight men. This is a very rare set, being the Marines from set 228 painted in active-service olive drab. They were still at the slope, but there was no sergeant with painted chevrons

Set 435, USA Aviation Monoplane, just like the RAF model, but painted khaki with US roundels rather than silver.

This completes the tally of basic United States sets during our period. The major development of the United States market during the late 1920s and early 1930s resulted in the production of a very large number of display sets and also a supporting cast of second-grade sets and figures, many of which are shown on page 156.

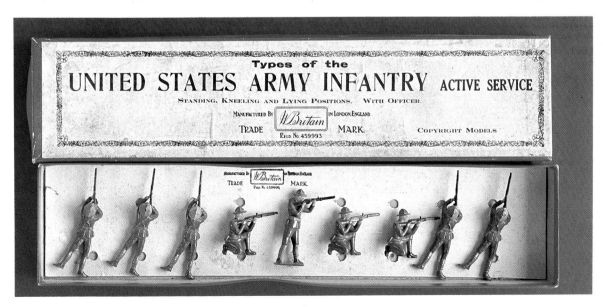

Above: All Britains' early models of United States troops were in blue uniforms. **Left to right:** the early set 91, US Infantry in their Montana hats (examples of their opponents, Spanish Infantry, are shown far right); the second-version set 91 is the infantry on guard, while the similar khaki figures are a special printing. At the back, the two sets of US Cavalry shown are also special paintings, done to order by Britains in the 1920s, using the Boer cavalry figure. On the right is the Beiser patent clipboard set 149, American Soldiers. **Left:** Box 1251, introduced the year after our period ends. This does not contain a true set, which would have the officer, who was the type that came with set 227. The standing firing figure is rare and was sometimes left out of this set. Similar troops in second-grade paint are illustrated on page 156, and it is interesting that these were available before the best-quality set was issued.

No. 91.   United States Infantry, 1/-

Above: Set 91 was the only set of United States troops in the 1915 catalogue, unless one counts the rather vaguely worded set 149 American Soldiers. This picture was used to illustrate the set in that catalogue, even though it shows the first version at the slope in Montana hats rather than the second version which was introduced about 1906, ie nine years before this catalogue was issued. The picture is very true to life, obviously faithfully copied from the real thing, since even the arms with rifles are shown at various angles, as the troops would normally appear in a box unless specially posed.

United States Troops: descriptions

Top row The basic US foot figures of 1927 are shown with their A series equivalents to the right: fig 1, set 227 infantry officer, fig 3 set 227 'doughboy', fig 5, set 228 marine. Fig 6 is the sergeant from the set showing his chevrons and fig 7 the A series figure. Fig 8 is from set 339, marines in service dress. Fig 10 is from set 230, blue jackets, and fig 12 is the A series Whitejacket. Fig 13 is the winter-dress West Point cadet from set 226, and fig 15 is the summer-dress painting from set 299.

2nd row All the figures in this row are in second-grade paint. Figs 1, 2 and 4 are early 'doughboys' based on the normal British infantry in gaiters firing. Figs 3 and 5 are an improvement on these outfitted in the more correct puttees. Some sets in the A series included fig 6, the drummer boy. Fig 7 is a W series small-size 'doughboy'. Fig 8 is W series US Cavalry, while fig 9 could be another version of this, although it is perhaps more likely to be an M series British cavalryman in service dress, number M 5. Fig 10 is an interesting A series US cavalryman in peak cap on an unusual horse not often seen.

3rd row Fig 1 is the full-dress version of set 91, in the white infantry helmet, probably pre-dating the version in the 'Boer' hat. Fig 2 is a US infantryman in khaki wearing a slouch hat. He is the same figure as the second-version men of set 91, but being in khaki he probably comes from an American Soldier Company set (see page 150). Fig 3 is an example of the machine gunner from sets 324 and 359, which was specially painted in US uniform with a brown peak to the cap and grey puttees.

Figs 4–10 show types of the USA aviation. Fig 4 is the officer in short coat from set 330, fig 5 the officer in overcoat from set 331, fig 6 the aviator in short coat from set 332, with fig 7 an A series equivalent, fig 8 the aviator in sidcot suit from set 333, and fig 9 the private in peak cap from set 334. Fig 10, based on the British RAF figure, is the odd one out, appearing after our period in the mixed USAF set 1904. Note the slightly darker khaki, lighter cheeks and absence of eyebrows in this last figure.

4th row Figs 1 and 2 show examples of set 229, the US Cavalry in service dress, based on the Scots Grey cavalryman. Where mounted infantry officers were called for, this figure seems to have been used with no change to the painting. Figs 3 and 4 are examples from set 276, US Cavalry in action. This was a new figure, which was also used for Mounties and South African mounted infantry. Fig 5 at the end of the row is the normal figure found representing US cavalry in the series.

Right: Boxed set of US Marines in service dress, set 399. The border and trademark are typical of the early 1930s. This set is one of the rarest of the regular line of issued United States sets, particularly difficult to find in its box. One imagines that it had nothing like the sales appeal of the full-dress set 228, even though it was still included in the catalogue from 1929 to 1940. Unlike the full-dress set, no figure had sergeant's stripes added. (Phillips, Glasgow)

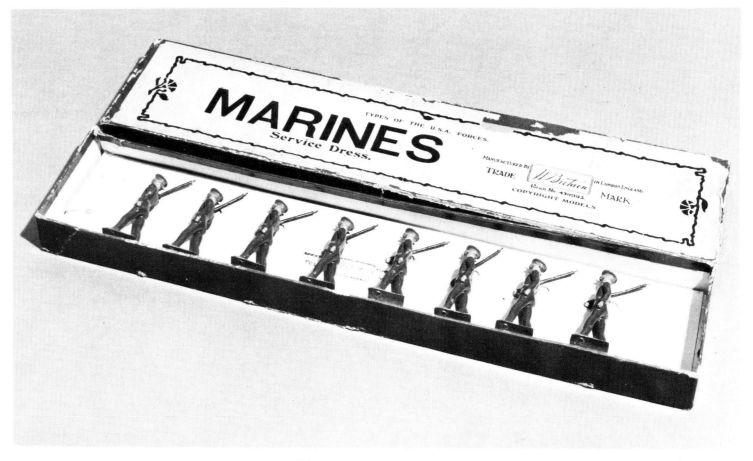

Left: US Girl Scout from set 238, compared with two of her transatlantic cousins, the British Girl Guides from set 1332, made after our period. This is interesting example of the United States version of a subject being made first. (Phillips, London)

Bottom left: Boxes for United States forces. Top to bottom: 1 Whisstock design for set 227. 2 Whisstock design for set 228. 3 Second-grade box for set 57a, *c.*1933. 4 – 6 Whisstock designs for sets 229, 230 and 299. 7 Whisstock design for set 194, overprinted with the set number 359 in order to serve as the box for the United States set of lying machine gunners, which were painted somewhat differently. 8 Another example of overprinting, this time rather more elaborately executed on a label current in the late 1930s for the Infantry in Action with Gasmask sets which were also issued as United States sets.

Below: United States of America Aviation Monoplane, set 435, which is in khaki with US markings. The box is that for set 433, the RAF Monoplane. Whether this box was used for both sets (ICP) or this is simply the wrong box is a matter for conjecture. (Phillips, Glasgow)

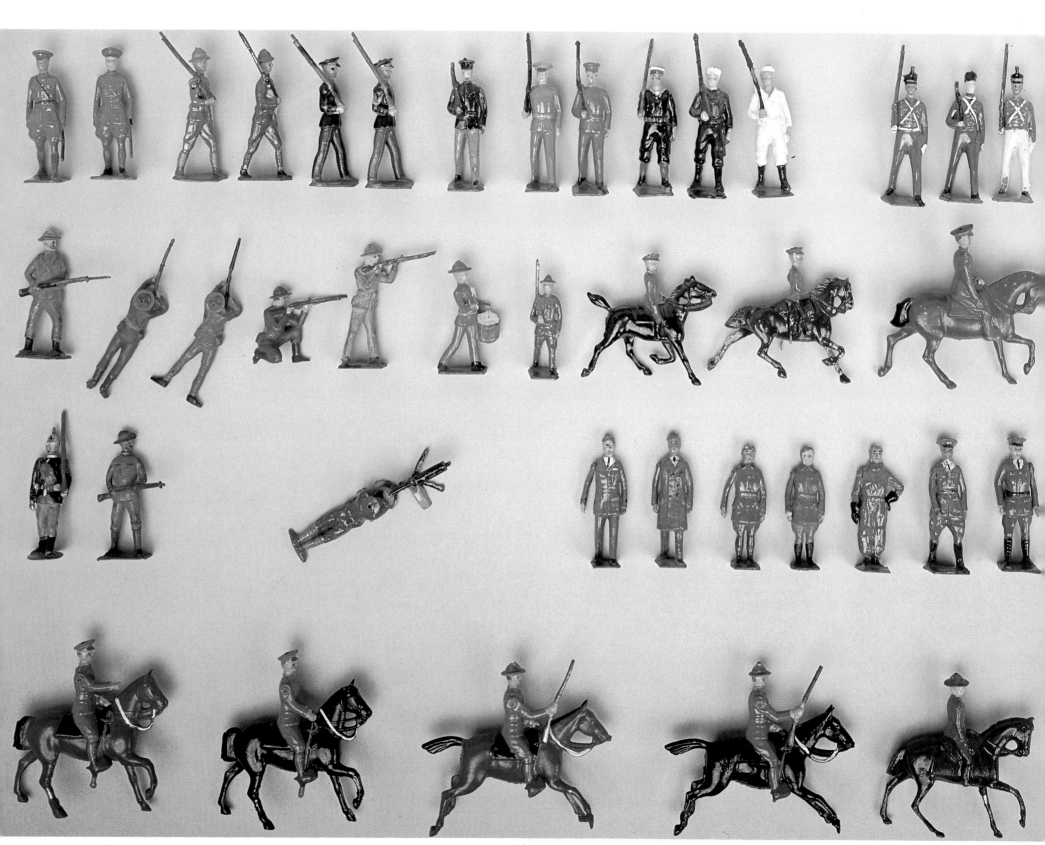

Examples of US troops, described on page 154.

Chapter 42
Cowboys and Indians

CW Beiser may well have been instrumental in initiating Cowboys and Indians at Britains. With the onset of moving pictures, Cowboys and Indians became a major feature of European children's play activity, and North American Indians are prominent, for instance, in H.G. Wells' book *Floor Games*, published in 1911. The interesting question is: why were the Indians made five years before the Cowboys? The gap between the two is large, given that they so obviously go together. A range of four basic sets with two displays was issued, the Indians in 1908 and the cowboys in 1913, and this range was extended with 31 other sets in the 1920s. Obviously they were one of the most popular lines. The illustration shows a wonderful *mêlée* of first and second grades and W series.

Set 150, North American Indians with chiefs on foot. This was the first set. The bases were dated 12.11.1907. There were six North American Indians standing on guard in a curiously disciplined stance, with two chiefs with tomahawks, all with fixed arms. The braves on guard came in the usual three-colour variation allowed for Britians' irregulars, in this case red, yellow or blue trousers. The chiefs were both painted with green coats and brown trousers. Later, two additional figures with movable arms were added to this set, one of a chief with a knife, the other of a medicine man, in place of two of the braves on guard.

Set 152, North American Indians mounted, five figures. At first this was all based on one cavalry figure dated 6.2.1908. This was one of the fullest gallop figures

Examples of Cowboys and Indians, described above and on page 158.

Britains ever produced, so nearly leaving the ground altogether that it needed a base to stand up. Three of the riders carried rifles, and two had tomahawks. The two with tomahawks had red coats; two of the riders with rifles had green coats, one yellow. A few years later, probably after the First World War, the two with tomahawks changed to a new galloping figure reminiscent of the mounted Arab. It was a shame that the Arabs did not also make use of the early galloping Indian.

Set 179, Cowboys mounted, five pieces. The mounted cowboy was another splendid horseman. Two carried lariats and three a pistol. As this set appeared in 1913, the figures never had a date – nor did the equivalent foot figure.

Set 183, Cowboys on foot, eight pieces. To start with, the foot figures all carried rifles, but later a new arm with a pointing pistol came in. Both these were movable arms as opposed to the fixed-arm Indians on foot.

In the A series a very spirited mounted Indian came with a crawling Indian and a crouching Indian with knife and tomahawk. The mounted Indian in the first version had a streaming horse's tail, but the later version had the tail moulded into the figure to minimize breakages. The two first-grade figures were sometimes also done in second grade. The mounted cowboy A series figure was a nice new idea, with the man turning round and firing his pistol at the pursuing Indians. On foot the cowboy was simply walking along holding a pistol. For the W series, probably introduced in 1933, the mounted A series figures were reduced in size almost exactly, as was the cowboy on foot, but a rather nice new Indian pointing with one hand came out. All these A and W figures are shown in the front of the illustration. Britains often used trees and tents in their mixed displays of the Wild West, and the range of trees (set 204) is shown in the background.

Britains seemed happy with the few models of Cowboys and Indians that it produced, just eight Cowboys and nine Indians including all the different sizes and grades in our period. Later, as with the Arabs, a larger diversity was forthcoming, to compete better with the more wildly animated models of competitors.

BOXES FOR COWBOYS AND INDIANS
Top to Bottom: 1 Whisstock design for set 150. 2 and 3 Early Typographical boxes for set 152. First marketed in 1908, the North American Indian boxes were issued with typographical labels for about five years, before the Whisstock design was used. On the other hand, the Cowboys may well never have had a pre-Whisstock label. 4 1930s pictorial design for set 179. By this time Cowboys and Indians were such big business that much care was devoted to new labelling. 5 Whisstock design for set 183. 6 The same design as 5, with modified trademark on the right, c.1935. 7 Label for W series Wild West boxes.

Above: AMERICAN HERO COWBOY AND INDIAN SET
As one would expect, Cowboy and Indian figures were especially popular in the United States of America. North American Indians entered Britains' list suspiciously soon after the start of their special relationship with CW Beiser, and it seems logical to suppose that he suggested these models to Britains. Several sets of Cowboys and Indians similar to the one pictured above are known to have existed, a number with different contents using this colour printed stand-up card insert and arrangements with the familiar patent clips. The figures have always been genuine Britains in the normal paint style for the figures, and the set often includes a Daisy pop-gun to knock the figures over with. Tying holes for a pop-gun were punched in the card in the illustration but cannot be seen in the picture as they are behind the front edge of the box. This particular set does not have very many figures in it, and one can imagine at least twice this number in some sets. An interesting feature of the label is that it states 'Manufactured by Selchow and Righter Co. "Makers of Parcheesi" New York, N.Y.' Whether this company was a residual legatee of the American Soldier Company, or possibly sub-licensed, is a question that needs further research. Assuming that the American Hero range of sets had sufficient sales, George Borgfeldt and Company, Britains' agents after 1927, might even have felt it worthwhile to go on supplying the necessary Cowboys and Indians. (Phillips, London)

Left: Group of labels from after our period, showing the development of Britains' labels during the 1930s and 1950s. Top to bottom: 1 Single-row box of Indians, set 152, with very detailed illustration typical of the limited number of new individual illustrated labels for sets which replaced some of the Whisstock labels between 1930 and 1941. 2 A two-row Wild West display set, with a label from the 1930s suitable for a variety of sets. A printed label with the actual set title and number would be glued to the end of the lid. 3 This Arabs of the Desert display box is one of the labels developed in colour for the post-Second World War range of sets. It was also used for the Eastern People display. 4 In the 1950s, Wild West displays usually had this label. Notice that the term 'Cowboys and Indians' had now won out over 'Wild West'.

Chapter 43
Latin America

Set 186, the Pride of Mexico, the Rurales, seven men and an officer. The set was brought out in 1914 to mark the fighting in Mexico at the time. They are shown in the centre of the illustration with broad-brimmed sombreros, brown coats and grey trousers. Specially made figures,

they had a separately made officer with a smaller hat, and are one of Britains' most sought after sets.

Within our period, the only other Latin American figures made were three basic sets each for Argentina and

Uruguay of infantry, cavalry and military cadets. As they were all first made at the same time in 1925, we may presume (ICP) than an export arrangement to these countries had been made, probably via an agent in Argentina, where there was an influential British

Latin American sets, described above and on page 161.

community. With these South American sets were also produced set 218, the Spanish Cavalry, and a new model for set 92, the Spanish Infantry (see page 125), and these figures were prominent in Britains' exports to Buenos Aires. Over the next few years, 17 combination and display sets featuring Argentinian, Uruguayan and Spanish troops were used, and the interest in this area of the world continued until 1941, extra sets being made outside our period. In the best traditions of exporting, the labels were in Spanish. In our picture, the Uruguayans are on the left and the Argentinians on the right, the order of sets from the left being:

Set 220, Uruguayan Cavalry, four men and an officer
Set 222, Uruguayan Infantry, eight men
Set 221, Uruguayan Cadets, eight men
Set 186, Mexican Infantry, seven men and an officer
Set 219, Argentine Cadets, eight men
Set 216, Argentine Infantry, eight men
Set 217, Argentine Cavalry, four men and an officer

The Argentinian troops are distinguished by the yellow tops to their shakos, while the cadets have thick white horsehair plumes based on a uniform taken from the Prussian Army. Both the Uruguayan and Argentine Cavalry sets were based on the same figure, an adaptation of the head-up trotting horse fitted out with a head with a large shako. Both sets carried lances with a blue and white pennon, while the officers had an outstretched sword arm.

The Uruguayan Infantry is probably the rarest of the seven sets. The Uruguayan Cadets were the most picturesque, a figure based on a uniform dating back to the Napoleonic Wars, and also long-lived, Britains' production continuing until 1954, when the set was replaced by set 2051 which contained a new figure. The Uruguayan Cadets in the picture are a post-Second World War painting, the one in front being in 1930s paint. The Argentine Cadets are a group of nine, collected from various different sets. The Argentine Infantry also are a post-Second World War painting with one earlier figure. The other four sets are c.1930, except for the Mexicans, c.1938. The colour details and paint style of all these sets did not alter much, but the facial details of the early sets show greyer flesh and brighter pink cheeks.

Interestingly, the arrival of British troops in South America sparked off a local industry copying Britains' figures. One of its products can be seen on page 60, 4th row, fig 5, marked Industria Argentina.

BOXES FOR LATIN AMERICAN SETS
Top to bottom: 1 Whisstock design for set 186, the only label with which this set appeared. 2 – 6 Typographical labels for sets 216, 217, 220, 221 and 223. All these have the later style of trademark, and so may well be revised labels from the 1930s, although in other respects probably retaining most of the typographical elements with which they were first issued. The titles are all in Spanish, as one would expect from sets primarily intended for export to Argentina.

SUMMARIES AND LISTINGS
Britains' Paris Office

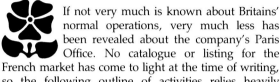 If not very much is known about Britains' normal operations, very much less has been revealed about the company's Paris Office. No catalogue or listing for the French market has come to light at the time of writing, so the following outline of activities relies heavily on ICP.

It would seem that the opening of the Paris Office in 1905 coincided with the initial production of sets 138 to 143 (see page 127). At first, the office was simply an agency for distributing these and other Britains' products, all of which were still made in London. The gentlemen who ran the Paris Office were Messieurs Landrieu and Rousseau, and very soon they started to ask Britains for additional lines to sell in France. One of these is the 'Infantérie à grande tenue', a new figure dated 1.6.1910 (illustrated on page 128). This is firmly marked 'Made in Great Britain' as well as *déposé* (registered), but never appeared in a catalogue for the British market. Small-size French infantry at the trail and at the slope were date-stamped 1.7.1912 and 9.9.1912 respectively, and these do not appear in the 1915 catalogue.

French distribution must have been small compared with that in Britain, since so few of the models have survived, and the scouring of Paris by eager collectors has not often produced any result. The Parisians, it seems, were well content to purchase from Mignot and the other established indigenous manufacturers. Another problem was the import duty levied by the French. On this subject Fred Britain said in December 1905:

> The cost of sending the toys to France and the payment of the tariff amount to 35 per cent of the value of the toys. We find we could move our factory to Paris and thus obtain a much larger profit over there, while the cost of production there is so much cheaper that we could send the toys back to this country and obtain a larger profit here than we do at present. But we are patriotic enough to stay where we are.

By late 1912 the situation had become insupportable, and Britains responded to the Frenchmen's pleas to set up production in France and thus make models at competitive prices. From 1912 to 1923, some Britains' models were produced in France, and production there seems to have continued throughout the First World War, factories being opened at Saint-Leu and Cosque, near Paris. The postcard Britains issued of George V looking at its stand at the British Industries Fair in 1922 shows the heading 'Britains Ltd, London and Paris' across the top of the stand. Possibly the great success of the Home Farm Series in 1923 led Britains to decide to consolidate its efforts at home, or else the conditions favourable to French production noted in 1905 had ceased by this time. Certainly Britains was thinking in terms of another London factory, and the Paris venture was closed in 1923, all the Paris moulds being brought back to London.

Because of the difficulties of finding Paris Office models, it is not yet possible to collate anything like a full list of those produced. They fall into two periods of production as follows:

1 British-produced models distributed by the Paris Office, 1905-12. This period includes some models made especially for the Paris Office, such as the 1910 'Infantérie à grande tenue' noted above. All models sent to France would have had to be lettered 'Made in Great Britain', but of course this is not necessarily a guide to what was actually sold in France. We can be certain that those which carried in addition the word *déposé* were offered through Paris.

2 French-produced models, 1912-23. The proliferation of models during this period indicates production of moulds in France. Indeed it may have been at this time that French manufacturers such as Mignot learned the secrets of hollowcasting, by which method they were certainly producing figures between the two world wars. All Britain's figures produced in France had to have the word *déposé* lettered on the base. At the conclusion of the Paris venture, numbers of moulds returned to London, all with the engraved *déposé* in the base. Britains continued to use some of these moulds in London for many years. The only conclusion, therefore, on finding figures marked *déposé*, is that at some time that type of figure was either offered or moulded in France. Only those figures marked *déposé* but without the words 'Made in England' or 'Made in Great Britain' added were actually moulded in France.

Most of the figures on offer through the Paris Office appear to have fallen into the following groups:

1 Depictions of the French Army in full dress
In addition to the sets in the British catalogue, these included:
Infantry of the Line in blue with yellow trim (page 128)
Mounted Saint Cyr Cadets at the halt with carbines
Mounted General with kepi on sway-backed horse
Mounted General based on the figure used for the British general officer. This must have been added to the range in 1922 (page 130).
Infantérie à grande tenue (page 130).
Supply wagon, with drivers in kepis.

2 Depictions of the French Army during the First World War
There was a large variety of figures in steel helmets, both cavalry and infantry. Most types were either in horizon blue or khaki. In addition, some infantry retained the kepi:
Standard marching figure, but all in horizon blue (page 129)
Lying firing (page 132)
Kneeling officer with binoculars (page 132)
Standing officer with binoculars
Standing and kneeling firing figures probably also existed.
In steel helmets:
Horizon blue: Officer on foot, based on chauffeur figure with sword or flag.
    Standard marching figure at slope
    Charging (page 129)
    Mounted officer, extended sword arm, cantering horse
    Trooper on horse at halt, short carbine.

Khaki: Standard marching figure at trail (page 129)
    Similar figure at slope
    Mounted officer to match, head-up trotting horse
    (It is possible that these types are meant to be Belgians and thus fall into group 4.)
    Zouave in khaki.

3 Countries neighbouring France
Italy: Bersaglieri in grey uniform (page 133)
    Italian Infantry, standard-bearer
    Mounted Lancer, all-grey uniform
Britain: Royal Horse Guard, the French Cuirassier figure painted appropriately. This may have been done in 1917 or 1918 when Britains in London were not making any models (page 132)
Spain: Dragoons (page 129) in various positions mounted and dismounted.

4 Participants in the First World War
Britain, all khaki with peaked caps:
    Officer based on the medical officer figure
    Marching, based on the chauffeur figure, with rifle at slope, or empty hand
    Lying firing, based on the French figure in horizon

blue with full trousers
Steel helmeted figure on guard, based on the CIV figure
Mounted figures in steel helmets, empty hands, on cantering or Scots Grey horse.
Russia, green infantry uniform:
Officer mounted at halt, on horse dated 18.8.1903
Colour-bearer on foot, marching
Bugler on foot, marching.
Japan, light blue coats:
Officer mounted at halt, on sway-backed horse
Marching at the slope, based on the chauffeur figure.

5 Small size

Examples of most known figures are illustrated on page 132. Their subject matter may correspond with the standard size. In addition, fixed-arm mounted Cuirassiers and Chasseurs have now been discovered.

To identify Paris Office figures you must know which figures were not in the regular list of British-made figures, and then recognize the greyish flesh tones used by the French painters. In order to compete with French manufacturers, many Paris Office sets included officers, colour-bearers and musicians. Other different figures were probably made during 1917 and 1918, when Britains in London was engaged in ammunition production. It is plainly impossible to sort out figures

which were made in England and then sold through the Paris Office (unless they were never on offer in England, like the Infantérie à grande tenue). And it would be hard to sort out figures which were part of the regular British list, but were painted in Paris (if indeed this was done). The one known boxed set definitely attributable to the Paris Office is a mixed cavalry box of Cuirassiers and Chasseurs à cheval, the box being covered in orange paper rather than the red normal in Britain.

Altogether, the Parisian episode of Britains' history is fascinating to the collector both because of its obscurity and because of the many models produced that differed from the normal British product.

Second-grade production

Early days and the X Series

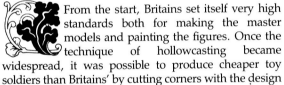From the start, Britains set itself very high standards both for making the master models and painting the figures. Once the technique of hollowcasting became widespread, it was possible to produce cheaper toy soldiers than Britains' by cutting corners with the design and paintwork, as well as producing them without such features as movable arms. To counter this cheap competition, Britains started to produce its own figures for sale singly or in sets with less painting detail and for a considerably lower price. Unfortunately, it does not seem to have included in the catalogues any of the sets of this type made before the First World War. I have seen two boxed sets of this period which have reference numbers, the labels being marked 4X 1st Dragoons and 8X 6th Dragoon Guards. These sets contained five cavalry with a different cavalryman as an officer. Similar sets, both of cavalry and infantry, had no reference number at all. For convenience, these pre-First World War figures are generally referred to as the X series. While most of the cavalry figures used were different models from the best quality, a number of the infantry were taken from fixed-arm types used in the regular best-quality sets; for instance, the volley-firing Foot Guard and the early standing and kneeling on-guard figures.

By and large, Britains was not very proud of the X series, and thus the famous trademark did not appear, the sets being sold anonymously. See labels on pages 50, 51 and 82.

A and C Series

The A Series was probably first produced c.1925 and

was simply a regularization of existing un-numbered sets produced for the cheaper market (ICP). Altogether, nearly 1000 sets had been produced by 1940, but these sets were made up of various combinations of relatively few models. By the end of our period in 1932, some 200 sets had been put together, and the Parade Series, initiated in the first-quality (see page 188), was being extended to second-grade sets.

Most of the figures that appeared in the A series were also available as single figures. In 1926, these figures were numbered 4, 4a, 4b, 4c etc, but this proved to be a rather confusing way of describing them. By 1931 they had been transferred into a 'C Series' – 1c, 2c, 3c and so on. By 1933, this series had reached 51c, although not all the numbers allocated were in the catalogue. In both the A and the C Series, numbers were dropped and added quite frequently to follow demand.

'Third-grade' figures

In spite of offering the A and C series, Britains must still have suffered competition from lower-quality manufacturers. In 1932 the P series was introduced, in which fewer different colours were used on the models. At this period they were only foot figures, and retailed for one penny each as opposed to a penny halfpenny for the C series. Most of the same models as the C series were used again and, when they first came out, the 21 figures from 1p to 21p were numbered in strict alphabetical order. Savings were achieved by not painting the base green, not painting the rifle brown, not painting in belts and not painting the eyes on the face. As a generalization, the C series might be called 'five-colour figures' and the P series 'three-colour figures'. Such is the power of competition that after the Second World War the 'five-colour figures' were not

revived, and the 'three-colour figures' became the normal second-grade offering. Before the Second World War, various Britains' figures were offered on the market simply painted in gold paint or, more rarely, in 'copper finish', which looked like silver. These figures, which might originally have been first- or second-grade castings, were a traditional offering in the souvenir market and for street traders. Britains never offered for sale unpainted castings in the toy trade, as these were known to be unhealthy for children to handle. No records were kept of which castings were sold painted gold, and sometimes there were some odd combinations of castings and arms.

Listing the second grades

Because of the very large number of sets containing different numbers or combinations of the same figures, I will simply list the individual figures that I know were produced in our period. Other information provided is the figures' respective catalogue numbers when offered as gilt, C series, P series or otherwise, together with the earliest A series set in which they appear, and a page reference to illustrations of the figure.

The figures are listed in alphabetical order, and it is interesting to note that Britains did the same when starting the P series. The Black Watch, which seems to contradict this, was known as a Highlander for P series purposes. The Gilt figures given a 3 number with a letter of the alphabet in the 1926 catalogue were also put into the C series, and their C series number is given in brackets. The headings X series, 1926, C series and P series follow in chronological order. Where a figure is known to exist, but no number is known, the word 'yes' appears in the column.

SECOND-GRADE FIGURES PRODUCED 1893-1932

Regimental or other title	In X Series	Gilt	A Series	1926	C Series	P Series	Page
Black Watch, slope	—	3a(2c)	19a	4d	2c	8p	77
Boy Scout	—	—	—	4s	29c	1p	148
Buffs (khaki) on guard, steel helmet	—	—	326a	4g	21c	2p	140
Buffs (review order), on guard	—	3j(5c)	25a	4l	23c	3p	81
Buffs (review order), oval base, on guard	Yes	Yes	—	—	—	—	85
Cavalry, service dress (peak cap), head-up spindly horse	—	—	5a	40d	11c	—	140
Cavalry, steel helmet, head-down spindly horse	—	—	4a	40f	13c	—	—
Cowboys, kneeling with revolver	—	—	296a	—	—	4p	157
Cowboys, mounted with revolver	—	—	138a	—	36c	—	157
Cowboys, walking with revolver	—	—	37a	4t	30c	5p	157
Dragoons, 1st Royal, fixed-arm pony-horse	Yes	—	—	—	—	—	52
Dragoons, 1st Royal, head-down spindly horse	4x	—	—	—	—	—	—
Dragoons, 1st Royal, head-level spindly horse	—	—	8a	—	—	—	52
Dragoons, 1st Royal, head-up spindly horse	4x	—	8a	40g	14c	—	33
Dragoon Guards, 6th, head-level spindly horse	8x	—	—	—	—	—	—
Dragoons, 2nd – see Scots Greys							
Dragoon Guards, 6th, head-down spindly horse	8x	—	—	—	—	—	49
Highlanders charging, rifle pointing down, with glengarry	—	3i(4c)	23a	4f	4c	—	140
Highlanders running, rifle level, with glengarry	—	—	—	4m	24c	7p	140
Horse Guards, head-down spindly horse	Yes	Yes	2a	40k	15c	—	33
Horse Guards, head-level spindly horse	Yes	Yes	—	—	—	—	—
Horse Guards, head-up spindly horse	—	—	2a	—	—	—	—
Hussars, 3rd, head-down spindly horse	Yes	—	6a	6a	—	—	—
Hussars, 3rd, head-up spindly horse	—	—	6a	—	16c	—	53
Infantry of the Line, firing, kneeling, peak cap	—	—	—	—	—	9p	140
Infantry of the Line, khaki gaiters, standing, peak cap	—	—	—	—	—	11p	140
Infantry of the Line, khaki, running, peak cap	—	—	17a	—	—	—	140
Infantry of the Line, lying feet together	—	—	—	—	—	10p	140
Lancers, 12th, head-down spindly horse	Yes	—	—	—	—	—	—
Lancers, 12th, head-level spindly horse	—	—	1a	40c	12c	—	57
Lancers, 12th, head-up spindly horse	Yes	—	—	—	—	—	—
Lancers, halt, with lance, movable arm	—	—	—	40a	8c	—	57

Regimental or other title	In X Series	Gilt	A Series	1926	C Series	P Series	Page
Lancers, halt, with sword, movable arm	—	—	—	40b	9c	—	—
Life Guards, 1st, head-down spindly horse	Yes	41(6c)	3a	40	7c	—	44
Life Guards, 1st, head-level spindly horse	Yes	Yes	—	—	—	—	33
Life Guards, 1st, head-up spindly horse	—	—	3a	—	—	—	44
Machine gunners, lying	—	—	—	—	—	12p	140
Machine gunners, kneeling, peak cap	—	—	—	—	—	13p	140
North American Indian, crawling	Yes	—	21a	4q	27c	15p	157
North American Indian, knife and hatchet	—	—	—	—	—	16p	157
North American Indian, mounted	—	—	75a	—	35c	—	157
North American Indian, chief on foot	—	—	50a	—	—	—	157
North American Indian, on guard	—	—	25a	4n	25c	17p	157
Rifles, running	—	3h(3c)	26a	4k	22c	18p	88
Royal Marine Artillery, slope, oval base	Yes	—	—	—	—	—	88
Sailors, Royal Navy, Straw Hat	—	—	18a	4p	26c	19p	88
Scots Greys, fixed-arm, pony horse	Yes	—	—	—	—	—	52
Scots Greys, head-level spindly horse	—	—	7a	—	—	—	52
Scots Greys, head-up spindly horse	Yes	—	7a	40c	10c	—	52
Scots Guards, volley firing	Yes	Yes	—	—	—	—	59
Somerset Light Infantry, kneeling on guard	Yes	—	—	—	—	—	85
Somerset Light Infantry, standing on guard, oval base	Yes	—	—	—	—	—	85
Sussex Regiment, fixed-arm, slope	—	3(1c)	42a	4c	18c	20p	81
Sussex Regiment, mounted officer, head-down spindly horse	—	—	42a	—	—	—	—
USA Cavalry, service dress	—	—	56a	—	17c	—	156
USA Cavalry, slouch hat	—	—	54a	—	51c	—	—
USA Infantry, 'charging', on guard	—	—	—	—	43c	—	—
USA Infantry, doughboy at slope	—	—	41a	—	32c	—	156
USA Infantry, kneeling firing, gaiters	—	—	—	—	41c	—	156
USA Infantry, lying firing, feet together, gaiters	—	—	—	—	42c	—	156
USA Machine gunners, lying	—	—	—	—	40c	—	—
USA Marine, review order, slope	—	—	49a	—	31c	—	156
USA Marine, service dress, slope	—	—	—	—	38c	—	156
USA Sailor, blue jacket, slope	—	—	53a	—	33c	—	156
USA Sailor, white jacket, slope	—	—	—	—	39c	—	156

Regimental or other title	In X Series	Gilt	A Series	1926	C Series	P Series	Page
USA West Point Cadet, summer dress, slope	—	—	—	—	37c	—	156
USA West Point Cadet, winter dress, slope	—	—	56a	—	34c	—	156
West Surrey Regiment, kneeling firing, gaiters	—	—	303a	—	—	—	—
West Surrey Regiment, lying firing, gaiters	—	—	303a	—	—	—	—
West Surrey Regiment, slope, oval base	Yes	—	—	—	—	—	85
West Surrey Regiment, standing firing, gaiters	—	—	20a	—	—	—	—
Worcestershire Regiment, standing on guard, oval base	Yes	—	—	—	—	—	85
Worcestershire Regiment, kneeling on guard	Yes	—	—	—	—	—	85
Zulu	Yes	—	22a	4r	28c	21p	105

Non-standard size second-grade figures

Britains also produced second-grade figures in sizes other than the standard. Even their standard second-grade figures tended to look a little smaller than the 'First Quality', but there were also two scales smaller than that. The W series was sets of figures in 45mm scale, and a few of these were also sold singly as part of the D series. Smaller yet was a series of very small cavalry in about 30mm scale. These had been incorporated into the W series by 1926, but originate from shortly after the turn of the century, having normally been produced in gilt only. Both these smaller sizes are described in on pages 166-8.

There were also two sizes larger than the standard, although only one of these comes within our period. The HH size was only produced in the late 1930s, but the H size was current in the 1915 catalogue, although not known as the H series until 1930. There were only three figures in the series, but they could be obtained in gilt or painted finish, listed as follows:

Figure	H series listing	1926 listing	In 1915 catalogue	Illustrated on page
Highlander gilt	1h	3b	No	77
Infantry gilt	2h	3c	Yes	—
Fusilier gilt	3h	3d	No	—
Infantry painted	4h	4	No	85
Fusilier painted	5h	4a	No	65
Highlander painted	6h	4c	Yes	77

Small-size troops

 As well as producing less well painted toy soldiers, Britains' competitors also tried to undercut Britains by producing smaller soldiers that used less metal and so cost less. As usual, Britains was quick to respond, producing before the First World War a series of sets numbered 1b to 26b, known to collectors as the B series. In this series of single-row sets, Britains offered four cavalrymen or seven infantrymen in a scale that started at 43mm and was increased in later versions to 45mm. The figures were painted in the same high quality as those in the standard scale, but the boxes retailed for only sixpence, half the price of the standard box, and Gamages offered

them at a mere fourpence halfpenny. Small-size troops were also made by the Paris Office (see page 163). Richards believed that the first small-size figures were produced in 1896. From then until 1901, eight boxes larger than the single-row sets described above appeared as part of the main standard-size numbering sequence. Presumably the single-row boxes started to appear at much the same time.

The first small-size cavalry figure was on a small trotting horse (1). This was soon supplemented by two types of cantering horse (2 and 3) and a somewhat larger walking horse (4). This group of figures was used separately or mixed for most of the cavalry sets, and as a

result is known collectively as the first version. The second version came with six different horses in a decidedly larger scale, all dated 1904 (5-10). In this version specific types were used for specific sets, as with the standard-size figures.

William Britain Junior's designs of horses definitely improved over the years, and some people consider that the second-version small-size horses are his best work. The dates on them indicate that they were made immediately after he had finished improving the standard-scale horses, which are dated 1901 to 1903, so that by the time he moved on to the small size his eye was in. After 1904, the beautiful horses created for the

Red Indian and Cowboy sets, followed by the magnificent General Staff set, 201, show that the improvement was continued.

The small-size infantry also came in two versions. The first version was an undated marching figure on an oval base, either at the slope (11 and 12) or at the trail (13 and 14), or a running figure (15 and 16) on a rounded wedge-shaped base dated 1.2.1901. From the start, infantry sets only contained one type of figure in a particular set, the officer being the same figure with gold facings, sometimes with the rifle removed. The second-version figures were also based on a series of marching men (17-19), all with 1912 dates, and a new taller running figure (20 and 21), which is undated and therefore probably originated in 1913.

These second-version infantry figures are quite rare, since they were only produced from 1912 to 1916. They did, however, reappear in second-grade paint in the W series (see below).

**LISTING OF SMALL-SIZE
FIRST QUALITY FIGURES**

Sets in the small-size included in the main catalogue sequences were as follows:

57 1st Dragoon Guards, 12 pieces, illustrated pages 33 and 49

58 1 row Scots Greys, 4 pieces
1 row Mounted Infantry, 4 pieces
1 row Royal Horse Guards, 4 pieces, illustrated page 44
Total: 12 pieces

84 1 row 2nd Life Guards, 4 pieces, illustrated page 44
1 row 7th Royal Fusiliers, 7 pieces
Total: 11 pieces

85 1 row 5th Dragoon Guards FSO, 4 pieces, illustrated page 116
1 row Scots Greys 4 pieces
1 row Scots Guards, 7 pieces
I row Northumberland Fusiliers, 7 pieces
Total: 22 pieces

86 2 rows Lancashire Fusiliers, 14 pieces

87 2 rows 13th Hussars, 8 pieces, illustrated pages 33 and 53

125 Royal Horse Artillery, full dress, 13 pieces, illustrated page 116

126 Royal Horse Artillery, active service, 13 pieces, illustrated page 116

Sets in the B series were as follows:
Sets marked * did not appear in any catalogue, but are all supposedly single rows of sets that appeared in the displays listed above.

1b 1st Life Guards, 4 pieces, illustrated page 44

2b* Royal Horse Guards, the Blues, 4 pieces

3b* 5th Dragoon Guards (active service), 4 pieces

4b* Scots Guards, slope, 7 pieces

5b* 1st Dragoon Guards, 4 pieces

6b 2nd Dragoons, the Royal Scots Greys, 4 pieces, illustrated page 52

7b* 2nd Life Guards, 4 pieces

8b* 7th Royal Fusiliers, 7 pieces

9b* 13th Hussars, 4 pieces

10b 11th Hussars, 4 pieces, illustrated pages 33 and 53

11b Japanese Cavalry, 4 pieces

12b 16th Lancers (active service), 4 pieces, illustrated pages 57 and 116

13b 17th Lancers, 4 pieces, illustrated pages 33 and 57

14b Russian Cavalry, 4 pieces, illustrated page 124

15b Mounted Infantry, 4 pieces, illustrated page 65

16b Coldstream Guards, slope, 7 pieces, illustrated page 69

17b Lancashire Fusiliers, 7 pieces, illustrated pages 37 and 65

18b Grenadier Guards, 7 pieces, illustrated page 69

19b Dublin Fusiliers, 7 pieces, illustrated pages 37 and 65

20b Manchester Regiment, 7 pieces, illustrated pages 37 and 81

21b Northumberland Fusiliers (active service), 7 pieces, illustrated page 37

22b Bluejackets, Royal Navy, 7 pieces, illustrated page 88

23b Cameron Highlanders (active service), 7 pieces, illustrated page 77

24b Whitejackets, Royal Navy, 7 pieces, illustrated page 88

25b Japanese Infantry, 7 pieces, illustrated page 124

26b Russian Infantry, 7 pieces, illustrated page 124

Other unlisted small-size figures were produced by Britains' Paris office, see page 132.

The W series

Between the two world wars, the only best-quality small-size sets that Britains continued to make were sets 125 and 126, the Royal Artillery gun teams. In order to continue offering a full range of cheaper toys, however, a number of the figures from the best-quality small size were continued in second-quality paint, and these formed the cheapest sets available in Britains range. The cavalry were adapted so that all the small second grade were with fixed arms (22-28). The infantry had never had movable arms in any case. The three types of miniature cavalry (see page 61) were also incorporated into the W series. Another early fixed-arm cavalryman, the Life Guard on the head-down horse (see page 64), was used by the Paris Office (see page 132). The toy soldiers in the W series until 1932 are listed below. The early sets of toy kitchen utensils have been omitted.

7w The Life Guards, 4 cavalry trotting

8w Hussars, 4 cavalry at the halt, illustrated page 53

9w Lancers, 4 cavalry trotting

10w Infantry of the Line, 6 men marching, illustrated page 81

11w Grenadier Guards, 6 men running, illustrated page 69

12w Highlanders, 6 men marching, illustrated page 77

13w The Life Guards, 6 gilt mini-cavalry, illustrated page 61

14w Hussars, 6 gilt mini-cavalry, illustrated page 61

15w Lancers, 6 gilt mini-cavalry, illustrated page 61

18w The Scots Greys, 4 cavalry at the trot, illustrated page 52

19w Sailors (Bluejackets) RN, 6 men at the slope, illustrated page 88

20w Sailors (Whitejackets) RN, 6 men at the slope, illustrated page 88

21w British Army Encampment with tent, 9 pieces

22w British Army Encampment with tent, trees and shrubs, 15 pieces

23w British Army encampment with tent, trees, shrubs and gun, 28 pieces

24w British Army Encampment with tents, trees, shrubs and guns, 42 pieces.

It is interesting to note that five British Army Encampment sets appear on page 15 of the 1915 Britains catalogue, numbered 01, 02, 04, 05 and 06. These are illustrated as containing second-grade figures, all in the small size except for 06, which contained standard-size figures but the same tents, trees, shrubs and guns as the other four. The four W series sets correspond closely in size with the 1915 illustrated sets, but presumably contained later version figures. (See also page 85.)

Set 41 was the highest number in the 1931 catalogue, and sets 25w to 41w inclusive were new sizes and combinations of figures appearing in earlier sets. New arrivals in 1933 are the US Cavalry and Infantry (see page 156) and the Cowboys and Indians (see page 157), and sets and combinations of these, together with more new sets of earlier figures, brought the tally of W series sets up to 65w by the end of 1933.

A number of the figures in the W series were also sold individually and numbered in a D series.

Figure type and sequence glossary

The purpose of this glossary

There is a twofold purpose to this glossary. First, to list the *types* of figure that Britains used widely, that is, as in more than two sets, and to group them together by posture. Second, to follow the *sequences* of improvements that Britains made to individual types of figure. The result is organized into 25 groupings, mostly containing sequences of a particular type, although individual multi-use figures may be included. NB As in the rest of this book, the sequences *only* cover models produced during the years 1893 to 1932.

SEQUENCING

Britains' product line remained very consistent throughout the entire period 1893 to 1966, and many sets stayed available from their first issue until near the end of production. As the business evolved, however, and in line with the company's aims of improving quality and value, the models making up a set changed from time to time – as Britains hoped, for the better.

A major change in a figure is known as a different *version*. In the context of a set, a change of version means a change in the figure making up the majority of the set rather than in auxiliary pieces such as officers or single musicians. In the early era, before the First World War, changes of version were relatively frequent, and the complete tally of different versions through which a figure went is known as a *sequence*.

Minor changes – in paint, arms, heads, under-base engraving or small parts of the main mould – are termed *variations*. It is generally up to the individual collector to decide for himself whether to describe a change as a version or a variation, and some changes are on the borderline. For instance, most figures changed from an oval to a square base between about 1908 and 1912, although no other changes were made to the figures at all. Because the oval base is so distinctive, however, it is quite normal to talk of 'the oval-based version'.

Similarly, there was usually no difference at all in the mould of models in the same set immediately before and after the Second World War, but as the paint style evolved after 1940 was markedly different from that which had gone before, principally in the absence of moustaches, the later figure is often referred to as 'the post-war version'. Variations are particularly useful in pointing to a date of manufacture, since, in combination with other matters discussed in Part Two (page 9) such as paint and parts, the date of a figure can often be accurately determined.

Types of figures are the basic postures used for Britains' models, eg marching or attention for infantry, and at the halt or at the gallop for cavalry. In the Type and Sequence Glossary that follows, all the types of figure used for more than one or two individual sets are illustrated in the sequences through which they went. Then the sets in which they appeared are listed, with a cross-reference to illustrations elsewhere in the book. It is soon apparent that the types of figures used in a widespread way is quite few, but between them they account for the contents of a remarkable number of sets. Some types introduced had no sequence since they were never changed. These are just shown as the single type with the list of sets using them.

The Glossary is arranged as follows:

MOUNTED FIGURES AND HORSES
(illustrated page 171)
Group 1 Household Cavalry at the walk
Group 2 Hussar at the canter
Group 3 Prancing-horse officer
Group 4 Dragoon at the walk
Group 5 Head-up trotting horse
Group 6 Horses at the gallop – full stretch
Group 7 Other galloping horses
Group 8 Horses at the halt
Group 9 Spindly horses
Group 10 Team horses
Group 11 Indian Empire cavalry

Group 12 Troops on camels.

INFANTRY
(illustrated page 175)
Group 13 Firing
Group 14 Officers with binoculars
Group 15 On guard
Group 16 Running and charging
Group 17 Marching at the slope
Group 18 Marching officers
Group 19 Highlanders marching
Group 20 Marching at the trail
Group 21 Indian Empire infantry
Group 22 Drill positions
Group 23 Musicians
Group 24 Seated figures
Group 25 Foreign soldiers.

GROUP 1 HOUSEHOLD CAVALRY AT THE WALK

Sequence: 1.2.3.4.

1 Germanic version, used from 1893 to 1897.
2 Normal Household Cavalry figure with tin sword and fixed arm, used from 1897 to 1902.
3 Normal Household Cavalry figure with movable arm, but horse still one-eared, used from 1902 to 1925.
4 Standard two-eared version, used from 1925 onwards.

Used in sets:
1 Life Guards, all four versions, pages 40 and 44.
2 Horse Guards, all four versions, pages 40 and 44.
3 5th Dragoon Guards, versions 1 and 2, pages 40 and 49.
72 1837 Life Guards, versions 2 and 3, page 44.
101 and 103 Household Cavalry Bands, were always mounted on a modified version 3, page 45.
Paris office, the Spanish Dragoons on page 129 are a repainted version 3 from set 72.
400 The Life Guards in Cloaks, are based on version 4, page 44.

GROUP 2 HUSSARS AT THE CANTER

Sequence: 1.3.4.

1 The donkey horse, so called because of its resemblance to that animal and its rather large head. It was a fixed-arm Hussar carrying a carbine, used from 1893 to 1903.
2 Movable-arm pony horse, so called because it was a rather smaller horse than the later norm; used from 1899 to 1903. An interesting variation is that some models had high pointed ears, whereas others did not, as illustrated here. There was also a fixed-arm variation of this model used as an X series Dragoon (2A).
3 Cantering horse, dated 12.2.1903. This model with an embossed date was used from 1903 to 1923.
4 Cantering horse, undated, used from 1923 onwards. The only difference between this and the dated figure is in the slightly larger rider's head and the long carbine, but these, the absence of the date and the evolving paint style are enough to justify it as a different version.

Used in sets:
12 11th Hussars, versions 1, 3 and 4. The pony horse may have been used for a short period, but not for long enough to count it as a standard version for this set, page 53.
13 3rd Hussars, versions 1, 3 and 4. An example of a pony horse 3rd Hussar is shown on page 53, but, as with set 12, this was not at all common, pages 33 and 53.
83 Middlesex Yeomanry, versions 1, 3 and 4. Until 1926 there were normally only two of this type in each set, the other two troopers coming from sequence 6. Thereafter, all four troopers were version 4. Page 53.
73 A full-dress version of the 17th Lancers was sometimes included in this set in the very early days, based on version 2.
81 17th Lancers in Ulundi foreign-service dress. The first version of this was from group 6, but from 1899 it was version 2 for a period before changing to group 5, although the trumpeter changed to versions 3 and 4, pages 97 and 104.
93(?) There was a variation of the Royal Horse Guards with carbines based on version 2. Whether this was a part of set 93 or not is unproven, but it seems the most likely possibility, page 44.
99 13th Hussars, versions 2, 3 and 4, page 53.
100 21st Lancers, versions 2, 3 and 4, pages 33 and 57.
115 Egyptian Cavalry, versions 2, 3 and 4, page 108.

The following figures were made with version 3 and continued with version 4:
135 Japanese Cavalry trooper, page 124.
138 French Cuirassier officer, page 132.
139 French Chasseur officer, page 132.
140 French Dragon officer, page 128.
144 Royal Field Artillery officer, page 89.
144a Royal Field Artillery officer in khaki, page 144.

153 Prussian Hussars, officer and troopers, page 133.
159 Territorial Yeomanry officer, page 140.
160 Territorial Infantry officer (only until 1916), page 140.
170 Greek Cavalry officer, page 125.
190 Belgian Cavalry officer.
Paris Office Officer of Spanish Dragoons, with throat plume, page 129.
The following figures were made only with version 4:
253 Mounted officer of the Welsh Guards, page 69.
438 Mounted officer of the Grenadier Guards, page 69.
The cantering horse remained one of Britain's most popular mounted types from 1932 until the end of production.

GROUP 3 PRANCING-HORSE OFFICER

The officer on the prancing horse is one of the most typical and evocative of Britains figures. My belief is that it was first created in 1893 or shortly afterwards as an officer for the donkey-horse Hussar sets, the horse being complete with throat plume. It was then realized that with a head change and the throat plume clipped off it could also be used for the Household Cavalry and Dragoon Guards.

Sequence: 1.2.3.

1 Fixed-arm figure with a tin sword, used from 1893 to 1907.
2 Reworked version 1 with a movable arm and a rectangular base instead of the original wedge shape. The reworking was probably done so that the figure would fit into CW Beiser's patent clip (see page 150). Used only from 1907 to 1910.
3 Entirely new version dated 19.10.1909, included in sets from 1910 onwards. From shortly after the First World War, the date was no longer shown underneath the base. The figure did not feature a throat plume for any set.

The following sets used all three versions:
1 Life Guards, page 44.
2 Royal Horse Guards, page 44.
3 5th Dragoon Guards, page 49.
12 11th Hussars (versions 1 and 2 with throat plume), page 53.
13 3rd Hussars (versions 1 and 2 with throat plume), page 53.
31 1st Dragoons (versions 1 and 2 with throat plume), page 52.
72 1897 Life Guards, page 44.
83 Middlesex Yeomanry (versions 1 and 2 with throat plume), page 65.
Only version 2 seems to have been used for the Beiser clip sets in the UK list, each of which had a mounted officer. These were sets 148, Royal Lancaster Regiment (page 106), and 149, American Soldiers (page 153). There was no real reason why the 1909 prancing horse should not have been fitted to these sets, except

possibly that the base was larger. However, I have never seen either of these officers on a 1909 pattern prancing horse, nor does the 1909 horse appear to have gone overseas to the American Soldier Company.

On page 49 there is an example of a version 2 officer for set 127, 7th Dragoon Guards, but it was not normal for this set to be provided with this type as an officer, and so that example must be counted as an unusual variation. After set 149, no new set during our period was introduced with a prancing-horse officer. However, the un-numbered 'red Territorials' were provided with one (see page 61).

GROUP 4 DRAGOON AT THE WALK

Sequence: 1.2.3

1 Fixed-arm figure with tin sword, used from 1895 to 1903. This figure was a slightly larger scale than normal.
2 Long-rein Scots Greys walking horse dated 1.11.1902, the first horse produced by Britains with two distinct, separately moulded ears. Used from 1903 to 1910.
3 Short-rein Scots Greys walking horse also at first dated 1.11.1902. This is simply the same as version 2, but with the reins moulded to droop distinctively less under the horse's neck.

Sets using all three versions:
31 1st Dragoons, page 52.
32 2nd Dragoons, Royal Scots Greys, pages 33 and 52. The only other guise in which all three versions appeared was as officers of the Foot Guards for sets 56 (Grenadier Guard) and 93 (Coldstream Guard), page 69. Sometimes, this Foot Guards officer figure was used to produce a set of Scots Greys, page 52, and sometimes the Scots Greys figure was used as an officer of the Foot Guards, page 69.

Sets using the second version:
When Britains first produced this version, they could well (ICP) have been so pleased with it that they tried it out in several sets, until other types of improved cavalry horses became available. This would account for the 5th Dragoon Guards variation, page 33, and the 3rd Hussars variation, page 53. Version 2 was also adapted for:
138 French Cuirassiers, page 132.
CFE Army Service Supply Column Officer, page 120.
229 US Cavalry in service dress, page 156.

Version 3 was used for:
175 Austrian Lancers, page 125.
218 Spanish Cavalry, page 125.
437 Mounted officer of the Gordon Highlanders, page 77.
Subsequently, after 1932, several new models appeared based on version 2, and certainly the French Cuirassiers often appeared with short reins, so the distinction between versions 2 and 3 has always been rather slight.

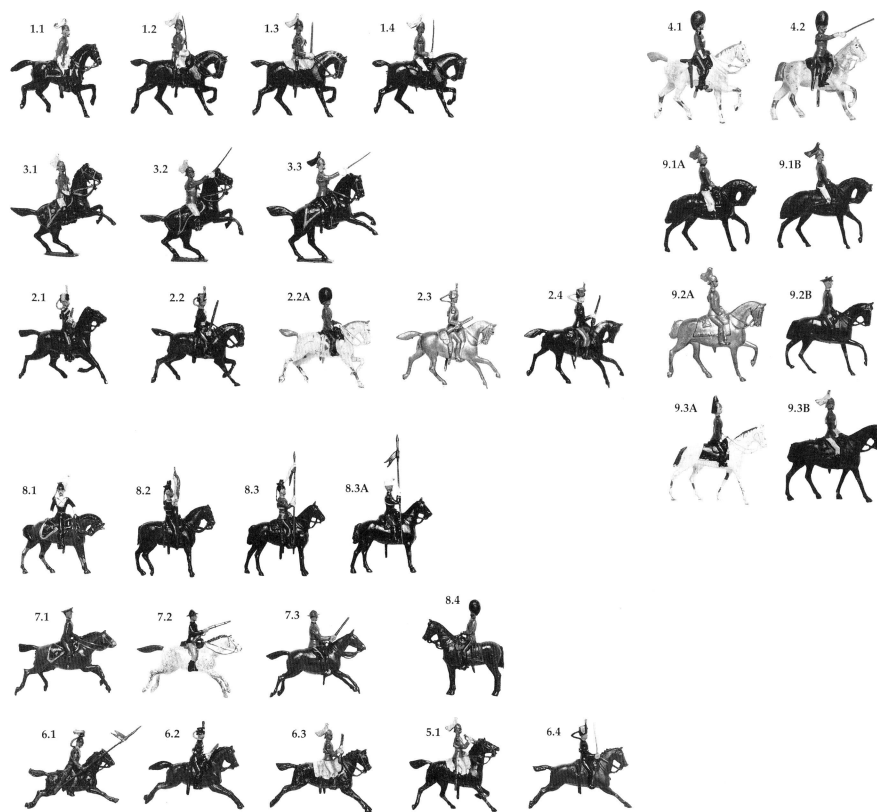
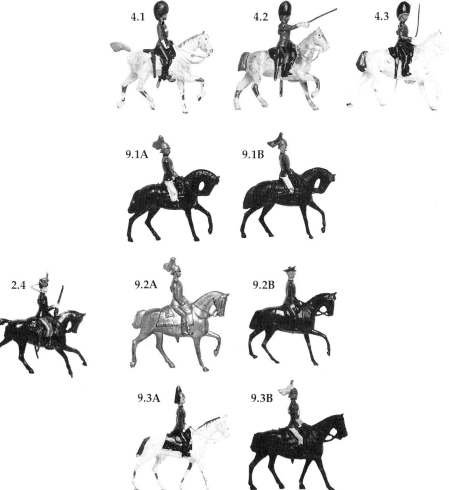

1.1 1.2 1.3 1.4 4.1 4.2 4.3

3.1 3.2 3.3 9.1A 9.1B

2.1 2.2 2.2A 2.3 2.4 9.2A 9.2B

9.3A 9.3B

8.1 8.2 8.3 8.3A

7.1 7.2 7.3 8.4

6.1 6.2 6.3 5.1 6.4

GROUP 5 HEAD-UP TROTTING HORSE, DATED 12.12.1902

This cavalry figure was made as one of the new, improved models for the mounted sets. Since it was not predominantly used to replace any particular previous figure, the type does not fit into any sequence, but stands on its own, as it was never further improved, although as usual the date was not shown after about 1924. It was a very popular figure with Britains, in use right through until 1966.

Used in sets:

3 5th Dragoon Guards, which had previously followed sequence 1, page 49.

8 4th Hussars, for the trumpeter only, page 53.

39 Royal Horse Artillery, for the mounted gunners with carbines, page 93.

39a Royal Horse Artillery in service dress, also for the mounted gunners, page 144.

43 2nd Life Guards, for the trumpeter only, page 44.

44 2nd Dragoon Guards, for the trumpeter only, page 49.

81 17th Lancers in Ulundi foreign-service dress, used for the troopers and trumpeter, page 105.

127 7th Dragoon Guards, used for the troopers, page 33.

128 12th Lancers, for the officer, page 57.

129 For the 13 troopers of the 1st Kings Dragoon Guards that appeared in this set, pages 48 and 49.

135 Japanese Cavalry, for the officer, page 124.

139 French Chasseurs à cheval. An adaptation of the type was done, equipping it with continental-style horse furniture and a blanket roll. The resulting model was given an extra date, thus reading '12.12.1902 & 9.5.1905'. Sometimes the same set would appear on the original horse with the English-style equipment, in which case it only had the single original date. This type was used for the troopers only, page 132.

159 Territorial Yeomanry, for troopers only, page 140.

170 Greek Cavalry, for troopers only, page 125.

176 Austrian Dragoons, page 125.

217 Argentine Cavalry, a modified figure, page 160.

220 Uruguayan Cavalry, identical to the Argentine in all but paint, page 160.

GROUP 6 HORSES AT THE GALLOP, FULL STRETCH

1 Plug-shouldered Lancer. Although this was the earliest Britains' horse at the full gallop, it is not really part of a sequence, in that it was only used from 1893 to 1895 and only for three unnumbered sets, of the 12th, 16th and 17th Lancers, pages 56 and 57. However, like the other versions in this sequence, all four of the horse's legs are extended outwards, as if the animal is about to do a belly flop. When these figures were first made, it was generally believed that the galloping action of a horse really did include this pose, and by the time

people generally knew better the pose had become traditional for Britains. The plug-shouldered Lancer was rather small compared with Britains' other figures, and the next galloping cavalryman was considerably bigger.

Sequence: 2.3.4

2 Rocking-horse figure, so called because the full stretch pose is like a traditional Victorian rocking horse. First made in 1896, it has the distinction of being the first Britains figure with the normal stud and loop style fitting for the movable arm. In use until 1902.

3 One-eared galloping horse, dated 1.1.1901. This was the earliest of the improved models brought in for any of Britains' standard cavalry types. It was phased in from 1901, and in use until about 1924. Perhaps the reason why it did not have two separate horse's ears was because William Britain Junior had not yet thought of this refinement. Certainly up to and including this figure, all Britains' cavalry horses had their ears moulded in one piece, but starting with the next new horse, the Scots Greys walking horse (see group 4), all the new standard-scale models except the 1906 wagon team horses had separately modelled ears.

4 Two-eared galloping horse. From 1924 onwards, the slight missing improvement was carried out.

Sets using versions 2, 3 and 4:

8 4th Hussars, page 33 and 53.

43 2nd Life Guards, page 44.

44 2nd Dragoon Guards, page 49.

49 South Australian Lancers, page 101.

81 17th Lancers, Ulundi foreign-service dress, page 105. Converted to pony horse then type 5 from 1899.

83 Middlesex Yeomanry, normally only two troopers, with all troopers in sequence 2 after 1928, page 53.

93 Royal Horse Guards with lances, and two trumpeters, which formed part of this large display set, page 44.

94 21st Lancers in Omdurman foreign-service dress, page 108.

Where the above sets contained a trumpeter, this was usually switched to a group 5 horse when this model became available in 1903.

The following sets used versions 3 and 4 only:

102 Foot Guards display, containing a mounted officer of the Irish Guards on the galloping horse, to go with a row of Guards running at the trail, page 69.

106 6th Dragoon Guards, for troopers only, page 49.

127 7th Dragoon Guards, for officer only, page 49.

129 for the officer of the 1st Dragoon Guards, pages 48 and 49.

From the issue of set 129 in 1906, Britains never again produced a new set using the full-stretch galloping horse, although Royal Horse Artillery mounted gunners were switched to this horse after our period. Otherwise, it preferred to use the more realistic type developed in

1927 (see group 7, version 3). Nevertheless, Britains did not discontinue the full-stretch galloping type, and all the sets described continued to use it until they reached the end of their production.

GROUP 7 OTHER GALLOPING HORSES

1 RHA officer's horse. This magnificent horse was created for the rather special set 39 in 1895, and was only used in that set for the officer, page 92. Apart from the khaki version of the same set, 39a, shown here, and page 144, the only other catalogued set to use it was 106, 6th Dragoon Guards, whose officer was also accorded the privilege of riding this spirited steed, page 33. The figure was fixed-arm, and used for these three sets throughout our period. Apart from this, it was a Britains' favourite for use as a special casting or painting in the 1930s.

Sequence: 2.3

2 Boer Cavalry horse, in use from 1898 to 1928, a fixed-arm figure with the arm holding a rifle or pistol.

3 US Cavalry in action horse, in use from 1928 onwards.

Only one set used a sequence from the above figures.

6 Boer Cavalry. This set was dropped from the catalogue long before version 3 was available, page 120.

38 South African Mounted Infantry used versions 2 and 3, page 121.

276 US Cavalry in action, the set for which version 3 was designed in 1928, with a movable arm with rifle, page 156. The same figure was also later used for the mounted Royal Canadian Mounted Police. US Cavalry specials of version 2 are shown on page 153.

GROUP 8 HORSES AT THE HALT

1 Lancer officer turned in the saddle. This archetypal Britains figure, almost certainly inspired by a Richard Simkin painting, was the officer used throughout our period for all sets of Lancers at the halt. These were:

23 5th Irish Lancers, page 56.

24 9th Lancers, page 33.

33 16th Lancers, page 57.

As well as these, it was used as the officer for the row of 17th Lancers in set 73, page 97, and sometimes appeared as an officer for the similar single-row set 81, page 105. The figure continued to be used until the end of production, the only figure with a tin sword to be so, and was probably of all Britains' figures the one in continuous use for the longest period, 1895 to 1966.

Sequence: 2.3

2 Cross-legged Lancer, so called because the rear left leg almost crosses the rear right, as if the horse is a little restless and having a bit of a scratch at a fetlock. The whole stance is both charming and typical of real life, more so, perhaps, than is strictly desirable for a toy soldier but then these touches of master modelling are one of the hallmarks of Britains.

3 Horse at the halt, dated 18.8.1903. This became the standard horse at the halt of the Britains army.

The three sets detailed under version 1 used the sequence of 2 and 3 for the four troopers in the set. As well as the Lancers, the following sets used version 3:

140 French Dragons, used for the troopers only. The horse was given continental equipment and used for European armies, being double dated 18.8.1903 & 9.5.1905, page 128.

165 Italian Cavalry (3A). Normally, this set used the adapted horse with continental equipment, but the earliest set I have seen is on the English pattern with just the single date, and this variation continued to turn up from time to time, page 133.

182 11th Hussars dismounted. The horse for this set was an adaptation of the horse at the halt without a rider, page 53, and is endlessly useful in displays. Britains also did a similar model without saddle or equipment, but just what this was intended for is not known.

190 Belgian Cavalry, used for the four troopers only. Sometimes appeared with English pattern equipment, as with set 165 above, page 125.

270 11th Hussars, used with Hussar heads for an officer and four troopers mounted at the halt, the other row of this double row set being the same as set 182, page 53.

315 10th Hussars, used for officer and four troopers, page 33.

316 RHA at the halt, used for the mounted officer, page 89.

317 RFA at the halt, used for the mounted officer.

318 RA service dress at the halt, used for the mounted officer.

4 Sway-backed horse at the halt, not part of a sequence, but the other multi-use horse at the halt. Since this figure originally appeared without embossing or date, and is of the one-eared variety, it must have been created before 1900, possibly as an individually sold figure of a general officer.

Used in sets:

111 Grenadier Guards at attention, used as mounted officer, page 69.

130 Display set of Scots Guards, used as general officer and mounted Guards officer, page 68.

131 Large display set, used as general officer, page 64.

132 Large display set, used as general officer, page 64.

The figure was also used for mounted officers by the Paris Office.

GROUP 9 SPINDLY HORSES

These are so called because they look distinctly thin in contrast with the standard best-quality models, particularly as seen in their spindly legs. They are the main type used for second-grade mounted figures, page

163, but they also had a limited use as mounted officers in the best quality, which are listed below. All models were fixed-arm and one-eared. The illustration (page 171) shows the three figures in use, the left-hand version (A) being the earliest, with slightly thicker legs, the right-hand (B) being introduced 1910 (dated 9.5.1910), possibly to reduce the amount of metal needed.

1 Head-down figure.

2 Head-level figure.

3 Head-up figure.

Figure 1 early version was used for best-quality officers until about 1911, after which figure 3 late version was used for the rest of our period. Sets in which these were used are as follows:

19 West India Regiment, page 101.

28 Mountain Artillery, page 108.

36 Royal Sussex Regiment, page 84.

In addition to these, a special variation of the later figure 1 was made with a base between the two rear hooves, in order to fit into Parade Series baseboards, and these were used both in the best quality and in the second grade. Examples of these figures are shown on pages 81 and 84. Known sets in which they were included are 447, West Surrey Regiment, 448, 7th Royal Fusiliers, and 480, Middlesex Regiment. See also page 188 for a detailed listing of the Parade Series.

GROUP 10 TEAM HORSES
(not illustrated)

The galloping team horse was used only for the RHA sets 39 and 39a during our period, and is therefore not dealt with here (see page 91).

Sequence: 1.2

1 Collar-harness walking team horses. These were always used in pairs, the one on the left carrying the driver, and the one on the right having none, but carrying a valise where the saddle would have been. Dated 14.3.1906 and used from then until 1924.

2 Light-harness walking team horses, used in pairs as version 1, but equipped with breast harness and without valises. This was a two-eared figure as opposed to the one-eared version 1. These team horses were used from 1924 until the end of production for all walking team applications except for the state coaches. Versions 1 and 2 were used in the following sets:

144 Royal Field Artillery, page 89.

145 Army Medical Corps Ambulance, page 112.

146 Army Service Corps supply wagon, page 112.

CFE Army Service Supply column, version 1 only, page 120.

144a RFA service dress, page 144.

145a RAMC ambulance in service dress.

146a RASC supply wagon in service dress, page 141.

These three team sets with khaki service dress drivers were issued in 1916.

Version 1 horses were also used to pull wagons of French, Spanish and no doubt other nationalities issued by the Paris Office, see pages 129 and 162.

203 Royal Engineers Pontoon Section, page 112.

Version 2 only was used in the following sets:

1 18 inch Howitzer with limber and 10-horse team, page 145. The introduction of this set was probably made the occasion for remodelling the team horses as version 2.

203a Royal Engineers Pontoon Section, service dress. Team horses at the halt were issued in 1929 with the three new artillery sets 316, page 89, 317 and 318.

GROUP 11 INDIAN CAVALRY FIGURE
(not illustrated)

In addition to being used for all the Indian Empire cavalry regiments, pages 100 and 101, this figure was also used for set 71, Turkish Cavalry, page 125. This was, as one might expect, a one-eared horse, but it was not remodelled, except for the later addition of lettering under the belly, and remained the same as it always had been until the end of production.

GROUP 12 TROOPS ON CAMELS
(not illustrated)

Sequence: 1.2

1 Camel with tail made of a short piece of wire, laid into the mould.

2 Camel with tail detailed as part of the mould.

The three sets containing troops on camels all used both versions, and they were:

48 Egyptian Camel Corps, page 108.

123 Bikanir Camel Corps, page 100.

131 As part of this giant display set, were nine British Camel Corps, page 108.

Normally the camels were exactly the same for all three sets, and the riders could be taken off separately. For a period in the 1920s and 1930s, however, the riders were lightly soldered to the camels. The Arab on camel, set 193, page 109, was a completely different, unique model.

GROUP 13 FIRING FIGURES
(not illustrated)

1 Volley-firing Foot Guard. Used exclusively for set 34, Grenadier Guards, page 69, but it seems correct to include it here since the set switched to the standing version 2 when this became available.

Sequence: 2.3

2 Firing figures, standing, kneeling and lying, also available in modified form as Highlanders in foreign-service helmets. Dated 1.7.1901.

3 In about 1932, Britains realized that the version 2 lying firing figure was rather odd – a feet together position which, if used in real life to fire a rifle, would have been disastrously unstable. A new prone firing position with the feet apart was designed and put into production at just about the end of our period (2A). Examples of these are quite rare (pages 69 and 81), since almost immediately afterwards, and as one of the characteristics of the next period of production, all the firing figures were given full trousers rather than the gaiters they had worn until 1934. The full-trouser figures are thus version 3, at which time minor alterations were also made to the Highland figures. The following sets used versions 2 and 3:

34 Grenadier Guards, standing, page 37.
89 Cameron Highlanders, standing, kneeling and lying, page 76.
90 Coldstream Guards, standing, kneeling and lying, page 69.
118 Gordon Highlanders, lying, page 77.
119 Gloucestershire Regiment, standing, with the model modified for Boer War service dress with puttees, pages 37 and 117.
120 Coldstream Guards, kneeling, page 37.
121 Royal West Surrey Regiment, standing, page 81.
122 Black Watch, standing, page 77.
124 Irish Guards, lying, page 69.
130 Scots Guards, standing, kneeling and lying, as part of a large display box, page 68.
156 Royal Irish Regiment, standing, kneeling and lying, page 81.
157 Gordon Highlanders, standing, kneeling and lying, page 77.

GROUP 14 OFFICERS WITH BINOCULARS

To accompany the firing sets, Britains issued officers with binoculars, presumably to observe the results of the shooting. Only sets with troops actually firing had one of these officers; sets on guard, for instance, only had marching officers. None of the officers with binoculars was so sensible as to lie down, so sets of prone troops were led by a kneeling officer. Looking again at the list of sets for group 13, standing officers were issued to sets 89, 90, 121, 122 and 130, while kneeling officers were issued to sets 89, 90, 118, 120, 124 and 130. Thus the three large sets, 89, 90 and 130, had both officers, but the 10-piece mixed-position firing sets 156 and 157 had neither, set 34 continued as it had started with a marching officer, and set 119 was not provided with an officer. In concert with the firing men, the officers were also given full trousers in 1934. Examples of the officers will be found under the same page references as in group 13. A noteworthy variation in the Highland officers was the smooth helmet worn by the very earliest examples, page 77. One of the mounted staff officers used the same binocular arms as these infantry officers. In later periods, officers with binoculars were used more widely. There were also

examples issued by the Paris Office, page 162.

GROUP 15 ON GUARD

Sequence: 1.2

1 Oval-based infantryman standing on guard, one of the very first infantry figures, created for set 16, issued in 1894. It was used in some sets in combination with a kneeling on-guard figure, which held the rifle more upright than the later figures and had a broad leaf-shaped bayonet. Early figures had a small base attached to the front foot, although later variations did without this support.
2 Square-based infantryman, dated 17.1.1910. It is assumed that the kneeling figure was also remodelled at this date, although the figure has no room for an embossed date to be shown. Immediately after our period, both these figures were remodelled with full trousers, in line with the firing figures.

Sets using versions 1 and 2:
16 East Kent Regiment, the Buffs, standing, pages 37 and 84.
17 Somerset Light Infantry, standing and kneeling pages 37, 81 and 84.
18 Worcestershire Regiment, standing and kneeling, pages 81 and 84.
29 Royal West Surrey Regiment, standing, as part of a larger display box, page 81.
131 East Kent Regiment, it is possible that examples of kneeling figures in yellow facings are Buffs from this large display set, used here in addition to standing figures.

Sets using modified figures:
104 City Imperial Volunteers, used a modified standing version 1 which may actually have been built from scratch, as it has its own date, 1.6.1900, page 121.
167 Turkish Infantry, used version 2 with a new head, page 125.
189 Belgian infantry, used a heavily modified version 2.
3 Officer on guard. This was modelled for set 104 and was a splendid figure with sword and pistol, much more suitable to go with on-guard figures than the marching officer usually supplied. At first, this officer only appeared with set 104, City Imperial Volunteers, page 121, but when other sets of on-guard figures with puttees appeared (see below) this officer was given to sets 26, page 117, and 91, page 152.
4 On guard with puttees. Dated 15.6.1906, this figure was probably developed as a US infantryman for the deal with CW Beiser, see page 150.
Used in sets:
26 Boer Infantry, as a second version, page 117.
91 US Infantry, also as a second version, page 152.
Associated with this figure is another figure of the same date, marching at the shoulder, also used in set 26, possibly in set 91 and with the on-guard figure in many

American Soldier Company sets, page 151 (4A).

GROUP 16 RUNNING FIGURES

Sequence: 1.2.3

1 Pigeon-chested figure, so called because the chest is pronounced as in a pigeon. The figure usually carried a rifle at the trail, but was also used as an officer with a sword arm, was introduced in 1899 and remained in use until about 1922.
2 Open-elbow figure, a new running figure with full trousers, and somewhat more upright than the pigeon-chested version. In this model, the fixed arm is held away from the chest so that there is an opening between the arm and the body. In use from about 1922 to about 1928.
3 Closed-elbow figure, yet another modification of the running figure, but here there is no hole between the fixed arm and the body, hence 'closed elbow'. This figure was used from about 1928 until the end of production.
Sets using running figures were as follows:
70 Scots Guards. There is major doubt about the existence of this set, as it has never been confirmed by a catalogue listing or the discovery of a box.
93 Coldstream Guards, as part of a large display, page 69.
96 York and Lancaster Regiment, probably the first single-row set to use the running figure. First version in khaki with smooth foreign-service helmet, as at the Battle of Omdurman, page 117, second version, still using version 1 of group 16, in standard Infantry of the Line uniform with spiked helmet, pages 37 and 81.
97 Royal Marine Light Infantry, page 88.
98 King's Royal Rifle Corps, pages 37 and 88.
102 Irish Guards, as a row in a mixed Foot Guards display box, page 69.
130 Scots Guards, as a row in this large display box, page 68.
148 Royal Lancaster Regiment. Version 1 was given a square base to fit the clips in which this set was packed, and the square base was used for version 1 figures in all sets from about 1907, page 104.
149 American soldiers, the companion set to 148, page 152.
171 Greek Infantry, page 125.
The above sets used all three versions except for sets 148 and 149, which only used version 1, since they were discontinued after 1916. The running figure was used for a set officer in sets 96, 97, 98, 148, 149 and 171. Sets 148 and 149 contained in addition three figures at the slope, trumpeter and standard bearer, all using the running figure, and the figure was used extensively for American Soldier Company sets, page 151.

Sequence: 4.5

4 Naval running figure, somewhat similar to the

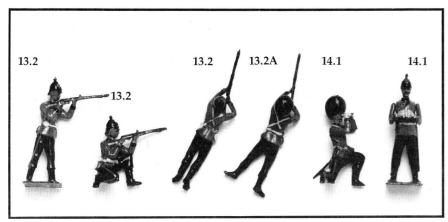

13.2 13.2 13.2 13.2A 14.1 14.1

16.1 16.2 16.3 15.1 15.2 15.1 15.2

16.4 16.5 17.1 17.2 17.3 17.4

18.1 18.2 18.3 20.1 20.2 24.1 24.2

23.1 23.2 23.3 23.4 23.5 23.6

22.1 22.2 22.3 22.3A 22.4

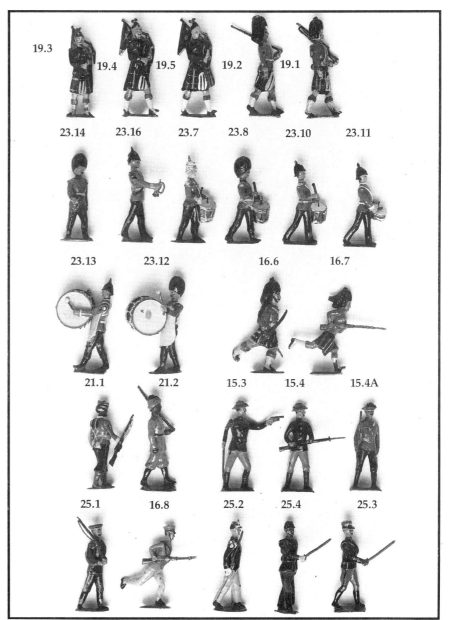

19.3 19.4 19.5 19.2 19.1

23.14 23.16 23.7 23.8 23.10 23.11

23.13 23.12 16.6 16.7

21.1 21.2 15.3 15.4 15.4A

25.1 16.8 25.2 25.4 25.3

infantry model, but actually preceding it in date of issue. In use from 1898 to about 1922.

5 Naval running figure, rather more upright than its predecessor and with a larger head. Used from about 1922 to the end of production.

Used in sets:

78 Bluejackets at the trail, page 88.

80 Whitejackets at the slope, although at the trail with version 5, page 88.

143 French Matelots, using a different head and arm, page 132.

The above sets all used both versions 4 and 5. The officer for sets 78 and 80 was a separately modelled running petty officer, also used for set 79, page 88.

Sequence: 6.7

6 Plug-handed Highlander, the other running figure made by Britains and used in several sets, and which pre-dates all the other versions detailed above. Issued 1893 and in use until 1904.

Used in sets:

11 Black Watch.

15 Argyll and Sutherland Highlanders.

77 Gordon Highlanders.

88 Seaforth Highlanders.

The figure is described in detail on page 39.

7 Charging Highlander, dated 17.12.1903, the figure that is sequential to the plug-handed Highlander for all the above sets except 77, pages 37 and 77. No further sets of charging Highlanders were introduced, so this fixed-arm figure remained limited to these three sets. The figure started with an oval base, and was converted to a square one in about 1910. The engravings underneath the base are particularly attractive, page 18.

8 Japanese charging figure, the only other multi-use charging figure made during our period (discounting the Zouave-Turco, page 132). It was only used for two foreign infantry sets during our period, although it was used for second-grade figures later. Issued in 1904, fixed arm on an oval base, which it retained throughout production. Used in sets:

134 Japanese Infantry, page 124.

173 Serbian Infantry, page 125.

There was no officer figure in these sets.

GROUP 17 MARCHING FIGURES

1 Fixed-arm valise pack, introduced in 1895, in use until about 1910. The rifle was carried on the right shoulder in the style of the German army, which may suggest that this figure was designed in Germany as part of the germanic group, since it was also rather out of scale (50 mm).

Used for sets

29 Royal West Surrey Regiment, as part of a larger

display set, page 81. This set continued with version 2 from 1897.

36 Royal Sussex Regiment, pages 37 and 84. This set skipped the next two versions in the marching sequence, resuming with version 4, and continuing to use version 1 until that time.

Version 1 was also extensively available as a second-grade figure.

Sequence: 2.3.4

2 Movable-arm valise pack, introduced 1897, in use until about 1905. This also was a rather small figure, but correctly had the movable arm at the slope on the left shoulder.

3 Box pack, dated 1.8.1905, taking its name from the square shape of the back pack. This figure was the full 54mm scale. In general use until about 1916.

4 1910 marching figure, dated 21.2.1910, and without pack or gaiters. The scarcity of figures actually bearing this date would lead one to suppose that the figure was not generally introduced for marching sets until after the First World War, although thereafter it became the most widespread basic marching type.

The following sets started with version 2 and remained, for the rest of their production in our period, with version 3:

7 7th Royal Fusiliers, pages 37 and 84.

9 Rifle Brigade, pages 37 and 88.

35 Royal Marine Artillery, page 88.

74 Royal Welch Fusiliers, page 84.

The following sets started with version 2 and changed to version 3 and then version 4 at the appropriate dates:

75 Scots Guards, page 69.

76 Middlesex Regiment, page 81.

82 Scots Guards Pioneers, with axes rather than a rifle, page 69.

93 Coldstream Guards, as part of this large display, page 69.

107 Irish Guards, pages 37 and 69.

The following sets started with version 2, but did not thereafter follow the marching sequence:

26 Boer Infantry, page 117.

91 US Infantry, Cuban War, page 152.

92 Spanish Infantry, page 125.

The only new set to use the box-pack figure was 154, Prussian Infantry, page 133, and this was only, it seems, on a temporary basis, the dating of which is uncertain. Sets so far discovered using version 4, dated:

36 Royal Sussex Regiment, page 81.

166 Italian Infantry, page 133.

The un-numbered red Territorial figure is a dated version 4.

After the First World War, the following additional sets were based on version 4:

177 Austrian Infantry of the Line, second version, page 125.

178 Austrian Foot Guards, second version, page 125.

253 Welsh Guards, page 37.

255 Green Howards, page 84.

438 Grenadier Guards, page 69.

GROUP 18 MARCHING OFFICERS

Sequence: 1.2.3

1 Bemedalled officer, a rather small fixed-arm figure originating in 1894. The nickname comes from the two medals prominently displayed on his chest, the only Britains officer to be awarded any; he did not carry a sword.

2 Wasp-waisted officer, so called because of his rather shapely waist. Introduced in about 1898, the figure had a movable right arm normally carrying a drawn sword. The wasp-waisted figure is quite rare, so, although it would be logical to expect to find it in sets between 1898 and 1905, it is more likely that the bemedalled figure was retained in use for some time.

3 Officer with gaiters, a new infantry officer dated 16.11.1905, brought out to complement the box-pack figure. This remained the standard infantry officer until the end of our period, after which a full-trouser figure with an empty-handed arm was introduced. Version 3 was a movable-arm figure holding an extended sword, and started on an oval base, which was changed to a square one in about 1908.

Sets using all three versions:

7 Royal Fusiliers, page 84.

9 Rifle Brigade, page 88.

16 East Kent Regiment, pages 81 and 84.

17 Somerset Light Infantry, pages 81 and 84.

18 Worcestershire Regiment, pages 81 and 84.

29 Royal West Surrey Regiment, page 81.

34 Grenadier Guards, page 69.

35 Royal Marine Artillery, page 88.

74 Royal Welch Fusiliers, page 84.

75 Scots Guards, page 69.

90 Coldstream Guards, page 69.

107 Irish Guards, page 69.

In addition, the bemedalled figure was used in the very early days of sets:

19 West India Regiment, page 101.

36 Royal Sussex Regiment, page 81.

The following sets used versions 1 and 2 only before dropping out of this sequence:

91 US Infantry, Cuban War, page 152.

92 Spanish Infantry, page 125.

Version 2 was used for a short period to provide the whole of set 76, Middlesex Regiment, pages 37 and 79, not just the officer, and the series from version 2 onwards was used to provide the standard-bearer in set 82, Scots Guards Pioneers and Colours, page 69. The version 3 officer was used in sets 166, Italian Infantry (although not exclusively, see page 133), and in set 255, Green Howards, page 84.

GROUP 19 MARCHING HIGHLANDERS

Sequence: 1.2

1 Box-pack Highlander, so called from the shape of the pack, dated 20.1.1901, thus preceding the ordinary box-pack figure (group 17) by over four years. In use from 1901 to about 1914.

2 Standard marching Highlander, introduced in about 1914, this figure being without a pack, the Highlander equivalent to the 1910 marching figure from group 17. The following sets used these figures:

77 Gordon Highlanders, which switched to version 1 from the plug-handed Highland figure (group 16) pages 37 and 77.

112 Seaforth Highlanders, which started with version 1, pages 37 and 77.

114 Cameron Highlanders in foreign-service dress, to start with in a smooth helmet, continuing with an adapted version 2, page 117.

449 Black Watch, Parade Series, page 77, which only used version 2.

Numerous display sets contained these marching Highlanders, and many special paintings were also done.

Sequence: 3.4

3 Oval-based piper. The sequence of Scottish pipers belongs here. The first figure was quite small, and in use from 1896 to about 1912. Although it was called the oval-based piper, a few were produced with square bases about 1912.

4 Square-based piper dated 1.3.1912, a taller figure, was used from 1912 until about 1935, after the end of our period, when another improved figure (illustrated as 5) was brought out with the plaid flying in the breeze. During our period, both 3 and 4 wore a glengarry cap with eagle feathers, rather than the full bonnet which appeared after our period for Scots Guard and Black Watch pipers.

Sets containing these pipers were:

69 Pipers of the Scots Guards, contained seven, page 69.

73 Large display, with four Gordon pipers, page 97.

75 Scots Guards, with one piper, page 69.

77 Gordon Highlanders, with two of version 3, but only one of version 4 after 1920, page 77.

88 Seaforth Highlanders, with two pipers, page 77.

89 Cameron Highlanders, with two pipers, page 76.

GROUP 20 MARCHING AT THE TRAIL

Sequence: 1.2

1 Slade-Wallace infantryman, so called from the pattern of equipment carried. The figure was usually provided with a trail arm on a movable right shoulder, and is dated 20.1.1901, the same as the box-pack Highlander. It was first used as a British infantryman in foreign-service dress.

2 Webbing equipment infantryman, first created as a British infantryman of the First World War, marching.

In use from 1916.

These two versions were used in sets:

109 Dublin Fusiliers, page 117.

110 Devonshire Regiment, page 117.

160 Territorial Infantry, page 140.

Two sets contained only version 1, which was oval-based until about 1910:

116 Soudanese Infantry, which remained as version 1 until 1947 when it ceased production, page 108.

CFE Army Service Supply Column, where the escorting infantry was based on this version, page 120.

One set was brought in with version 2:

195 British Infantry in Steel Helmets, page 140.

GROUP 21 INDIAN EMPIRE INFANTRY

Sequence: 1.2

1 Indian Army infantry with pack. This special figure, the first Britains infantryman with a movable right arm, was created for the purpose. In the use from 1896 to about 1924, starting on an oval base, but probably given a square base after the First World War.

2 Indian Army infantry without pack, usually with movable right arm at the slope, whereas version 1 was usually at the trail. Version 1 was revived for later sets after our period, one of the few early figures so used. Otherwise from about 1924 all Indian infantry sets used version 2.

Sets using both versions:

64 7th Bengal Infantry (being half of a two-row display set), page 101.

67 1st Madras Native Infantry, pages 100 and 101.

68 2nd Bombay Native Infantry, pages 100 and 101.

GROUP 22 DRILL POSITIONS

Sequence: 1.2

1 At attention in gaiters dated 20.1.1901, a figure initially given an arm with a rifle held more at ease than at attention. Early examples had a truly round base.

2 At attention, full trousers, introduced from about 1925. This had a rifle held in to the side in a true at-attention pose. For a short period, version 1 was issued with the new arm.

Sets using these two versions were:

102 Coldstream Guards, as one row of a mixed display set of Foot Guards. One figure carried a flag, page 69.

111 Grenadier Guards, page 69.

113 East Yorkshire Regiment, pages 37 and 81.

130 Scots Guards, as one row in a large display box, page 68.

Version 1 was also used as follows:

117 Egyptian Infantry, page 108, version 2 was never

used with this set.

148 Royal Lancaster Regiment, the gunners in this set were version 1 fitted with ramrods, page 104.

149 American Soldiers, as **148**, page 152.

As a red Territorial, page 61.

In various C.E.T. and Co sets, page 136.

By the Paris Office, page 129 and page 162.

By the American Soldier Company, page 151.

3 Present-arms early figure. This was introduced by Britains in 1923, using a drill position current at the time in which the feet turned out at about 45 degrees from the heels. The more familiar figure with one foot in advance of the other (3A) was introduced in 1937, with further sets than the two that used the version 3:

205 Coldstream Guards, page 69.

206 Warwickshire Regiment, page 37.

4 At ease, introduced 1929, being a truly at-ease figure compared with the rather uncertain attention attitude of version 1. Used in sets:

314 Coldstream Guards, page 69.

329 Sentry with sentry box, page 68. The sentry was sometimes a Grenadier, but more usually a Scots Guard.

I have also seen on two occasions a set of seven Grenadier Guards at ease with a marching officer in brown gloves, possibly a variation of set 314, page 69.

GROUP 23 MUSICIANS

Infantry bands are described in chapter 23, and illustrations of all the musicians in the various sequences below will be found there, as will detailed descriptions of the figures concerned. Here I simply list the sequences with the date on which the figures were introduced. Because the various figures in the band were changed at differing dates, a particular set can usually be dated quite closely.

Drum majors
Sequence: 1.2

1 Oval-based, fixed-arm	1895
2 With baton movable at wrist	1913

Band musicians
Sequence: 3.4.5

3 Slotted-arm	1895
4 Movable-arm gaitered	1911 dated 1.5.1911
5 Movable-arm full-trousered	1913 dated 1.5.1911

After the First World War version 5 no longer had a date embossed under the base.

Boy fifer

6 Unique figure	1929

Side-drummers
Sequence: 7.8.9.10

7 Pigeon-toed	1895

8 Heel and toe — about 1899
9 Square-based (not illustrated) — 1909
10 Full-trousered — 1934
11 Thin side-drummer — 1929

Bass-drummers
Sequence: 12.13

12 Fixed-arm — 1895
13 Movable-arm — 1909 dated 8.12.1908

Buglers
Sequence: 14.15.16

14 Boy bugler, oval base — 1895
15 Boy bugler, square base — 1909 (not illustrated)
16 Adult bugler — 1920.

Side-drummers and buglers were used in sets, apart from the Drum and Bugle set 30, as follows:
16 East Kent Regiment, one of each, pages 81 and 84.
17 Somerset Light Infantry, bugler, pages 81 and 84.
18 Worcestershire Regiment, drummer, pages 37 and 84.
29 Royal West Surrey Regiment, two of each, page 81.
34 Grenadier Guards, drummer, page 69.
90 Coldstream Guards, one of each, page 69.
93 Coldstream Guards, two buglers in addition to the band included in the display box, page 69.
130 Scots Guards, four drummers and four buglers, page 68.

255 Green Howards, drummer, page 84.
480 Middlesex Regiment, two drummers, not illustrated.
Other Parade Series sets may also have had musicians. The musicians belonging to regimental sets have facings matching the regiments'.

GROUP 24 SEATED FIGURES

Sequence: 1.2

1 Legs together, introduced 1895 for the RHA team at the gallop.
2 Legs apart, a rather larger figure with the legs more widely separated and without a moulded cross-strap. This figure was introduced in about 1924.
These seated figures were used on limbers, bucket seats on guns and on wagons as follows:
39 Royal Horse Artillery, first version only, page 92. Seated figures on this set were discontinued after 1906.
144 Royal Field Artillery, version 1 only, page 89.
144a RFA service dress, version 1 only, page 144.
145 Army Medical Corps Ambulance, page 112.
145a RAMC service dress.
146 Army Service Corps, page 112.
146a RASC service dress, page 138.
CFE Army Service Supply Column, version 1 only, page 120.

GROUP 25 FOREIGN TROOPS

These are the figures created for foreign army sets which were used for more than one other occasion.
1 Russian Infantry type, originally made for set 133, was first issued dated 16.1.1904 and used for:
133 Russian Infantry, page 124.
172 Bulgarian Infantry, page 125.
174 Montenegrin Infantry, page 125.
2 Fixed-arm French officer dated 9.5.1905, originally made for set 142, was used for:
142 French Zouaves, page 132.
Various Paris Office figures, see chapter 44.
166 Italian Infantry, as modified with movable arm (illustrated page 133).
3 French officer with blanket roll, dated 18.3.1909, probably first created for the Paris Office, was occasionally used for:
141 French Infantérie de Ligne, page 128.
142 French Zouaves.
167 Turkish Infantry, page 125.
4 Prussian officer, dated 16.2.1908, first created for set 154, was used for:
154 Prussian Infantry, as the officer, page 133.
177 Austrian Infantry of the Line, page 125.
178 Austrian Foot Guards, page 125.

All other first-quality figures were only used in one, or at the most two, sets apart from single-row set figures repeated in display sets.

Chronological and numerical index of sets

This index lists all the set numbers in the main military sequence from 1 to 500. The information is set out under yearly headings from 1893 to 1932. If it appears that a set was not issued in strict chronological order, a reference is made to the actual year of production, and the full entry is given at the point in the sequence at which the set is most likely to have been issued.

Full details are given of all those sets which contained new models, these usually being single-row sets (see Chapter 6). Display sets and sets duplicating previously used figures are very briefly detailed, with information only on the type of set. Further information on these sets is readily available from the catalogues and set listings mentioned in the Bibliography (see page 6). As far as I know, no figures other than those already described in their 'set of first use' were used in those sets not fully described in this index.

The following information is given for each set (with the exceptions noted above):
Number and title
Latest year of production; some sets continued to be produced well past our period
Type of box label used on single-row sets, where known, denoted as follows: T, typeset; P, pictorial; W, designed by Fred Whisstock. More than one symbol is given if more than one type was used.
Reference to the chapter in which the set is more fully discussed.
Usual contents found during our period including a short summary of changes of version until 1932.

Anomalies in early set numbering

Why was it that, of the sets produced early in Britains' career, five were never numbered, and why were some of the sets that were given early numbers obviously not first made until some years later?

My hypothesis is as follows: if the sets were produced in a certain order, then among the Britain family they might have been known by that order, the first set, the second set, etc. As the range developed, so these numbers would have become established, so that when, in about 1898, it became necessary to issue an official numbered list, Britains naturally used the numbers to which it was accustomed. But this meant that there would be gaps where sets had been discontinued in the meantime. Those gaps would then be filled by the next production sets to be created.

On this basis (ICP), I would expect that *all* the germanic figures were produced first, using moulds designed by outsiders (possibly German contacts). Indeed, Alfred Britain, in an interview with a Mr Grubb, a journalist, in 1910, said that he had had the first mould made. I believe, therefore, that the first William

Britain-designed figures were the donkey-horse Hussar and the cross-legged Lancer, followed by the infantryman on guard and the officers to match these sets.

Now it so happens that if we follow Richards in saying that numbers 4 and 5 were given to sets of the germanic Life Guard painted gilt, then there are just five non-sequential catalogue numbers, 6 to 10, before the Black Watch, set 11, which is the final germanic type. The un-numbered sets of germanic figures were the Scots Greys, the Fusiliers and the 12th, 16th and 17th Lancers. Maybe these were the original sets number 6 to 10. In this event, the Fusiliers would have been truly the first version of set 7.

If these sets were current throughout 1894 and dropped in 1895, this would explain why the other two regiments of Lancers, the 5th and 9th, were issued as sets 23 and 24, while a new set of 16th was only issued as set 33, a year later. Previously the 16th Lancers would have been represented by the germanic set.

The reason why the Scots Grey, Fusilier and Lancer germanic figures were discontinued was, of course, that they were not of the correct scale to fit the rapidly evolving scheme of things whereby the figures created by the genius of the Britains family were all of a constant scale and appearance. The other germanics, the Life Guard and the plug-handed Highlander, would, for the time being, pass muster.

The above hypothesis does not account for the other early non-chronological sets 14, 20, 26, 35, 38 and 65, but these too should be accounted for by items withdrawn before 1898. Would that we knew what they were!

1893

1 1st Life Guards 1966 TPW Ch 14 and 15
Officer on prancing horse and four troopers. Germanic to 1897, fixed-arm to 1902, one-eared to 1925, then standard two-eared

2 Royal Horse Guards 1966 TPW Ch 14 and 15
As set 1

3 5th Dragoon Guards 1941 TP Ch 14 and 16
As set 1 to 1903, then officer on prancing horse and four troopers on head-up trotting horse dated 12.12.1902

4 Reputedly gilt Life Guards
Unknown; does not appear in any known catalogue

5 Reputedly gilt Life Guards
As set 4

6 Boer Cavalry see 1895

7 Royal Fusiliers see 1897

8 4th Hussars see 1896

9 Rifle Brigade see 1897

10 Salvation Army Men see 1906

11 Black Watch 1966 TW Ch 24
Plug-handed officer and six men to 1904, then eight fixed-arm charging dated 17.12.1903. Square base from c.1909

12 11th Hussars 1941 TPW Ch 18
Officer on prancing horse and four troopers with carbines. Donkey horse to 1903, then cantering horse dated 12.2.1903

13 3rd Hussars 1941 PW Ch 18
As set 12

14 Salvation Army Women see 1906

15 Argyll and Sutherland Highlanders 1941 T Ch 24
As set 11

It seems that, having completed trials of the hollow-casting production method the previous year, the Britain family went into production early in 1893. The earliest soldiers were those in sets 1 – 15 except for the gaps indicated. Originally these may well have been filled by sets that never received an official catalogue number (see above). During 1893, the new Britains soldiers were accepted by a number of outlets, including Gamages. Prices were one shilling per box, except in Gamages, where the price was discounted to tenpence halfpenny, discounting being a well-known feature of that establishment.

1894

16 East Kent Regiment 1941 TW Ch 25
Officer, bugler, drummer and seven standing on guard. Oval-based to 1910, then new square-based figure dated 17.1.1910

17 Somerset Light Infantry 1966 TW Ch 25
Officer, bugler, four standing and four kneeling on guard. Oval-based and early kneeling figure to 1910, then new figures

18 Worcestershire Regiment 1941 TW Ch 25
Officer, drummer, four standing and four kneeling on guard. As set 17

19 West India Regiment 1941 P Ch 30
Mounted officer, eight men marching, shoulder arms. Oval-based to c.1925, then same figure with square base

20 Russo-Japanese display see 1905

21 Display set British Army 1941
Four rows, including sets 1, 12, 16 and 19

22 Display set British Army 1941
Four rows, including 2, 11, 18 and 23

23 5th Lancers 1932 PW Ch 19
Officer turned in saddle, four troopers at the halt. Cross-legged horses to 1903, then at-halt figure dated 18.8.1903

24 9th Lancers 1966 PW Ch 19
As set 23

In 1894, Britains produced its first display boxes, probably at the urging of Gamage, who had a good trade for more expensive items. Each display set simply consisted of four existing sets. Display sets were priced at four shillings, except in Gamages, where they were three shillings and threepence. The production of set 19, the West India Regiment, at this time was probably a result of the regiment's participation in the 3rd Ashanti War (1893-4). In 1894 Kaiser Wilhelm II received the colonelcy of the 1st Dragoons, an event celebrated by Britains with a special model (see Chapter 21).

1895

25 Soldiers to shoot 1916 T Ch 21
Four kneeling firing figures with hollow rifle-barrels

26 Boer Infantry see 1897

27 Band of the Line 1955 T Ch 23
Twelve musicians, slotted-arm to 1911, then movable-arm

28 Mountain Artillery 1966 TW Ch 28
Mounted officer, six gunners, four mules and gun. Officer, men and mules changed to larger size c.1924

29 Display set – British Army 1941
Large box containing 41 pieces, including sets 1, 13, 24, 28 and the West Surrey Regiment, with officer, two buglers, two drummers, five at the slope and five standing on guard. Changes as sets 16 and 36, except that the marching figure used valise-pack and box-pack figures from 1897 to 1910

30 Drums and Bugles of the Line 1966 TW Ch 23
Drum-major, bass-drummer, two side-drummers and four buglers. Buglers changed from boy to adult figure c.1920. For other figures, see Type and Sequence Glossary, page 177

31 1st Dragoons, the Royals 1941 TW Ch 17
Officer on prancing horse and four troopers with swords. Tin sword to 1903, then Scots Grey horse dated 1.11.1902

32 2nd Dragoons, Royal Scots Greys 1966 TW Ch 17
Officer and four troopers all on same type horse, as set 31

33 16th Lancers 1952 TW Ch 19
As set 23

34 Grenadier Guards 1941 TW Ch 22
Eight men standing firing, marching officer and drummer. Volley-firing figure to 1901, then firing figure dated 1.7.1901

35 Royal Marine Artillery see 1897

36 Royal Sussex Regiment 1941 TW Ch 25
Mounted officer and eight men at the slope (six after 1910). Fixed-arm marching figure to 1910, the movable-arm figure dated 24.2.1910

37 Full Band of the Coldstream Guards 1959 T Ch 23
Twenty-one musicians, slotted-arm to 1911, then movable-arm

38 Dr Jameson and the African Mounted Infantry 1941 T Ch 32
Officer with pistol and four troopers with rifles. Fixed-arm to 1927, then change to US Cavalry in action figure, the set then having no officer

6 Boer Cavalry 1910 T Ch 32
As set 38, but discontinued c.1910

39 Royal Horse Artillery 1965 T Ch 28
Until 1906, six-horse team at gallop, limber and gun with four seated gunners and mounted officer. From 1906, gunners given horses and ride separately. In 1924, light-harness horses introduced

39a R.H.A. in Khaki see 1916

40–42 Display sets of the British Army, two rows for two shillings.

The Chitral campaign in India took place in 1895, and during the last few weeks of the same year the famous 'Jameson Raid' happened in South Africa. Jameson surrendered to the Boers on New Year's Day, 1896. It is very much a matter of conjecture whether Britains brought out sets 6 and 38 before, during or after this event, although it would at least be logical to suppose that the set of Boer Cavalry was brought out at the same time as the Mounted Infantry. We know that the Royal Horse Artillery set was produced for Christmas 1895, and the horse for the officer of that set bears a marked resemblance to the horses for sets 6 and 38.

By this time a pattern seems to be developing, whereby the sets for the year were produced in two 'seasons', the first in the spring and the second in the autumn for the Christmas market, the display boxes being numbered after the end of the year's production. Often, innovations were introduced at the beginning of the year, and the first set in 1896, the 2nd Life Guards, set 43, has the first stud-and-loop style movable arms.

43 2nd Life Guards 1941 PW Ch 15
Four troopers at the gallop with carbines and a trumpeter. Rocking horses to 1901, one-eared horse to 1925, then two-eared horse

44 2nd Dragoon Guards (Queen's Bays) 1952 TW Ch 16
As set 43, but carrying lances

8 4th Hussars 1952 TW Ch 18
As set 43, but carrying swords

45 3rd Madras Cavalry 1941 P Ch 30
Four troopers with swords and a trumpeter. No different versions

46 10th Bengal Lancers 1941 T Ch 30
Four troopers with lances and a trumpeter. No different versions

47 1st Bengal Cavalry 1966 T Ch 30
Four troopers with swords and a trumpeter. No different versions to 1932

48 Egyptian Camel Corps 1941, revived 1957-66 T Ch 31
Six men on camels for two shillings. Wire-tailed camel until c.1922, then moulded tail

49 South Australian Lancers 1941 T Ch 30
Four troopers at full gallop with lances, and an officer. As set 43; slouch hat changed to spiked helmet c.1898

50–56 Display sets of the British Army, two rows for two shillings or three rows for three shillings

57 and 58 Small-size display sets see page 168

59 Display set: double row of Scots Greys

60–63 Display sets of Indian Army Cavalry, either two or three rows of the same regiment. These boxes contained both a trumpeter and an officer

64 Display set: 2nd Madras Lancers
Four troopers with lance and a trumpeter
7th Bengal Infantry 1941 Ch 30
Seven infantry at trail with officer. Cavalry – no different versions; infantry – at trail until c.1924, then new figure at slope without pack.

65 Russian display set see 1905

66 1st Bombay Lancers 1966 P Ch 30
Four troopers with lances and a trumpeter. No different versions to 1932

67 1st Madras Native Infantry 1941 TW Ch 30
Seven infantry at the trail with officer. Sepoy at trail until c.1924, then new figure at slope without pack

68 2nd Bombay Native Infantry 1941 TW Ch 30
As set 67

There was renewed activity in India in 1896, including the campaign in Malakand by the Malakand Field Force. This may well account for Britains' outburst of activity with Indian Empire regiments. The Indian Cavalry figure arrived as the second movable-arm model and the Indian sepoy as the third; this was the first infantry figure modelled in what later became the standard way. The Egyptian Camel Corps was also an interesting innovation, particularly as the men were removable from the camels.

Assuming the numbering is in strict chronological order, then 1896 saw the arrival of the small size figures with sets 57 and 58. These models had movable arms from the start, and for the present featured only cavalry. For more information on small-size figures, turn to page 166.

1897

69 Pipers of the Scots Guards 1941 TW Ch 23
Seven pipers, small early model to 1912, then taller figure dated 6.3.1912

70 The contents of this set, if it existed, have never been confirmed. Reputedly, it contained Scots Guards running at the trail, in which case it should belong to the 1899 issues.

71 Turkish Cavalry 1941 TW Ch 34
Four lancers and an officer. No different versions

72 Life Guards 1837 and 1897 P Ch 15
Five troopers and an officer of each type, total twelve pieces. Same changes as set 1 during the period of production

73 Large display set of the British Army 1965 Ch 29
First version included full-dress 17th Lancers, and a general officer

74 Royal Welch Fusiliers 1965 PTW Ch 26
Officer, goat and six men marching at the slope. Valise-pack type to 1905, then box-pack type marching figure

75 Scots Guards 1966 PTW Ch 22
Officer, piper and six men at the slope. As set 74 to c.1911, then the 1910 marching figure

76 Middlesex Regiment 1963 TW Ch 25
Officer and seven men at the slope. Versions as set 75

7 Royal Fusiliers 1941 PTW Ch 26
Officer and seven men at the slope. As set 74

9 Rifle Brigade 1916 TW Ch 26

Officer and seven men at the slope. As set 74. Bayonets not fixed

26 Boer Infantry 1913 T Ch 32
Eight men at the slope. Valise-pack type to 1906, then on-guard or shoulder-arm types dated 15.6.1906. (Although both these latter types were used for this set, I have not seen mixed sets.)

35 Royal Marine Artillery 1963 PTW Ch 27
Office and seven men at the slope. Versions as set 74

77 Gordon Highlanders 1966 TW Ch 24
Two pipers and six men at the slope. Plug-handed type to 1901, then box-pack Highlander dated 20.1.1901 to 1913, then standard marching figure without pack

78 Royal Navy Bluejackets 1941 TW Ch 27
Petty officer and seven men running at the trail. Early figure changed to slightly thicker model, c.1920

79 Royal Naval Landing Party 1963 TW Ch 27
Petty officer and eight men running with limber and gun. Two shillings and sixpence. Figure·changed to later one, c.1920

80 Royal Navy Whitejackets 1941 TW Ch 27
Petty officer and seven men running, as set 78, but early version at the slope

81 17th Lancers in Ulundi foreign-service dress 1941
Trumpeter and four lancers in white foreign-service helmets. Rocking-horse figure to 1899, then pony horse to 1903, after which the head-up trotting horse dated 12.12.1902 was used

82 Scots Guards colour and pioneers 1959 TW Ch 22
Officer with colour, and seven pioneers with axes. Versions as set 75, but with arms with axes rather than rifles

The main event of 1897 was Queen Victoria's Diamond Jubilee, celebrated on 20th June. Souvenir set 72 was probably issued in good time. Greece and Turkey were at war between 17 April and 18 September, which may explain set 71, although it would have made sense for some Greeks to have been represented also. The marching and Royal Navy sets may well have been suggested as much-needed troops for the Jubilee celebrations. From now on, marching infantry were Britains' most common type of set. The boundary I have suggested here between 1897 and 1898 production is not necessarily correct, as there is nothing about the sets in the sequence at this point to suggest where the new year starts.

1898
83 Middlesex Yeomanry 1941 TW Ch 18
Officer on prancing horse and four troopers with

carbines. Mixed rocking horse and donkey horse until 1903, then one-eared horse at gallop and cantering horse dated 12.12.1903. After c. 1930, sometimes all on cantering horses

84–87 Small-size display sets

88 Seaforth Highlanders 1941 Ch 24
Fourteen charging and two pipers. Plug-handed to 1903, then fixed-arm charging figure

89 Cameron Highlanders firing see 1901

90 Coldstream Guards firing see 1901

91 United States Infantry, Cuban War 1941 T Ch 41
Seven men with officer. Valise-pack to 1906, then on-guard with slouch hat, dated 15.6.1906

92 Spanish Infantry, Cuban War 1941 TW Ch 34
Seven men with officer. Valise-pack at trail to 1925, then new figure at slope, no officer

93 Large display set of Coldstream Guards and Royal Horse Guards 1941 Ch 22
Included Royal Horse Guards galloping with lances. Versions as set 44

94 21st Lancers in Omdurman foreign-service dress 1941 T Ch 31
Four lancers and trumpeter. Versions to 1915 as 4th Hussars, set 8, but with foreign-service helmet. After 1916, steel helmet used

Small-size infantry were introduced in this year. Special events included the Spanish-American war, in which most action was seen in Cuba, hence sets 91 and 92; the Battle of San Jacinto took place on 1 July. On the other side of the world, the British were reconquering the Sudan. On 2 September the Battle of Omdurman was fought, in which the 21st Lancers and the York and Lancaster Regiment distinguished themselves, hence set 94 and, a little later, set 96.

1899
95 Japanese display set see 1905

96 York and Lancaster Regiment 1941 TW Ch 32
Seven men running at trail with officer. Pigeon-chested figure, foreign-service dress to c.1908, then full dress with square base to 1922. Open-elbow running figure until c.1928, then closed-elbow type

97 Royal Marine Light Infantry 1941 TW Ch 27
Seven men running at trail with officer. Pigeon-chested figure, red coat, white helmet to c.1908, then square base, blue helmet to 1922, opened- and closed-elbow types as set 96, changed to blue coat c.1932

98 King's Royal Rifle Corps 1952 TW Ch 26
Seven men running at trail with officer. Pigeon-chested with spiked helmet to c.1901, then busby. Figure versions as sets 96 and 97

70 Scots Guards Ch 22
If this set of running figures ever existed, it would have been issued at this point

99 13th Hussars 1941 TW Ch 18
Four troopers with swords, and officer. Pony-horse to 1903, then as set 12

100 21st Lancers, full dress 1941 T Ch 19
Four lancers and trumpeter. Pony-horse to 1903, then horse changed as 11th Hussars, set 12

101 Band of the 1st Life Guards 1965 Ch 15
Twelve mounted musicians, slotted-arm to 1911, then movable arms. Blue and gold uniform to 1916, then gold and red

In this year Britains introduced the pony-horse cavalry figure, and also the running infantryman. Set 96, the York and Lancaster Regiment, was probably introduced to go with the 21st Lancers, set 94, in the Sudan campaign, rather than for the Boer War. The Boer War started in October of this year, but the first set of Britains' Boer War figures came out in 1900.

1900
102 Display set of Foot Guards see 1901

103 Reputedly the **Band of the Royal Horse Guards,** but no entry in any known catalogue. A red and gold uniformed twelve-piece band sometimes found in a box 101 could be this set

104 City Imperial Volunteers 1941 P Ch 32
Nine men on guard with officer. No version changes, officer alone went to square base

105 Imperial Yeomanry 1941 T Ch 32
Five troopers. Fixed-arm trotting horse dated 1.6.1900, slouch hat. No version changes

Britains seems to have reduced considerably its output of new sets during 1899 and 1900, although this was just a pause before a very large production in 1901. Other matters may have been claiming the company's attention, probably because of the competition that it was undoubtedly facing by now. The second-grade and small-size lines were developed at this time, and the principle of dating each new figure was established. At about this time, too, the catalogue was first produced, with numbers for each set, and a dominant position in the market place against German imports was being established.

Once more, it is not clear whether set 108, for instance, was first produced in 1900 or 1901, although set 106 contained horses dated 1.1.1901. The Boer War lasted throughout 1901, and Britains' models of participants continued to be introduced to the range.

1901

106 6th Dragoon Guards 1941 TW Ch 16
Four troopers with carbines and an officer. Galloping horse, versions as set 43, starting with horse dated 1.1.1901

107 Irish Guards at the slope 1941 TW Ch 22
Seven men and an officer. Versions as set 75

108 6th Dragoons, Boer War service dress 1941 T Ch 31
Five troopers, as set 105, but with foreign-service order helmet. No version changes

109 Dublin Fusiliers, Boer War service dress 1941 TW Ch 32
Eight men marching at the trail, Slade Wallace equipment, smooth helmet to c.1904, then helmet with pugaree. In 1916, change to figure with 1908 webbing equipment. In all versions, trousers were a lighter colour than the coat

110 Devonshire Regiment, Boer War service dress 1941 TW Ch 32
Eight men marching at the slope, until c.1907, thence at the trail. Other version changes as set 109. In all versions, colour of coat matched trousers

111 Grenadier Guards, attention 1941 TW Ch 22
Six men with mounted officer. Round base dated 20.1.1901 to c.1907, then square base to 1925, when new at-attention figure was introduced

112 Seaforth Highlanders, slope 1941 TW Ch 24
Eight men, as second-version Gordons, set 77, with subsequent changes

113 East Yorkshire Regiment, attention 1941 TW Ch 25
Eight men, all versions as set 111

114 Cameron Highlanders, slope Boer War service dress 1947 TW Ch 32
Eight men, as second-version Gordons, set 77, but with smooth foreign-service order helmet, then from 1902 with pugaree, new marching figure c.1913

115 Egyptian Cavalry 1966 TW Ch 31
Four Lancers and an officer. Pony-horse to 1903, then horses and versions as set 12

116 Soudanese Infantry 1947 T Ch 31
Eight men at the trail, as set 109 but wearing fez, square base, c.1908, but then same figure until end of production

117 Egyptian Infantry, attention 1941, and 1957-9 TW Ch 31
Eight men, as set 111 but wearing fez. Version changes as set 111, but new at-attention figure not used

118 Gordon Highlanders, lying firing 1941 TW Ch 24
Nine men, with kneeling officer with binoculars. Men in foreign-service order helmet with pugaree, dated 1.7.1901

119 Gloucestershire Regiment standing firing 1939 TW Ch 32
Ten men with puttees, no officer, oval base to c.1908, square base thereafter

120 Coldstream Guards kneeling firing 1966 TW Ch 22
Nine men with kneeling officer with binoculars

121 Royal West Surrey Regiment, standing firing 1941 TW Ch 25
Nine men with standing officer with binoculars. Square bases from c.1908

122 Black Watch standing firing 1941 TW Ch 24
Nine men with standing officer with binoculars. Square bases from c.1908

123 Bikanir Camel Corps 1941 T Ch 30
Three men. Versions as Egyptians, set 48

124 Irish Guards lying firing 1941 TW Ch 22
Nine men with kneeling officer with binoculars

125 and 126 Small-size artillery teams

89 Cameron Highlanders firing 1941 Ch 24
Large box of firing Highlanders, changes as in single-row boxes

90 Coldstream Guards firing 1962 Ch 22
Large box of firing Guards, changes as in single-row boxes

102 Display set of Foot Guards Ch 22
Includes Irish Guards running, six men with mounted officer, changes as set 96 with Foot Guard head. Also Coldstream Guards at attention, seven men with one man holding colours, changes as set 111

Queen Victoria died on 22 January 1901, and the Boer War continued throughout this year on a guerilla warfare basis, and part way into 1902. Britains completed its line of toy soldiers for the Boer War in 1901, and also produced two more boxes of Egyptian troops and one of Soudanese, with which the Imperial side at Omdurman and the Soudan campaign could be depicted. This begs the question why no Arab troops

were made to depict the enemy at this stage, although this may simply reflect the continued imports of numbers of Heyde and other German-made 'enemy troops'.

During this year Britains introduced the new Slade Wallace type marching infantryman, with the derived Highlander, the infantryman at attention, all the standard firing troops, and the small-size gun teams. In other words, this was a very active year for the release of new models. By the end of the year, all the issues that appear in the earliest listing available – Gamage's catalogue of 1902 – were in production, although it is possible that some of the sets listed above for 1901 were not in fact released until 1902.

1902

Given that all the above sets were issued in 1901, this would leave nothing new for 1902, so one might suspect that a number of the sets were not issued until a year later. The small-size artillery horses, for instance, were dated 1.11.1901, and so might well not have appeared until the new season. In the meantime, however, the appearance of inactivity is again misleading, since William Britain Junior was now embarking on an intensive period of redesigning most of the cavalry and infantry figures to the new standard of modelling achieved with the Boer War figures. Also, a number of souvenir items were made with an eye to the Coronation of Edward VII, which took place on 9 August 1902 (see page 62.) New model activity can be seen by referring to the list of dated figures on page 16.

1903

127 7th Dragoon Guards 1941 TW Ch 17
Four troopers on head-up trotting horse dated 12.12.1902. Officer on one-eared horse dated 1.1.1901. Troopers carry slung lances, officer outstretched sword

128 12th Lancers 1941 TW Ch 19
Four troopers with slung lances on cantering horse dated 12.2.1903, officer on head-up trotting horse dated 12.12.1902

129–132 Large display sets, see 1906

Most of the remodelled standard-size horse figures were introduced in 1903, and existing cavalry sets were mostly reissued with these new models. Later in the year, the first of the remodelled foot figures, the charging Highlander dated 17.12.1903, was created, appearing in the appropriate sets in 1904. The two new sets made during 1903 both used the new horses.

1904

133 Russian Infantry 1939 TW Ch 33
Officer and seven marching at slope and trail, new

figure dated 16.1.1904. Oval base to *c.*1910, then square base

134 Japanese Infantry 1941 T Ch 33
Eight men charging, new figure dated 16.1.1904. Some early figures have a smaller head. Always oval-based

134 Japanese Cavalry 1939 T Ch 33
Officer and four troopers as set 128, but with Japanese caps, troopers carrying carbines

136 Russian Cavalry, Cossacks 1966 TW Ch 33
Officer and four Lancers, new figure dated 7.3.1904

The major event in this year was the outbreak of the Russo-Japanese war. The attack on Port Arthur took place on 8 February 1904, followed by the Battle of the Yalu on 30 April, the surrender of Port Arthur on 2 January 1905, the Battle of Tsushima on 27 May 1905 and the Treaty of Portsmouth on 6 September 1905.

Britains produced figures for playing this war in both standard and smaller sizes (see Chapter 33.) One puzzling factor in the chronology is that the Russian and Japanese infantry figures were dated 16.1.1904, nearly a month before the war broke out. Maybe the tensions in the Far East were so noticeable that it was fairly easy to decide on the next interesting models. The display sets for the Russians and Japanese must have been made rather later than the single-row sets, as I have a listing that shows the latter but not the former. Another venture started in 1904 was the football teams (see page 149).

1905
20, 65 and 95 Russo-Japanese Displays
These sets used up earlier numbers in the sequence which for some reason had not previously been used

137 Army Medical Service 1941 T Ch 31
Senior Medical officer, two doctors, four nurses, six stretcher-bearers, three stretchers and eight wounded in three different types. All dated 20.3.1905. Oval bases, but stretcher-bearers changed to square bases, *c.*1912

138 French Cuirassiers 1966 T Ch 35
Officer and four troopers with swords. Early version has small extra plume. Dated 1.11.1902 & 9.5.1905, based on Scots Grey horse

139 French Chasseurs à Cheval 1948 TW Ch 33
Officer and four troopers with carbines, dated 12.12.1902 & 9.5.1905, based on set 127 but with kepi and plume. Early version has short carbine, to *c.*1913

140 French Dragons (Dragoons) 1941 T Ch 35
Officer and four lancers at the halt dated 18.8.1903 & 9.5.1905, based on Lancer at-halt figure. Early version to *c.*1912 with plug carbine

141 French Infantérie de Ligne 1941 TW Ch 35
Marching figure, full-trouser, oval-base or gaitered, both dated 9.5.1905. Early sets sometimes contained officer and seven men, otherwise just eight men at the slope

142 French Zouaves 1966 TW Ch 35
Seven charging figures with fixed-arm walking officer, oval bases, dated 9.5.1905. From *c.*1912, square base, no officer

143 French Matelots 1949 T Ch 35
Eight sailors running at the slope, sometimes with paper label dated 20.3.1905. From *c.*1912, square base and at the trail

Apart from the ambitious set 137, which required the design of seven completely new models, 1905 was notable for the setting up of the Paris Office (see page 162). From this stems the preoccupation in the main list with types of the French armed forces. In the second half of the year, the new designs for standard full-dress marching British Army infantry and officers were worked out, so this was not at all a year without progress.

1906
144 Royal Field Artillery 1941 T Ch 28
Six-horse team, limber, gun and mounted officer. First version had four seated gunners. From *c.*1920 the two seated on the gun were removed, as were the seats. From 1924, the horses had light harness

144a as 144, but Service dress see 1916

145 Army Medical Corps Ambulance 1959 T Ch 31
Four-horse team, wagon with tilt and two seated drivers. Light harness from 1924

145a as 145, but Service dress see 1916

146 Army Service Corps Wagon 1959 T Ch 31
Four-horse team, open wagon and two drivers. Light harness from 1924

146a as 146, but Service dress see 1916

147 Zulus of Africa 1959 T Ch 31
Eight running, various weapons. Oval bases to *c.*1912. Dated 23.5.1906

10 Salvation Army men *c.*1908 Ch 40
Five men, two cornets and standard. Dated 3.5.1906

14 Salvation Army women *c.*1908 Ch 40
Three women with empty hands, three with timbrel and two with newspaper. Dated 3.5.1906

129 Large Cavalry display, including 1st Dragoon Guards 1941 Ch 16
1st Dragoon Guards on head-up trotting horse dated 12.12.1902

130 Large display of Scots Guards

131 Very large display including British Camel Corps and Worcestershire Regiment 1932
British Camel Corps as Bikanir Camel Corps with Mountain Artillery head. Worcestershires at slope and running at trail with white helmets and white facings

132 Very large display, which had no new figures in it as far as I know, except possibly kneeling Buffs.

Horse-drawn transport was introduced to Britains' army in 1906, with a welcome new gun team and a reorganization of the Royal Horse Artillery team so that the gunners rode separately instead of being shaken to pieces sitting on the limber and gun. The Zulus of Africa were the first real colonial 'enemy' troops produced apart from the Boers, and were the last with oval bases in their first version. Talks were going on at this time with CW Beiser about his patent-hinge system of packaging, which would necessitate rectangular or 'square' bases (see pages 150–1). Two new figures with square bases were designed, dated 15.6.1906, specifically with the United States market in mind.

The Salvation Army figures were also designed in this year, appearing in Gamages' 1906 Christmas Catalogue, and taking up two more previously vacant early set numbers, 10 and 14. Also probably with Gamages in mind, four very large sets were introduced. Of these 129 and 130 may have been ready for the 1905 Christmas season, but were not on the 1904 list.

Late in 1906, William Britain Senior died. The firm was left in his will to his eldest child Emily. The Britain brothers clubbed together to buy her out, and it seemed likely (ICP) that they raised the money by forming Britains into a limited company and using the shares as security. The deal probably took most of the next year to complete, and Britains was incorporated on 4 December 1907.

1907
148 Royal Lancaster Regiment Display tray and game 1916 T Ch 31
Mounted officer, foot officer, colours, trumpeter, three at trail, three at slope, two gunners and gun

149 American Soldier Display tray and game 1916 T Ch 41
As set 148

These were probably the only new sets issued during 1907, which is not surprising under the circumstances. Britains was searching for new directions and stability, as evidenced by Alfred Britain's experimental figures (see page 62). By the end of the year, several other new figures had been made ready for issue early in 1908, and things generally were back on course. It is noticeable that the interest in subjects North American was continued with the next set, the North American Indians.

1908

150 North American Indians on foot 1966 TW Ch 42
Two chiefs with tomahawk, six braves on guard, dated 12.11.1907

151 Royal Naval Volunteer Reserve 1941 T Ch 27
Petty officer and seven men marching at the shoulder, dated 12.11.1907

152 North American Indians mounted 1966 TW Ch 42
Three chiefs mounted with rifles, two on different horse with tomahawk

153 Prussian Hussars 1941 T Ch 36
Officer and four Lancers. Horse based on trotting horse dated 12.2.1903, remodelled and given second date 16.2.1908

154 Prussian Infantry 1941 TW Ch 36
Officer and seven men at the slope. New model dated 16.2.1908. Sometimes issued as the box-pack figure dated 1.8.1905

155 Railway station staff
Station-master, ticket-collector, porters, trolleys and luggage

156 Royal Irish Regiment, firing 1941 TW Ch 25
Four standing, three kneeling and three lying firing

157 Gordon Highlanders firing 1941 TW Ch 24
Same composition as set 156

158 Railway station staff and passengers
As set 155, with engine-driver, stoker, policemen and passengers

Although this does not seem a long list of sets for an entire year, a large number of completely new figures was required, especially for the railway sets.

1909

159 Territorial Yeomanry 1941 TW Ch 38
Officer and four troopers with swords, based on head-up trotting horse dated 12.12.1902

160 Territorial Infantry at the trail 1941 TW Ch 38
Before 1916, mounted officer and six men at trail based on Slade Wallace equipped figure dated 20.1.1901. Then

new foot officer, and seven men with webbing equipment

161 Boy Scouts 1941 Ch 40
Scoutmaster and eight marching scouts

There seems to have been very little activity in this year, although a Britains' leaflet with a photographic treatment of the new lines from this year has survived. The only other dated figures from this year, apart from the Boy Scouts and Scoutmaster, are the French officer and blanket roll based on the same figure as the Scoutmaster, and the new prancing-horse officer. It may also have been in this year that Britains brought out its book on war-gaming, and time may have been spent liaising with the new Boy Scout movement that was rapidly gaining in popularity. Preparations were most likely also being made for the introduction of the new on-guard and marching figures as well as the completion of further Boy Scout and civilian figures.

1910

No new sets appear to have been issued in 1910, although we cannot be certain what might have been happening on the second-grade or licensing sides. Improved on-guard and 1910 marching figures were issued, thus causing new versions of several sets. Various Paris figures were also being developed, and the new Boy Scout figures are dated late in this year and were probably issued early in 1910. Edward VII died on 6 May and preparations for the coronation of George V would certainly have been seen as a sales opportunity. Production in London at this time is estimated at about 200,000 figures a week, ten million in the full year.

1911

162 Boy Scout Encampment 1941 Ch 40
Tree and gate, ten hurdles, Scoutmaster, three marching, six standing and two kneeling scouts

163 Boy Scout signallers 1959 Ch 40
Five signallers

164 Bedouin Arabs mounted 1966 TW Ch 31
Three with scimitar, two with jezail, mounted on horses dated 17.7.1911

The next four sets may also have come out in 1911, since the Italian-Turkish conflict broke out on 29 September 1911, the Italians seizing Libya. But it is perhaps more likely that Britains' response was delayed until early in the next year. The Agadir incident also took place in 1911, and, probably more important for Britains' sales, the coronation of George V, on 22 June.

1912

165 Italian Cavalry 1941 TW Ch 36
Officer and four Lancers at the halt, based on set 140, French Dragons, with Italian kepi

166 Italian Infantry 1941 TW Ch 36
Officer and seven men at the slope based on marching figure dated 24.2.1910, with Italian kepi

167 Turkish Infantry 1941 W Ch 34
Officer and seven men on guard, based on figure dated 17.1.1910. No officer in set after 1916

168 Civilians
Eight assorted figures

169 Bersagliere 1959 T Ch 36
Eight marching, slung arms, dated 27.7.1912

The date of the Bersagliere tends to confirm that the other Italian and Turkish types were issued earlier in this year. The chronology of sets is confused by the fact that Gamages' catalogue for Christmas 1913 does not include some of the sets one would expect in that year, and yet illustrations of them do appear in the original Gamages' catalogue. It was in 1912 that Britains probably set up independent production facilities in Paris. The new improved small-size infantry figures are dated 1912.

1913

170 Greek Cavalry 1941 T Ch 34
Officer and four troopers with carbines, on the cantering horse dated 12.2.1903

171 Greek Infantry 1941 T Ch 34
Officer and seven men running at the trail. Probably the same version changes as set 96

172 Bulgarian Infantry 1939 T Ch 34
Officer and seven men marching at the trail, as set 133, Russians, but with Bulgarian kepi

173 Serbian Infantry 1934 T Ch 34
Eight men running, based on set 134, Japanese Infantry, with Serbian cap

174 Montenegrin Infantry 1934 T Ch 34
Officer and seven men marching at the trail, based on set 133, Russians, with Montenegrin cap

175 Austro-Hungarian Lancers 1941 T Ch 34
Officer, trumpeter and three troopers with swords, based on Scots Grey horse dated 1.11.1902

176 Austro-Hungarian Dragoons 1941 T Ch 34
Officer, trumpeter and three troopers with swords, based on head-up trotting horse dated 12.12.1902

177 Austro-Hungarian Infantry of the Line 1941 T Ch 34
Officer and seven men at the slope, based on Prussian officer figure from set 154. After 1916, based on 1910 marching figure

178 Austro-Hungarian Foot Guards 1941 T Ch 34
Officer and seven men at the slope as set 177, but with blue kepi and trousers. Same second version

179 Cowboys, mounted 1966 W Ch 42
Five mounted figures, two with lassoo and three with pistol

179 is the highest set number shown in the 1913 Gamages catalogue, and so was probably the last set to be issued in this year. The Cowboys are the first of the new figures issued under the new copyright law, which did not require the date of origination to be shown in order to establish copyright. All other sets first issued in this year were based on existing models.

The Balkan wars continued during 1913, having broken out with renewed vigour in 1912 with the formation of the Balkan League. The participants – Bulgaria, Serbia, Greece and Montenegro – attacked Turkey on 17 October 1912, and provided Britains with the opportunity of producing these sets in 1913.

1914
180 and 181 Large Boy Scout Displays These included the trek cart

182 11th Hussars dismounted with horses 1964 W Ch 18
Officer, three men and four horses

183 Cowboys on foot 1964 W Ch 42
Eight men walking with rifles, later with pistols or rifles, four of each

184 Cowboy display

185 Wild West display

186 Mexican Infantry 1941 W Ch 43
Officer and seven men marching, slung rifles

187 Bedouin Arabs on foot 1960 W Ch 31
Eight men at slope with jezails

188 Zulu Kraal 1941 W Ch 31
Two huts, two palm trees and seven Zulus

It is not very certain in which precise year 1914 and 1915 sets were issued. Assuming that the 1915 catalogue (see page 13) really was issued late in 1915 (which the appearance of the next three set numbers in the new lines list for 1916 tends to confirm) then the start of the First World War on 4 August was probably not reflected in Britains' list until 1915. On the other hand, the title of

set 160, Territorial Infantry, had changed to 'British Expeditionary Force Infantry' in the 1916 listing, and one would expect it to have changed in 1915 as well. The 1914 and 1915 set issue lists given here are the best compromise that I can reach.

1915
189 Belgian Infantry 1941 T Ch 34
Eight men on guard, figure with greatcoat

190 Belgian Cavalry 1959 T Ch 34
Officer trotting and four troopers at the halt with carbines

191 Turcos 1941 T Ch 35
Eight men charging, using the Zouave figure

1916
192 French Infantérie de Ligne steel helmets 1941 TW Ch 35
Eight men marching at the slope in greatcoats

193 Arabs of the Desert, on camels 1941 T Ch 31
Six on camels, with jezails

194 Machine Gun Section, lying 1941 TW Ch 38
Six men with guns

195 Infantry of the Line, steel helmets 1959 TW Ch 38
Officer and seven men at the trail, new figure with webbing equipment

196 Greek Evzones 1966 T Ch 34
Eight men in red jackets at the slope

197 Gurkha Rifles 1959 TW Ch 30
Eight men at the trail

39a Royal Horse Artillery, service dress Ch 38
144 Royal Field Artillery, service dress Ch 38
145a Army Medical Corps Ambulance, service dress Ch 38
146a Army Service Corps Wagon, service dress Ch 38
All these sets of horse-drawn vehicles were exactly the same as their full-dress counterparts, but painted in khaki uniforms and given heads with peaked caps

For a full discussion of the 1916 listing and the First World War in general, see pages 13 and 135. Britains had great plans to depict many types from the conflict, but were prevented first by the onset of 'total' war, which involved the company in war rather than in toy production, and second by the horrific nature of the war itself, which made people reluctant to buy any toy that reflected the conflict at all realistically (see for example page 142).

The only interesting feature of 1916 is that the

artillery and wagons were all issued in khaki service dress, using their original catalogue numbers with an 'a' suffixed. Shortly after this, the switch to armaments production prevented any further soldier sets being brought out until the end of the war. The period from 1919 is shrouded in mystery, the next known catalogue being dated 1926. The dates of first issue over the next few years are therefore uncertain.

1919
It was to be expected that after the trauma of the war it would take time to rebuild stocks of existing lines to a reasonable level. It may be that only one set was issued in 1919.

198 Machine Gun Section sitting 1941 W Ch 38
Four gunners with four separate guns. First issue had Maxim guns, later changed to Vickers

1920
199 Motor Machine Guns 1938 W Ch 39
Three motor cycle combinations with machine guns and gunners as a sidecar

200 Dispatch riders 1938 W Ch 39
Four dispatch riders on motor cycles

201 Officers of the General Staff, mounted 1959 W Ch 21
One general with binoculars, one without, and two aides de camp

202 Togoland Warriors 1959 W Ch 37
Eight warriors with bows

203 Pontoon Section, Royal Engineers, full dress 1939 W Ch 31
Four-horse team with wagon, pontoon boat and two roadway sections. A collar-harness first version of this was issued until c.1924, after which the team wore light harness

203a Pontoon Section, Royal Engineers, service dress, this was probably issued in about 1928

204 Assorted trees

The above sets are a guess at what might have been issued in 1920.

1921
205 Coldstream Guards, present 1941 W Ch 22
Officer and seven men. During our period these had both heels level and touching

206 Warwickshire Regiment, present 1941 W Ch 25

Officer and seven men, as Coldstreams Guards, set 205

207 Officers and Petty officers of the Royal Navy 1941 W Ch 27
Two admirals, two midshipmen and four petty officers

208–210 Various Cowboys and Indian displays

It would seem logical to leave a fair chronological gap here while Britains developed the Home Farm, which was launched early in 1923. The whole of 1922 and 1923 may quite possibly have been taken up with designing the new civilian models. In addition, in 1923 the Paris office and factories were closed down. I assume that the introduction of new toy soldier sets resumed in 1924.

1924
211 18-inch Heavy Howitzer with ten-horse team 1941 T Ch 39
This rather improbable set contained ten light-harness horses, the riders being in Royal Field Artillery full dress

212 Royal Scots 1966 W Ch 24
Eight men at the slope

213 Highland Light Infantry 1941 W Ch 24
Eight men at the slope. Although similar, this figure is a different mould from the Royal Scots, set 212

214 Royal Canadian Mounted Police, winter dress 1941 W Ch 30
Eight men at the slope

215 French Infantérie in steel helmets firing 1941 T Ch 35
Four each standing, kneeling and lying, with two kneeling machine gunners

This batch of sets includes several new models. At this time, too, the new light-harness team horses replaced the old collar-harness version.

1925
216 Argentine Infantry 1949 T Ch 43
Eight men at the slope

217 Argentine Cavalry 1959 T Ch 43
Officer and four Lancers

218 Spanish Cavalry 1941 T Ch 34
Officer and four troopers with swords, based on the Scots Grey horse

219 Argentine Military Cadets 1941 T Ch 43
Eight men at the slope

220 Uruguayan Cavalry 1959 T Ch 43
Officer and four Lancers. The same model as the Argentinians was used

221 Uruguayan Military Cadets 1952 T Ch 43
Eight men at the slope

222 Uruguayan Infantry 1941 T Ch 43
Eight men at the slope

223 and 224 Arab displays

This group of sets was presumably created to take advantage of an export opportunity to Argentina and Uruguay, the Spanish troops also being popular there. The opportunity was taken to make a new model of the Spanish infantry for set 92.

1926
It seems likely that the Hunting and Racing Colours series were issued in this year, as they appear in the catalogue that seems to correspond with 1926, while the sets that I have attributed to 1927 do not. The Hunting series comprised sets 234, 235 and 236, and the Racing Colours were numbered 237.

1927
225 King's African Rifles 1959 W Ch 30
Eight at the slope

226 West Point Cadets, winter dress 1941 W Ch 41
Eight at the slope

227 US Infantry, service dress 1948 W Ch 41
Officer and seven at the slope in 'doughboy' hats

228 US Marines, blue uniform 1966 W Ch 41
Sergeant and seven at the slope

229 US Cavalry, service dress 1959 W Ch 41
Five at the walk with empty hands, on Scots Grey horses.

230 US Sailors, Bluejackets 1941 W Ch 41
Eight at the slope

231–233 USA forces display

234–236 Hunting Series – see 1926

237 Racing Colours – see 1926

238 USA Civilians, Girl Scouts 1932 Ch 41
Eight girl scouts

239 Motor Patrol and Road Signs AA

240 Royal Air Force 1941 W Ch 39
Two officers with six men

241 Chinese Infantry 1941 T Ch 33
Eight Chinese with knives

242 US Infantry with mounted officer
Combination of earlier figures

243 Hunting Series

244–252 A series of seven-piece sets containing three mounted and four foot figures from earlier sets
1927 is noteworthy for two new departures, the new sets for the United States market (see page 150), and the start of production of many new sets in different numbers of figures in order (ICP) to increase the domestic market. Sets 244–252 made up the first experiment, and over the next few years a variety of sets was made for sale at different prices so as to overcome the economic uncertainties of the depression.

1928
253 Welsh Guards at the slope 1941 Ch 22
Mounted officer and seven at the slope

254 Bluejackets and Whitejackets 1941 Ch 27
Five Bluejackets and four Whitejackets at shoulder arms

255 Green Howards 1941 Ch 55
Officer, standard-bearer, drummer and six marching at the slope

256 and 257 Wild West displays

258 Infantry in steel helmets and gas masks 1941 W Ch 38
Eight marching at the trail

259–269 USA forces displays

270 11th Hussars, mounted and dismounted at the halt 1941 Ch 18
Two-row display box with a set 182 and an officer and four troopers mounted at the halt, empty-handed, unavailable in any other set

271 Skinner's Horse 1934 W Ch 30
Trumpeter and four Lancers

272–275 Wild West displays

276 US Cavalry in action 1941 Ch 41
Five at full gallop with carbines

277 and 278 Wild West displays

279 and 280 USA forces displays

281–283 Eight-piece displays with tent

284–288 USA forces displays

289 Boy Scouts and US Girl Scouts display

290 and 291 USA forces displays

292 Arab display

293 Boy Scouts and US Girl Scouts display

294 and 295 USA forces displays

296 Arab display

297 and 298 Wild West displays

299 West Point Cadets, summer dress 1966 W Ch 41
Eight at the slope, as set 226, but with white pants

300 Arab display

301–304 Eight-piece displays with tent

305–311 Ten-piece mounted and foot displays

It is not at present certain exactly which sets were issued in which years between 1927 and 1932. In each of these years there was frantic activity, with new sets being produced, sets of different sizes duplicated, and display sets issued with different combinations or numbers of previous figures or accessories such as tents.

1929
312 Grenadier Guards in greatcoats 1966 W Ch 22
Officer and seven at the slope

313 Team of Royal Artillery Gunners 1941 W Ch 38
Four standing and four kneeling at attention, khaki and peaked caps

314 Coldstream Guards at ease 1941 W Ch 22
Eight at ease (new figure)

315 10th Royal Hussars 1941 W Ch 18
Officer and four at the halt, mounted, empty hands

316 Royal Artillery (late RHA) gun team at the halt 1941 Ch 28
Six-horse team, limber, gun and mounted officer

317 Royal Artillery (late RFA) gun team at the halt 1941 Ch 28
Six-horse team, limber, gun and mounted officer

318 Royal Artillery gun team at the halt with team of gunners 1941 Ch 38

Six-horse team, limber, gun, mounted officer, standing officer with binoculars, three standing and three kneeling gunners in khaki and peaked caps

319 Police, mounted, foot and traffic 1941 W Ch 40
One mounted, two directing traffic and four standing

320 Royal Army Medical Corps doctors and nurses 1941 Ch 31
Two doctors and six nurses

321 Drum and Fife Band of the Line 1941 Ch 23
Seventeen musicians

322 Drum and Fife Band of the Coldstream Guards with rank and file 1941 Ch 23
Seventeen musicians with eight marching at the slope

323 Large USA forces display, including Artillery and Dispatch Rider

324 Large USA forces display

325–328 Wild West boxes

329 Sentry box with Foot Guard Sentry 1962 Ch 22
To start with a Grenadier sentry, then normally a Scots Guard

330 USA Aviation, officers in short coats 1939 T Ch 41
Eight officers

331 USA Aviation, officers in overcoats 1939 T Ch 41
Eight officers

332 USA Aviation, flying kit, short coats 1939 T Ch 41
Eight aviators

333 USA Aviation, flying kit, Sidcot Suits 1939 T Ch 41
Eight aviators

334 USA Aviation, privates, peaked caps 1939 T Ch 41
Eight privates

335 USA Aviation, review order Possibly never in catalogue.
Sixteen in peaked caps, marching at the slope

336–337 **USA Aviation displays**

338 British Infantry in gas masks, marching, display

339 and 340 USA forces boxes

341 Machine gunners display

342 and 343 Argentine forces displays

344 and 345 Small mixed boxes, British Army

346–350 Small boxes of USA forces with tent

351 **Mixed box of USA Aviation**

352–354 **Small USA forces displays**

355 and 356 **Small British Army displays**

357 and 358 **Small Wild West displays**

359 USA Machine Gun section, lying 1941 W, overprinted. Ch 41
Six gunners, as set 194 in US colours

360 Togoland Warriors

361–385 **Assorted USA and French forces displays**

386 **Royal Canadian Mounted Police, dismounted**

387 **Togoland Warriors**

388 **French Infantry in khaki**

389–392 **Ten-piece sets of infantry**

393-398 **Six-piece sets of cavalry**

Until set 325, with very few exceptions, all the numbered sets appeared in the catalogue. It would seem (ICP) that in 1929 Britains changed its numbering policy, possibly to avoid internal confusion, or muddles when customers reordered. Hitherto, only sets appearing in the general catalogue were numbered, and special sets done to order were un-numbered. After 1929, any set made for a commercial customer above a certain quantity was given a main series number, although these numbers did not necessarily appear in the catalogue. This change in policy would explain the very large gaps in the catalogued sets. The contents of the missing sets can only be discovered by referring to the factory records kept by Britains. It should be remembered, however, that there do exist sets made for Hamleys, in particular, in the 1930s and 1940s, without any number whatever, so the reasons for allocating a number are not fully known. All set numbers for which an entry has *not* been found in a catalogue are shown in italics.

1930
399 US Marines, active-service order 1941 T Ch 41
Eight marching at the slope, as set 228, but painted in olive drab

400 The Life Guards, winter dress 1966 W Ch 15
Four with swords in cloaks, and officer with empty hand

401–406 **Spanish and South American forces displays**

407–409 **Royal Navy displays**

410–416 **South American forces displays**

417–420 **Gordon Highlanders displays**

421 and *422* **North American Indian displays**

423 Boy Scouts

424 West Point Cadet display

425 Spanish forces display

426 Ideal Flower Support

1931
427 French forces display

428 USA Police 1932 only (in catalogue) Ch 41
As set 319, but with peaked caps

429 Guards in winter dress display

430 Life Guards display

431 Scots Guards display

432 German Infantry in steel helmets 1966 Ch 36
Officer and seven marching at the slope

433 Royal Air Force Monoplane 1947 P Ch 39
Monoplane with removable pilot and box making up into a hanger

434 see 1932

435 USA Aviation Monoplane 1947 P Ch 41
As set 433, in US colours

In 1931 a new 20,000-square foot factory, known as the North Light building, was erected in Walthamstow, east London, and the entire production of the Home Farm range was moved there.

1932
434 Royal Air Force Monoplane with six aircraftsmen

436 USA Aviation Monoplane with six aircraftmen

437 see 1933

438–459 Parade series, see below for full listing.

This book was planned to finish in 1932, when Britains completed the first 500 numbers of the main catalogue sequence. This almost works exactly, but, as usual with Britains, there are a few loose ends. Sets 437 and 460 to 500 were not in the 1932 catalogue, and those that are not in the Parade Series are listed below under 1933. After 500, the next military number was 1201, and so 500 makes a convenient point to end our survey of early Britains. To complete the 40 years, however, numbers 1201–1203 appeared in the 1932 catalogue, as follows:
1201 Gun of the Royal Artillery 1967 P
This was a new model of an 18-pounder gun, and replaced the RA gun hitherto used by Britains for all its gun teams
1202 Carden Loyd Tank with Driver 1932 only P
This model tank had a wide observation slit and rubber tracks
1203 Carden Loyd Tank with Driver, Gunner and Machine Gun 1941 P
The same as 1202, but with a narrow slit to hold the gun, and a gunner to sit in the second seat

THE PARADE SERIES

The major innovation of 1932 was the production of the Parade Series, completed, with the addition of A series Parade sets, in 1933. As all the best-quality Parade Series boxes are numbered before 500, they are listed in full below. Numbers 479–490 do not appear in the 1932 catalogue, and were introduced in 1933. The series was discontinued after 1934.

The feature of these Parade Series sets was that, instead of the figures being tied down flat in the boxes, their bases were inserted in a cardboard baseboard so that the figures were standing up. A tall box lid that fitted inside the rim of the lower tray of the box completed the packaging. The box was sufficiently tall to allow the figures to remain standing when it was closed. The baseboard complete with soldiers could be lifted out of the lower tray of the box, and the soldiers thus moved about without further effort by the section or platoon, beautifully spaced. To promote this effect, the baseboard was coloured green.

Like most other attempts by Britains to introduce packaging gimmicks, the Parade Series was not popular enough to remain in production long. It was discontinued after 1934, and hence is a rarity for collectors. Parade sets were also produced in the second grade, but only in 1933 and 1934, after our period. Until the Britains' factory listings are issued, the composition of many of the Parade sets will remain unknown. Among the larger sets there were a few figures not hitherto produced, or else painted in different uniforms. A new mounted figure was also made with a base that fitted the baseboards slots.

Parade series listing

438 Grenadier Guards
9 figures

439 Middlesex Regiment
9 figures

440 7th Royal Fusiliers
9 figures

441 Gordon Highlanders
9 figures

442 British Infantry khaki
9 figures

443 West Point Cadets, winter dress
9 figures

444 US Marines
9 figures

445 US Infantry, service dress
9 figures

446 Scots Guards
13 figures

447 Royal West Surrey Regiment
13 figures

448 7th Royal Fusiliers
13 figures

449 Black Watch
13 figures

450 British Infantry, khaki
13 figures

451 West Point Cadets, winter dress
13 figures

452 US Marines
13 figures

453 US Infantry, service dress
13 figures

454 West Point Cadets, summer dress
9 figures

455 West Point Cadets, summer dress
13 figures

456 US Sailors
9 figures

457 US Sailors
13 figures

458 US Infantry and Cavalry, service dress
13 figures

459 US Infantry and Cavalry, service dress
9 figures

479 US Marines and Sailors
18 figures

480 The Black Watch with pipers and mounted officers
18 figures

481 Middlesex Regiment, buglers, drummers and
mounted officers
18 figures

482 Gordon Highlanders with pipers and mounted
officers
26 figures

483 US Infantry, foot and mounted officers
18 figures

484 West Point Cadets, winter and summer dress
18 figures

485 US Infantry, foot and mounted officers
26 figures

486 US Infantry and Cavalry with foot officer
22 figures

487 US Infantry and Cavalry with foot officer
24 figures

488 US Marines and Sailors
26 figures

489 West Point Cadets, winter and summer dress
26 figures

490 Middlesex Regiment, buglers, drummers and
mounted officers
26 figures

The Grenadier Guards and the Black Watch had not
previously appeared before this series as marching
figures. The problem of introducing mounted figures

into these sets was solved by casting a special spindly
head-down type horse with a base cast in between the
two rear hooves. An adaptation of this figure appears to
have been used for all the mounted officers and 'cavalry'
mentioned in the set titles, although these sets were so
short-lived that I have not seen enough of them to verify
the exact contents of each set.

Sets numbered below were not produced until 1933.

437 Officers of the Gordon Highlanders 1941 T
One mounted, four on foot

460 Colour Party of the Grenadier Guards 1941 W,
overprinted. Ch 22
Two officers with drawn swords, two colour bearers
and three sergeants at the slope

461 Display of German infantry

462–464 Displays of the wild West

465–475 Displays of the USA forces

476 Display of Arabs

477 Display of the British Army

478 Display of French forces

479–490 Parade Series. See above for full listing

491–495 Displays of the USA forces

496 Gordon Highlanders

497 Royal Scots

498 USA Cavalry

499 USA Infantry

500 Life Guards, winter dress

London=Made Metal Soldiers.

THE following strikingly handsome Presentation Cases have been added to our List to meet the requirements of those of our customers who wish for a large assortment of London-made Metal Soldiers enclosed in one box.

This collection embraces the whole range of our well-known copyright models, with all latest additions, both cavalry and infantry, in their various positions and attitudes, and are beautifully decorated and packed with special care in strong wooden cases, the sizes and contents of which are enumerated below.

No. **131**. Containing : The Royal Horse Artillery, Mountain Battery, Camel Corps, Scots Greys, 11th Hussars, 5th Dragoon Guards, 17th Lancers, 2nd Life Guards, Horse Guards, full Band of the Coldstream Guards, the Scots Guards, lying, kneeling, and standing firing, the Gordon Highlanders with Pipers, the Worcestershire Regiment, Bluejackets and Whitejackets with 4.7 naval guns, and General Officer, totalling 275 pieces of cavalry and infantry. Size of case 3 ft. 9 ins. by 1 ft. 11 in. by 6 ins., with two inside trays. Price **90**/- each.

No. **132**. Containing : The Royal Horse Artillery, 2nd Dragoons (Scots Greys), 11th Hussars, 12th Lancers, 2nd Life Guards, Horse Guards, 7th Dragoon Guards, full Band of the Line, the Seaforth Highlanders with Pipers, Welsh Fusiliers with Goat, the Coldstream Guards, standing, lying, and kneeling firing, the East Kent Regiment, Mule Battery, 4.7 Naval Gun, and a General Officer, totalling 167 pieces of infantry and cavalry. Size of case 2 ft. 10 in. by 1 ft. 7 ins. by 6 ins., with two inside trays.
Price **62**/- each.

No. **73**. Containing the following regiments—The Royal Horse Artillery, 2nd Life Guards, 17th Lancers, Royal Welsh Fusiliers, Scots Greys, Band of the Line, the Gordon Highlanders, and a General Officer. Size of case, 2 ft. 2 ins. by 1 ft. 3 in. Price complete, **25**/-

No. **129**. Containing the 12th Lancers, 2nd Dragoons (Scots Greys), 1st Dragoon Guards, 11th Hussars and 2nd Life Guards, totalling 70 pieces of cavalry. Size of case 2 ft. 1 ins. by 1 ft. 5 ins. by 3 in., with one inside tray.
Price **15**/- each.

No. **130**. Containing a splendid collection of the Scots Guards, marching, running, standing-at-ease, standing, lying, and kneeling firing, together with Pipers, Drum and Bugle Band, Colours and Pioneers, mounted and unmounted Officers. Size of case 2 ft. 1 in. by 1 ft. 5 in. by 3 ins., with one inside tray, totalling 118 pieces of infantry.
Price **15**/- each.

No. **93**. This presentation case consists of a complete company of Coldstream Guards, with officers, Full Band, Colours, and Pioneers, with a Squadron of Royal Horse Guards, with Trumpeters, etc. Packed in well-made wooden framed box, with tray to lift out. Size of box 2 ft. by 1 ft. 1 in.
Price complete, **12**/-

DESCRIPTIONS OF LARGE SETS
Left: A reduced reproduction from the 1915 catalogue, where Britains described the contents of their large sets of the time. Unfortunately the quantity and poses of the figures are not fully explained, and so the contents of set 132 in particular are not well known, since no boxed set has come to light in recent years.

General index

The general index gives all significant references in the book to subjects, regiments, the more important types of figures and portrayals of national armies other than British. References in *italic* indicate that the reference is part of a picture caption. References in **bold** type are to illustrations. The symbol □ indicates that a box label is illustrated. **Bold** type with the symbol □ signifies figures with their box.

Acknowledgements

Putting together the information to go with the toy soldiers has depended on discussions and correspondence with collectors and dealers for 20 years or more. The toy soldier collecting world is a particularly friendly one and my thanks must go to everyone who has been generous with information and hospitality.

In particular Ken Pizey was kind enough to lend me the specific models of European armies that I no longer own, and Colin Barber and Ken Grace lent me vital figures at crucial moments. Among the photographs, Phillips Auctioneers' supplied a generous number of prints, and Britains Ltd kindly gave permission for the use of their copyright catalogue material, and allowed us to take photos of Alfred Britain's models.

Finally, my wife Avryll typed up a large part of the manuscript in her best super secretary style, and my children Elizabeth and Philip sometimes agreed that soldiers should come first on the agenda.